Great
Lakes

Mid-
Atlantic

England

CH CAGO
THEATRE

BATH HOUSE

Southern
Interior

South
Atlantic

BAKING *across* AMERICA

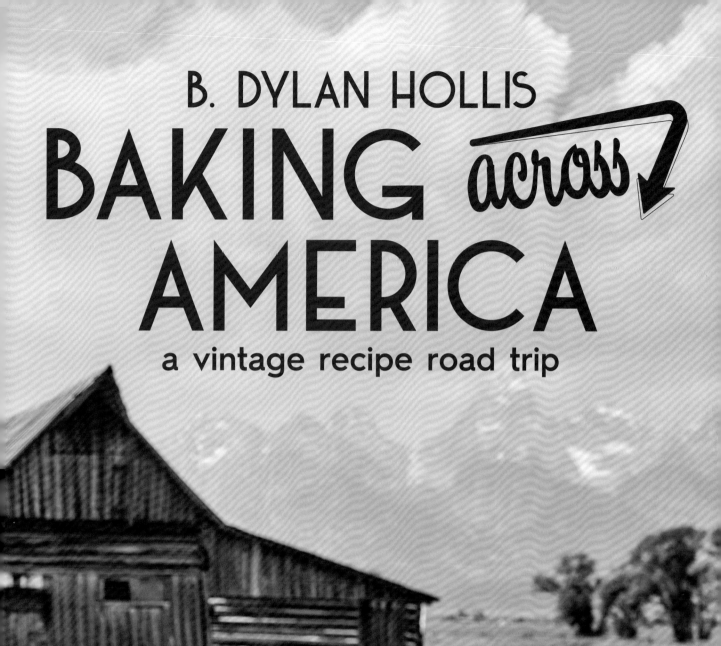

B. DYLAN HOLLIS

BAKING *across* AMERICA

a vintage recipe road trip

Publisher Mike Sanders
Executive Editor Alexander Rigby
Art & Design Director William Thomas
Editorial Director Ann Barton
Primary Photographer Mackenzie Smith Kelley
Baking Assistant Kailey Stalder
Associate Editor Brandon Buechley
Editorial Assistant Resham Anand
Illustrator Brandon Campbell
Studio Photographer Kelley Jordan Schuyler
Food Stylist Lovoni Walker
Recipe Tester Ashley Brooks
Copy Editor Kate Rowe
Proofreaders Mira S. Park, Lisa Starnes, Tiffany Taing
Indexer Celia McCoy

First American Edition, 2025
Published in the United States by DK Publishing
1745 Broadway, 20th Floor, New York, NY 10019

The authorized representative in the EEA is Dorling Kindersley
Verlag GmbH. Arnulfstr. 124, 80636 Munich, Germany

Copyright © 2025 B. Dylan Hollis
DK, a Division of Penguin Random House LLC
25 26 27 28 29 10 9 8 7 6 5 4 3 2 1
001-340521-MAY2025

A catalog record for this book
is available from the Library of Congress.
ISBN 978-0-7440-9760-3

DK books are available at special discounts when purchased
in bulk for sales promotions, premiums, fund-raising, or
educational use. For details, contact SpecialSales@dk.com

Printed and bound in China

www.dk.com

This book was made with Forest
Stewardship Council™ certified
paper – one small step in DK's
commitment to a sustainable future.
Learn more at
www.dk.com/uk/information/sustainability

To my mother, Shawn

How could I ever begin to repay
the one who's granted me each night and day?

CONTENTS

South

Introduction...9
Why *Baking Across America*?.....................10
How to Use This Book...............................14
Distinct Ingredients of America...............16
Pie Crust..17

Northeast

NEW ENGLAND.............................20
Culture Capital: Boston.........................22
Boston Cream Pie......................................25
The Toll House Inn Chocolate Chip Cookies.....28
Cranberry Loaf...31
Joe Froggers...32
Lowbush Blueberry Buckle.........................35
Whoopie Pies...36
Cider Doughnuts..39
Maple Creemee Pie...................................40
Snickerdoodles...43
Almond Joy Bars.......................................44
Coffee Milk Cheesecake............................47

MID-ATLANTIC..............................48
Culture Capital: Pittsburgh....................50
Strawberry Pretzel Salad...........................53
Irish Potato Candy.....................................56
Shoofly Pie..59
A New York Cheesecake.............................60
Waldorf En Stase......................................63
Red Velvet Cake..64
Black & White Cookies...............................67
Black Magic Tomato Cake..........................68
Aunt Sallie's Frozen Cream.......................71
Berger Cookies...72
Culture Capital: Washington, DC...........74
Watergate Cupcakes.................................77

SOUTH ATLANTIC.........................82
Culture Capital: Savannah.....................84
Sorghum & Honey Pecan Pie......................87
Peach Cobbler...90
Hush Puppies..93
Key Lime Pie...94
Piñón...97
Spoon Bread...98
Chess Pie..101
Moravian Spice Cookies..........................102
Hummingbird Cake..................................105
Benne Wafers..106
Charleston Chewies.................................109

SOUTH GULF.................................110
Culture Capital: New Orleans..............112
Beignets..114
Bananas Foster..119
Calas...122
Pralines...125
Texas Sheet Cake....................................127
Buttermilk Pie..128
German's Chocolate Cake.........................131
Mississippi Mud.......................................132
Mobile Bay Peanut Butter & Chocolate Chip Pie...137
The Prized Lane Cake...............................139

SOUTHERN INTERIOR.............142
Culture Capital: Hot Springs...............144
Possum Pie..147
Searcy County Chocolate Rolls.................151
The Vanilla Wafers of North Little Rock.....152
Fried Pies..155
Nashville Goo Clusters.............................156
Bourbon Bread Pudding...........................159
Jam Cake..160
Black Walnut Bread.................................163

Midwest

GREAT LAKES......................166
Culture Capital: Chicago....................168
Atomic Cake..171
The Brownie..175
Lemon Fluff..177
Hoosier Pie..181
Buckeyes..182
Bumpy Cake..185
Cherry Winks..186
Mackinac Island Fudge..........................189
Kringle...190
Bundt Pound Cake.................................193

GREAT PLAINS............................194
Culture Capital: Omaha.......................196
Kool-Aid Pie...199
Butter Brickle Bricks.............................202
The Runza...204
Smörbakelser..206
Povitica..209
Gooey Butter Cake.................................212
Dirt Cake...215
Blarney Stones..216
Kuchen...219
Butter Brickle Cake................................220
Honey Rough Riders..............................223

West

MOUNTAIN WEST.......................226
Culture Capital: Yellowstone............228
Huckleberry Scones...............................231
Outdoorsman Bars.................................234
Chokecherry Homestead Muffins.........237
Laramies..240
S'mores Crack...243
Huckleberry Ice Cream.........................244
The Pride of Deseret.............................247
Sunshine Granola....................................248
Palisade Peaches n' Cream Pie.............251
Bizcochitos..252
Hatch Chile & Cheddar Apple Pie......255

SOUTHWEST...................................256
Culture Capital: Palm Springs..........258
Chiffon of Grapefruit............................261
Polvorones Rosas....................................264
Date Cream...269
Mojave Nuggets......................................270
Piñon Tart...273
Prickly Pear Cheesecake........................274
Dateland Iced Oaties..............................277
Silver Miner's Pie...................................278
Pastel Vasco..281
Chocolate Haupia Pie............................282

PACIFIC NORTHWEST............284
Culture Capital: Seattle.....................286
Mapleine Dreams....................................289
Nanaimo Bars...292
Seattle Coffee Crèmes...........................297
Ice Cream Potato...................................298
Potato Macaroons...................................301
Bing Bars..302
Baked Alaska...305

Conclusion..306
Acknowledgments...................................308
Credits..310
Index..312
About the Author....................................320

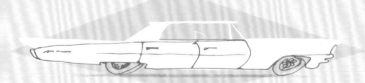

INTRODUCTION

What you have here is a celebration—an ode to America's towns, cities, and countryside, brought to living color by the treasured bakes that render them extraordinary. From little Laramie, Wyoming, to the busy avenues of Boston, Massachusetts, this book charts a sugared path through the heartland in a manner never before attempted. It's a rather grand approach to the whimsy of pies and cakes, but a deserving one if you consider that making a dessert is nothing less than crafting a smile. From all corners of these United States, we will find boundless and exciting ways to deliver just that. *Baking Across America* is a jubilee; a darn-good, old-fashioned party of recipes that is sure to rouse your neighbors to their feet and gather them around whatever table you set.

I'd like you to consider every state's recipe as an endearing postcard, stamped and signed with all the charms each holds dear. Some are beautiful, others are indulgent, and a curious few defy classification. But never before has the USA felt so splendid as when explored through these one hundred recipes of coast-to-coast joy. Why not take a load off and see the sights? I reckon you'll find our road ahead brimming with sweet tales and rich histories.

WHY BAKING ACROSS AMERICA?

Too often, outsiders lambast Americans for not leaving the confines of their nation. As a foreigner myself (from Bermuda), I took note of just how many US citizens had never left the country. It wasn't until I spent my college years in the US that I realized the average American has little need to trek afar, as the vibrancy offered within their borders proves enough to astound even the most travel-hungry of wayfarers.

I recall the first road trip I took from Fort Collins, Colorado to Scottsdale, Arizona. In a single day, I began on the bare high plains, ascended through towering snow-capped mountains, motored down through the pines alongside river-carved canyons, and was spat out into the sun-drenched desert of Utah. The slab-sided, ochre hues of Moab slowly gave way to the dusky sands and watchful cacti of the Sonoran Desert, and I was left utterly dizzy by just how much variety I beheld in a few hundred miles.

With variety in vista came variety in food. I ping-ponged from the alpine sensibilities of fondue and hot cocoa to the desert's spread of chiles and prickly pear. This was a trip that made me look at my collection of yesteryear's community cookbooks in a very different light. Where I had once organized them by decade, I began reading them by state, and boy, what a wild and wacky adventure that kicked off.

The buttermilk obsessions of Texas would fascinate while the unhinged and unbridled "salads" of Minnesota would abhor. I thumbed through the recipes of the South with such disbelief at their tonnages of butter that I wondered if there were enough cows on earth to satisfy their bottomless appetite. From New England's Amish curiosities to California's reverence for the date, it was soon apparent to me that this country had a cavalcade of unique desserts deserving of deeper exploration. Would it not be a learned adventure to visit the epicenters of these dishes? I knew as much. And so, with my shelves of vintage cookbooks soon laid out by region and a grand road trip mapped from coast to coast, there was only one thing left to do: begin *Baking Across America*.

With a title like *Baking Across America*, our scope was clear. We wanted to actually tour the nation with boots-on-the-ground ambitiousness so that we might give you an earnest representation of America through her recipes. The outcome is that half of the dishes in this book were physically baked and shot on location—across nineteen different states and the District of Columbia. We traveled to every region in America with our suitcases packed to the brim with baking supplies, ingredients, and camera equipment, all in the name of the sweetest road trip the 21st century has so far seen.

From the start, my eyes were wide open as we began our journey in Savannah, Georgia. Beneath the Spanish moss, we baked *Sorghum & Honey Pecan Pie* and walked Forsyth Park with *Peach Cobbler* in hand. The southland would see us rouse the Alabama state capitol as we clambered up its marble steps with *The Prized Lane Cake*, only a day before we beckoned the mighty Mississippi with its namesake chocolate dessert. We carried on all the way to the bayous of New Orleans, where our noses were powdered by *Beignets* and our public transportation rights were revoked as we were thrown off a trolley car for disrupting the peace with a tray of *Pralines*. Little Rock, Omaha, and Topeka all witnessed our sugar-laden assault, and we even fended off the ghosts of Missouri's past when we made *Dirt Cake* in a 19th-century mansion on Independence Avenue in Kansas City.

Baking, photographing, and tasting these desserts in their most befitting locations gave full credence to what makes them special and why the locals prefer them. I'd never fully understood *The Brownie* until I savored it in its birthplace, right in the gilded lobby of Chicago's Palmer House, where it first graced patrons some 130 years ago. This is not to be confused with the Parker House in Massachusetts, where I carried the famed *Boston Cream Pie* through the lobby and out onto the Freedom Trail. I learned completely of Seattle's clamoring for coffee as I bobbed and weaved through Pike Place Market. I crossed Pittsburgh's many yellow bridges and waded through West Virginia's Berkeley Springs. Poolside in Palm Springs, California and geyser-side in Yellowstone, Wyoming, we baked up to the Tetons and down to the stone effigies of our nation's capital in Washington, DC. All in the name of upholding what makes America sweet: its people, its places, and its desserts.

Clockwise from top left: Pittsburgh, Savannah, Palm Springs, and Laramie.

HOW TO USE THIS BOOK

This cookbook can be enjoyed in many more ways than what is typical. Sure, it is a collection of remarkable bakes and sweets that is deserving of its use as a kitchen reference. But from the outset, I wanted *Baking Across America* to read like an adventure that captures the essence of the United States' many marvelous locales. Stories and tales from the lower forty-eight and their satellites offer this book as a colorful travelogue, while the original cartographic illustrations alongside the stupendous photography offer an up close reverie to this journey. You will see descriptions of the photographs shot on location, which include where we captured the action on the road. This nation is a tapestry of varied enthusiasms, and from the hot and spicy streets of New Orleans to the haunted mansions of Missouri, this book will place you right in the heart of each state's action, armed with the means to enjoy that which makes the locals proud.

BAKING ARMAMENTARIUM

When choosing a recipe, be sure to read the method in its entirety beforehand. Take note of ingredients that require certain temperatures, and know that substitutions are seldom guaranteed to end well. Ensure your oven is true to temperature by use of a separate oven thermometer, and if you are using an electric oven, be aware of those which heat with a top element. These are known to cook the surface of baked goods far faster than others, and a careful eye or a repositioning downward of your oven rack may be required. The variability with which each oven bakes means baking times aren't always the be-all and end-all. The use of secondary measures to ensure a baked good is done is good practice, like the toothpick test you will see in many of the methods. In *Baking Across America*, all butter is assumed to be salted unless otherwise specified.

The Toasting of Nuts

Many recipes in this book call for toasted nuts. It is good practice to toast nuts, as doing so allows not only their full flavor to flourish, but also for their crunch and snap to remain apparent when baked within cookies and quick breads. To toast nuts, use the following method:

1. Preheat the oven to 350°F (180°C) and spread the required quantity of nuts over an ungreased baking sheet. Nuts are toasted whole and dry. If you have bought nuts in their shells, remove the shells before toasting. Peanuts, however, may be toasted in their shells for an earthier flavor.

2. Toast for 5 to 10 minutes until fragrant. Smaller nuts, or those in pieces, are generally done at 5 to 6 minutes, while larger nuts may require the full 10 minutes. Remove from the oven and let cool on the pan before chopping and incorporating into their accompanying recipe.

The Scalding of Milk

Scalding milk is a crucial step for yeast-leavened bakes, ice creams, and custards. Scalding deactivates proteins in the milk that would otherwise challenge gluten formation, adversely affecting structure and crumb. For ice creams and custards, scalding helps prevent ice-crystal formation caused by these same proteins, in addition to aiding in the cohesive incorporation of eggs and other ingredients. In the simplest terms, to scald milk is to heat it slowly in a saucepan to 180°F (82°C), or just below boiling. We do not boil the milk, as this causes coagulation, skin formation, and curdling. In lieu of a thermometer, heat the milk until it steams and small bubbles form around the sides of the saucepan.

The Beating of Egg Whites & Heavy Cream

Many recipes in this book call for egg whites to be beaten stiff. This is a scary prospect for many, but the undertaking is rather simple should you adhere to a few basic principles. For one, it's a good idea to have a stand mixer or a handheld electric mixer. This will allow you to beat the egg whites stiff in a matter of minutes as opposed to business days. Secondly, your apparatus and bowl (ideally one of metal or glass) should be utterly clean and free of residue, oils, and soaps. Any contamination will bar you from ever reaching stiff peaks. Contamination from the yolk of the egg will do the same. Thirdly, do not underestimate the time required to reach stiffness. It may take upward of 10 minutes of sustained beating. If beating egg whites with added sugar, be sure to add the sugar slowly as the recipe dictates. Peaks are only sufficiently stiff when the beaten mixture stands proud and perpendicular when lifted, with only minor curling.

For whipped cream, the stakes are lower. Of most importance is the temperature of your heavy cream: very cold. For use within recipes, the cream should be beaten only until it stands proud and glossy without collapsing. Note that this is stiffer than whipped cream used for garnish, where a looser texture like that of sour cream is preferred. If you beat your cream to the point of graininess—where it loses its gloss and starts to clump—you have gone too far. It may be acceptably rescued by adding a few tablespoons of unbeaten cream and slowly beating it back to smoothness. Heavy cream, whipping cream, double cream, and full cream all denote creams suitable for whipping, and can be considered interchangeable.

DISTINCT INGREDIENTS OF AMERICA

If you are baking from this book outside of the United States, you may encounter ingredients that are not readily available for purchase. Many of these products helped define America's 20th-century baking landscape and should be sourced whenever possible. However, I will offer you acceptable substitutions to some of these spangled mainstays:

Graham Crackers & Graham Cracker Crumbs

The graham cracker is a biscuit made from graham flour, a product invented by 19th-century health-reformer Sylvester Graham. It is distinct from whole wheat flour only in the varied coarseness of the milled bran and germ. This cracker has been immensely popular with Americans, but not elsewhere.

- To substitute graham crackers and their crumbs, digestive wheat biscuits, malted milk biscuits, or tea biscuits can be finely ground and effectively used.

Jell-O, Flavored Gelatin Mixes & Instant Pudding Mixes

Flavored gelatin was pioneered by Jell-O in New York around the turn of the 20th century. It is a ready-made powder of sugar, gelatin, and flavoring, activated by boiling water and chilled to set.

- To substitute for flavored gelatin mix, international brands like Hartley's or Aeroplane Jelly produce powders that can be used in the same proportions and manner. Look for names like "Jelly Crystals" or "Jelly Powder."

Flavored pudding mixes come in many varieties, once again popularized in America by Jell-O. For the purposes of this book, instant mixes are the only ones used, as opposed to those that require cooking.

- To substitute for instant pudding mixes, international brands like Bird's or Angel Delight produce instant custard mixes in powdered form that do not require cooking. Look for names like "instant custard powder" or "instant pudding crystals."

Cool Whip & Whipped Topping

A head-scratcher for non-Americans, whipped topping is a pre-fluffed, sweetened, and flavored whipped-cream alternative packaged similarly to ice cream. Invented by General Foods as Cool Whip in 1966, it took America by storm with its convenience, affordability, and low lactose content.

- To substitute whipped topping, the easiest method is whipping cream stiff and then measuring by its whipped volume to incorporate it into the chosen recipe. Some sweetness will be lost, but this is generally negligible. To more closely mimic the splendid, processed taste of whipped topping, the international brand Dream Whip produces a powder that can be whipped according to its instructions, measured by its whipped volume, and then incorporated the same way.

Corn Syrup & Molasses

Corn syrup is a 19th-century clarified glucose syrup manufactured from cornstarch that possesses sweetness without flavor. Its use in our book is primarily as a sweetener or as a product by which the crystallization of other sugars within candies, coatings, and frostings is prevented.

- To substitute for corn syrup, use golden syrup or honey.

Molasses is a dark, bitter, and complexly flavored sugar syrup that is a direct byproduct of the sugar-refining process. It can be found in the United States in its regular, unsulphured form. Though not used in this book, sulphured and blackstrap varieties offer tangy and more bitter flavors respectively.

- To substitute for molasses, use black treacle or dark treacle.

PIE CRUST

There will be pies in this book that call for a prepared pastry as part of their greater recipe. And while I feel that this buttery, flaky pastry deserves the right to be featured multiple times alongside them, its recipe will instead wait for you here with eagerness.

SINGLE CRUST FOR 9-INCH (23CM) PIE

1⅓ cups (185g) all-purpose flour

Pinch of salt

½ cup (115g) butter or vegetable shortening, cold and cubed

4–6 tbsp cold water

DOUBLE CRUST FOR 9-INCH (23CM) PIE

2⅓ cups (325g) all-purpose flour

¾ tsp salt

1 cup (225g) butter or vegetable shortening, cold and cubed

6–8 tbsp cold water

METHOD

1. Combine the flour and salt in a large bowl. Using a pastry cutter or two knives, cut half of the butter into the flour until the mixture is uniform. Then, add the remaining butter and repeat until the largest pieces are the size of peppercorns. Add the water and mix until the dough forms a ball. If the mixture does not hold its shape when squeezed in the hand, additional water may be added. Form a disk of dough resembling a hockey puck (for double crust, divide and form two disks), wrap in plastic wrap, and chill for at least 30 minutes.

2. Turn the disk onto a lightly floured board, and with a floured rolling pin, roll out from the center of the dough to form a circle that extends at least 2 inches (5cm) beyond the rim of your pie pan. While rolling the disk of dough, turn occasionally and lightly flour beneath to prevent sticking. This step will be repeated should you need a double-crust pastry.

3. Once the size is adequate, fold the dough gently in half over your rolling pin and center it into the pie pan before patting into place to form the bottom crust. Trim the edges evenly, leaving roughly a 1-inch (2.5cm) overhang beyond the rim. For a single-crust pastry, the overhang may be gently folded over the edge of the pie pan, or it may be fluted or crimped. For a simple crimp, gently press the tines of a fork into the dough to seal it to the edge of the pie pan.

Northeast
NEW ENGLAND · MID-ATLANTIC

New England

Here is a land of tradition and pride,
fiercely independent, with history its guide.
You'll find good bakes where you least expect,
and roads, it appears, they often neglect.
Like a brash great-uncle, blunt and true,
New England calls you a fool but still bats for you.
The coasts here are quaint, and inland sleep forests
that wake with fall colors in the fullest chorus.

BOSTON

Walking Boston, Massachusetts, is a striking exercise in witnessing the birth of this nation in stone and brick. And I do recommend walking, as driving these paths that were originally paved for horse and carriage is an equally impressive exercise in not soiling one's pants. In Boston Common, where I fed pigeons and lazily circled its ponds, it's easy to forget that its grounds stand as the oldest public park in the United States, and that beneath my feet was the same soil that the British camped on before the bloody battle of Lexington and Concord in 1775. Boston is history you can touch, and history you can eat. The Parker House, a grand hotel founded in 1885, which invented the famous Parker House rolls and the beloved *Boston Cream Pie*, played host to us as we sampled espresso martinis and the very dessert that was born within its walls. If there were ever another city that deserves the title of the nation's capital, it would be Boston. It thrives on yesteryear, and—infrastructure notwithstanding—it melds itself into modernity with revolutionary ease. Whether on the Freedom Trail or within the city's reformative halls, Beantown is New England's historic heart.

The Boston Latin School mosaic at Old City Hall, School Street, Boston.

BOSTON CREAM PIE

CAKE • 10-INCH CAKE
PREP: 50 MINUTES • BAKE: 30 MINUTES • CHILL: 1 HOUR

Boston is a city of firsts. It's home to the nation's first public school, first park, and first recorded UFO sighting, which took place in 1639 when colonial governor John Winthrop saw a great pig-shaped light in the sky. Obviously, it's a city whose degree of historical importance cannot be exaggerated. I personally find Boston so important because it's home to the *Boston Cream Pie*. And while many become outraged when they find out it's a cake and not a pie, I say get over it. The Battle of Bunker Hill took place on a completely different hill, and the Tea Party never once included teapots, doilies, or rowdy children.

The dessert features an old-fashioned sponge, crème pâtissière, and a thin coating of ganache. It tastes as beautifully Bostonian today as it did in 1856 when it was invented by Augustine Anezin at the Parker House. Though locals seldom indulge in the treat, they won't deny its legacy. Whenever public occasions need to be marked or visitors long to be welcomed, it's the *Boston Cream Pie* that's reached for.

FILLING
5 eggs, beaten
2 cups (470ml) whole milk
¼ cup (35g) cornstarch
1 cup (200g) granulated sugar
2 tsp vanilla extract
3 tbsp butter

CAKE
7 eggs, separated into yolks and whites
1 cup (200g) granulated sugar
½ tsp baking powder
¼ cup (55g) butter, melted and slightly cooled
1⅓ cups (185g) all-purpose flour
½ tsp cream of tartar
½ tsp salt

TOPPING
1 cup (170g) semisweet chocolate chips
½ cup (120ml) heavy cream

FILLING METHOD

1. In a large saucepan, thoroughly whisk together the milk and the cornstarch until few lumps remain. Cook over medium-low heat to scald. Once steaming and simmering around the edges, use a ladle or spoon to slowly pour about ½ cup of the hot mixture into the beaten eggs while whisking to temper them. Whisk the tempered eggs back into the saucepan.

2. Increase the heat to medium and begin slowly whisking in the sugar. Switch to a spatula or a spoon and stir constantly until the mixture noticeably thickens. Do not boil. This should take about 5 minutes, but it may take longer. Remove from the heat and stir in the vanilla extract and the butter until melted and uniform.

3. Transfer the filling through a sieve and into a heat-proof bowl, allow to cool slightly, and cover by placing plastic wrap atop the vessel and pressing it directly onto the surface of the filling. Refrigerate while preparing the cake.

RECIPE CONTINUES . . .

CAKE METHOD

4. Preheat the oven to 350°F (180°C) and lightly grease a 10-inch (25cm) cake pan.

5. In a large bowl, vigorously whisk together the egg yolks, sugar, and baking powder until all graininess is lost. Whisk in the melted butter, ensuring the butter is not too hot so as to not cook the eggs.

6. Fold in the flour until barely combined. Set aside.

7. In the bowl of a stand mixer fitted with a whisk attachment, or in a large bowl in tandem with a hand mixer, beat the egg whites, cream of tartar, and salt to stiff peaks. Thoroughly mix ⅓ of these beaten egg whites into the batter before gently folding in the remaining ⅔.

8. Turn into the prepared pan and bake for about 30 minutes, or until a toothpick inserted into the cake's center can be removed cleanly. Allow the cake to cool in the pan for 10 minutes before turning it out onto a wire rack to cool completely to room temperature.

ASSEMBLY & TOPPING METHOD

9. Once the cake has completely cooled, use a cake leveler or a sharp serrated knife to laterally slice the cake in half, making two 10-inch (25cm) rounds. If your cake is presenting too crumbly or soft, it may benefit from 1 hour of refrigeration to make this process easier.

10. With the two cake rounds ready, combine the chocolate chips and heavy cream in the top of a double boiler filled with simmering water. Once melted, stir until uniform. Reduce the burner to its lowest setting to keep warm.

11. Prepare a suitable place to assemble the cake, keeping in mind how it will be served. Ideally, use a cake stand with a cake board.

12. Lay down the bottommost round of the cake and spread the chilled filling atop. Allow the filling to abut the edges, but focus any excess in the middle. Center and place the second cake round over the filling.

13. Evenly spread the chocolate overtop of the assembled cake, allowing some drips down the sides. By design, the *Boston Cream Pie* need not look perfect, and both the filling and topping may drip.

14. Refrigerate for a minimum of 1 hour before slicing. Keep refrigerated when not serving.

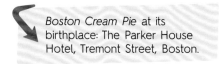

Boston Cream Pie at its birthplace: The Parker House Hotel, Tremont Street, Boston.

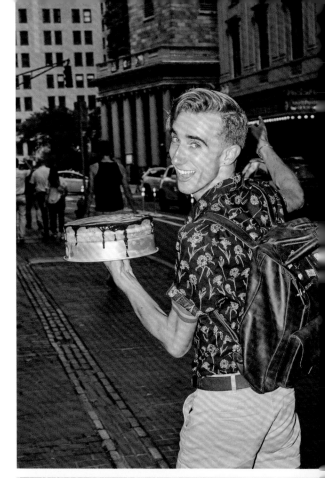

The Freedom Trail, Boston.

THE TOLL HOUSE INN CHOCOLATE CHIP COOKIES

COOKIE • 5 DOZEN
PREP: 20 MINUTES • BAKE: 10 MINUTES

There's no recipe more important to the baking legacy of the United States than the chocolate chip cookie. Its ubiquity has transcended borders just as its versatility has spawned global appeal. It is an icon of the Stars and Stripes, and one that can be traced right to its birthplace in Plymouth County, Massachusetts.

The Toll House Inn in Whitman, though not an actual toll stop, became a beloved rest area on the Old Stage Road—a historic route connecting Weymouth to New Bedford, now part of Route 18. In 1938, Mrs. Ruth Wakefield changed history at the inn's kitchen when she whimsically added broken bits of a semisweet Nestle chocolate bar into her butter-cookie dough. The candy bar failed to melt and mix completely, creating pockets of gooey chocolate that set the state of Massachusetts and the greater world on fire. The clamor for the cookies, which Wakefield called "Toll House Chocolate Crunch Cookies," was so loud that Nestle offered her a lifetime supply of chocolate in exchange for her recipe and endorsement in 1939.

Like the time I fell asleep on the beach, the Toll House Inn burned to a crisp in 1984. But its legacy continues on through Nestle's semisweet chocolate chips—a product invented specifically for Wakefield's cookie craze. Here, I invite you to bake the icon as it was in 1938, featuring gobs of melty chocolate chunks, baked crispy instead of chewy, and portioned smaller than the beloved cookie we know today.

INGREDIENTS

1 cup (225g) butter, softened
¾ cup (150g) granulated sugar
¾ cup (165g) brown sugar
2 eggs, beaten
1 tsp vanilla extract

2¼ cups (315g) all-purpose flour
1 tsp baking soda
1 tsp salt
14oz (400g) semisweet chocolate bar (3½ [4oz] Baker's bars)

METHOD

1. Preheat the oven to 375°F (190°C) and grease a baking sheet with a thin layer of shortening or nonstick cooking spray. Do not grease with butter.

2. In a large bowl, cream together the butter, granulated sugar, and brown sugar until light and fluffy. Mix in the beaten eggs, followed by the vanilla extract.

3. In a separate large bowl, combine the flour, baking soda, and salt. Mix into the creamed mixture until barely combined.

4. With a sharp knife, chop the chocolate bar into small chunks, leaving some pieces fairly large. Add to the dough and mix well.

5. Drop by level tablespoon or small cookie scoop (#60) onto the prepared baking sheet, allowing 2 inches (5cm) between each, and bake for roughly 10 minutes, or until the edges of the cookies have thoroughly crispened. Allow to cool briefly on the pan before freeing with a turner or offset spatula and transferring to a wire rack to cool completely. Wipe away any cookie debris from the pan before baking subsequent batches, regreasing the pan as needed.

Faneuil Hall Square, Boston.

Slices of *Cranberry Loaf* at the Public Garden, Boston.

CRANBERRY LOAF

QUICK BREAD • 9×5-INCH LOAF
PREP: 15 MINUTES • BAKE: 1 HOUR • COOL: 1 HOUR 15 MINUTES

To be completely transparent, I used to think Martha's Vineyard was named after or somehow related to Martha Stewart. It just fits her vibe. Turns out, it was actually named by 17th-century British explorer Bartholomew Gosnold after either his daughter or his mother-in-law, Martha. Long before that, the land now attributed to Martha and much of southeastern Massachusetts was home to the indigenous Wampanoag. It was their knowledge of wild cranberry harvesting that introduced the now-jellified star of American Thanksgivings to the pilgrims.

Not only did Massachusetts host the first (admittedly problematic) Thanksgiving, but it also has become one of the nation's top producers of cranberries. Wareham in Plymouth County is the state's cranberry capital, and when the bogs are flooded each autumn, farmers waist-deep in red luster get to work on packaging up all that defines the start of the yuletide. The Wampanoag Tribe of Gay Head even has its own Cranberry Day, when wild cranberries are foraged on Martha's Vineyard to celebrate harvest traditions. We collectively thank Massachusetts for their cranberries and for all their wise recipes that take advantage of them, like this simple, moist and de-lovely cranberry quick bread.

INGREDIENTS

¼ cup (60ml) vegetable oil

2 eggs

1 cup (200g) granulated sugar

1 tsp vanilla extract

Zest of 1 orange

1 cup (250g) sour cream

2 cups (280g) all-purpose flour

1 tsp baking powder (use ¾ tsp if baking at or above 5,000 feet)

½ tsp baking soda

½ tsp salt

1½ cups (165g) fresh cranberries, halved

1 tbsp orange zest, for glaze

3 tbsp orange juice, for glaze

1½ cup (180g) powdered sugar, for glaze

METHOD

1. Preheat the oven to 350°F (180°C) and thoroughly grease a 9×5-inch (23×13cm) loaf pan.

2. In a large bowl, thoroughly whisk together the oil, eggs, sugar, vanilla extract, orange zest, and sour cream until smooth.

3. In a separate large bowl, combine the flour, baking powder, baking soda, and salt. Add to the wet ingredients and whisk together until uniform. Mix in the cranberries.

4. Turn into the prepared pan and bake for 50 to 60 minutes, or until a toothpick inserted deep into the loaf's center can be removed mostly dry with minimal crumbs. Let the loaf cool in the pan for 15 minutes before turning out onto a wire rack to cool completely to room temperature before glazing, at least 1 hour.

5. To make the glaze, whisk together 1 tablespoon orange zest, 3 tablespoons orange juice, and the powdered sugar. The glaze should be thick, yet pourable. More powdered sugar may be added to thicken, or water added to thin. Pour the glaze over the completely cooled loaf. Once the glaze has hardened, cut and serve by the slice.

JOE FROGGERS

COOKIE • 12 LARGE COOKIES
PREP: 25 MINUTES • CHILL: 1 HOUR • BAKE: 11 MINUTES

It's not often you encounter a cookie the size of a lily pad. For one, lily pads aren't exactly common enough to enable quick or efficient comparison. Secondly, a cookie this large poses some logistical challenges in eating. But that's precisely how the legend of *Joe Froggers* goes: tavern cookies the size of the lily pads on the pond near Joseph and Lucretia Brown's tavern in Marblehead, Massachusetts.

Joe was born into slavery but came to own his salt-shack tavern after enlisting in the Revolutionary War in 1776—a service for which freedom was likely granted. History hasn't forgotten him, his wife, nor the giant, spiced molasses cookies that made "Black Joe's Tavern" famous. The story of this African American couple who owned a business and had to navigate the landscape of the late 18th century holds deep significance. It's a story that has been revived by the Old Sturbridge Village and the town of Marblehead, Massachusetts, and now by you, as you cheer Joe and Lucretia with these moguls of molasses.

INGREDIENTS

¼ cup (45g) vegetable shortening, or lard

½ cup (100g) granulated sugar

½ cup (170g) molasses

¼ cup (60ml) dark rum

2¼ cups (315g) all-purpose flour, divided

½ tsp baking soda

½ tsp salt

1 tsp ground ginger

1 tsp ground allspice

¼ tsp ground cloves

METHOD

1. In a large bowl, cream together the shortening and the sugar until light and fluffy. Beat in the molasses, followed by the rum.

2. Add in 1½ cups (210g) of the flour, the baking soda, salt, and spices. Beat to a uniform paste. Add the remaining 1 cup (140g) flour and mix briefly before switching to your hands and kneading in the bowl until a cohesive dough is formed.

3. Gather and shape the dough into a rough disk, cover with plastic wrap, and refrigerate for a minimum of 1 hour.

4. When ready to bake, preheat the oven to 375°F (190°C) and line a baking sheet with parchment paper.

5. Unwrap the chilled dough, lightly flour a work surface, and roll the disk out to a uniform ¼-inch thickness (0.6cm). Using a large cookie cutter (4 inch/10cm), punch out the cookies and carefully transfer to the baking sheet using a thin spatula. Allowing room for spreading, 6 may baked at a time on a full-size baking sheet.

6. Bake for roughly 11 minutes, or until the cookies have noticeably puffed and their edges are defined. Allow to cool briefly on the baking sheet before transferring to a wire rack to cool completely. Punch the remaining dough and bake in the same manner, gathering and re-rolling once, if necessary.

LOWBUSH BLUEBERRY BUCKLE

BAR • 9×9-INCH PAN
PREP: 20 MINUTES • BAKE: 50 MINUTES • COOL: 1 HOUR

When I initially heard of the Barrens, I imagined it as some craggy hellscape. Maine never struck me as an apocalyptic place, and as far as I know, no bombs have ever been dropped on the Pine Tree State to render it a wasteland. Rest assured, I soon found out that Maine's Barrens are in fact blueberry barrens: rough, rolling expanses devoid of good soil and with very few trees or vertical features, except for the opportunistic and revered lowbush blueberry.

Carpets of green in the spring followed by hues of deep blue in the summer make these barrens anything but, and as the landscape transforms, Mainers in towns like Machias and Jonesboro go hog wild with stained fingers and buckets filled to the brim. Many in Maine shift to a diet of 100 percent berries during this period, and those with any sense take the reserves of these lowbush lovelies and bake mountains of goodies. They're unmistakably tart, complex, and quite literally pop in the mouth when eaten. Bake them into the East Coaster's homestyle buckle, and these royal bars put the wild blueberry in a class beyond compare. So, after you've had your fill of the fresh berries, preheat the oven and prepare to taste the Maine difference.

TOPPING

1 cup (110g) fine graham cracker crumbs

½ cup (110g) brown sugar

1 tsp ground cinnamon

½ cup (115g) butter, cold and cubed

CAKE

¼ cup (55g) butter, softened

¾ cup (150g) granulated sugar

1 egg

1 tsp vanilla extract

2 cups (280g) all-purpose flour

1 tsp baking soda

¼ tsp salt

¾ cup (190g) sour cream

2 cups (300g) wild Maine blueberries, or any small variety (thaw and drain if using frozen)

TOPPING METHOD

1. In a medium bowl, combine the graham cracker crumbs, brown sugar, and cinnamon. Using a pastry cutter or two knives, cut the butter into the dry ingredients until the mixture is a uniform, grainy consistency, like that of wet sand. Set aside and move on to making the cake.

CAKE METHOD

2. Preheat the oven to 350°F (180°C) and thoroughly grease an 9-inch (23cm) square pan.

3. In a large bowl, cream together the butter and granulated sugar. Beat in the egg, followed by the vanilla extract.

4. In a separate large bowl, combine the flour, baking soda, and salt. Working quickly, fold into the creamed mixture, alternating with the sour cream and the blueberries.

5. Turn the batter into the prepared pan and evenly sprinkle the topping over the top. Bake for about 50 minutes, or until the topping has thoroughly browned and a toothpick inserted into the buckle's center can be removed cleanly, save for any blueberries. Allow to cool completely to room temperature in the pan set on a wire rack, at least 1 hour. Cut into squares and serve from the pan.

WHOOPIE PIES

SANDWICH COOKIE • 1½ DOZEN
PREP: 30 MINUTES • BAKE: 10 MINUTES

COOKIES

½ cup (90g) vegetable shortening, or lard

1 cup (220g) brown sugar

2 eggs

1 tsp vanilla extract

2 cups (280g) all-purpose flour

1 tsp baking soda

½ tsp salt

½ cup (60g) natural cocoa powder

1¼ cups (295ml) buttermilk

FILLING

¾ cup (135g) vegetable shortening

2 tsp vanilla extract

¼ tsp butter extract

4½ cups (540g) powdered sugar

¼ cup (60ml) water

COOKIE METHOD

1. Preheat the oven to 375°F (190°C) and line a baking sheet with parchment paper.

2. In a large bowl, whisk together the shortening, brown sugar, eggs, and vanilla extract until smooth and creamy.

3. In a separate large bowl, combine the flour, baking soda, and salt. Sift in the cocoa powder and mix to distribute. Add to the creamed mixture alternately with the buttermilk. Mix until smooth and uniform.

4. Drop by rounded tablespoon or cookie scoop (#50) onto the prepared baking sheet, allowing about 3 inches (8cm) between each. For perfectly smooth whoopie pies, the batter may be piped onto the sheet with a piping bag. Bake for 8 to 10 minutes, or until the cookies have lost their wet appearance and their edges appear defined. Allow the cookies to cool briefly on the baking sheet before carefully transferring to a wire rack with a turner or offset spatula to cool completely to room temperature before filling.

FILLING & ASSEMBLY METHOD

5. Add the shortening to the bowl of a stand mixer fitted with a paddle attachment or a large bowl in tandem with a hand mixer. Beat the shortening until it lightens, followed by the vanilla and butter extracts.

6. Beat in the powdered sugar and the water in alternate additions, 1 cup and 1 tablespoon at a time, respectively. Once all the sugar and water are incorporated, beat on high speed for 2 minutes until white and fluffy, scraping down the bowl intermittently.

7. Transfer the filling to a piping bag. The type of tip is unimportant. Pipe an appreciable amount of filling to the center of a cookie's flat bottom. Keep the tip of the bag barely touching the surface, and pipe without moving the bag until a uniform dollop is formed. Sandwich together with another cookie to make each whoopie pie. Repeat until all cookies are used. Keep covered in a cool place. These need not be refrigerated.

The whoopie pie is a symbol of New England, much like base-ball and the ease with which profanity is doled out to nearby motorists. So when the state of Maine declared *Whoopie Pies* their official treat in 2011, it likely dropped the jaws of thousands of Bay Staters and Pennsylvanians, who soon took up arms to defend a dessert they saw as unclaimable. To mediate, I'd venture that Mainers do have a long-standing love affair with the whoop-ies, and their larger, heftier pies have a surefire place in their state's culinary history.

Labadie's Bakery in Lewiston, Maine, boldly asserts they've been making *Whoopie Pies* since 1925, and some accounts place that date as early as 1918, making them the first to commercialize and popularize the beauties. A white, sugary, soft filling snugly positioned between pillowy chocolate cakes make *Whoopie Pies* unquestionably delicious. Not a day goes by in the Northeast without someone sitting down to take a bite out of this cloudlike New England creation.

New Hampshire

CIDER DOUGHNUTS

DOUGHNUT • 2½ DOZEN
PREP: 1 HOUR 30 MINUTES • COOK: 35 MINUTES

It's difficult to be upset with the end of summer when it means the arrival of apple season in New Hampshire. Though I detest the vexing whine of the Sisyphean leaf blower as it pierces the autumn quiet, at least it heralds good news: falling leaves mean falling apples too.

Apple time in the Granite State is a big deal, even more so since it overlaps with the changing of the leaves. New Hampshire practically becomes a pilgrimage site for throngs of apple pickers and leaf peepers alike. Amid the chaos of children neck-deep in fruit barrels and selfie-obsessed pumpkin spicers, these orchards are the best places to experience apple cider in its highest form. Yes, it's good by the glass, but it's even better in a warm, deep-fried, cinnamon-sugared doughnut. They're a huge part of the NH harvest season, and despite the unchanging, old-fashioned recipes, these fluffy doughnuts manage to foreshadow all the fresh and exciting prospects of the coming winter each year. New Hampshirites are fully aware of how good they've got it, and they'll continue smiling as long as the apples keep a-comin'.

INGREDIENTS

2 cups (470ml) fresh apple cider

¾ cup (180ml) apple cider vinegar

1 cup (200g) granulated sugar

3 eggs, beaten

¼ cup (55g) butter, melted

1 tsp vanilla extract

4 cups (560g) all-purpose flour, plus 1 cup (140g) in reserve

1 (¼oz/7g) packet or 2¼ tsp active dry yeast

3 tsp baking powder

1 tsp baking soda

1 tsp ground nutmeg

1 tsp salt

Canola, corn, or peanut oil, for frying

1 cup (200g) granulated sugar mixed with 4 tbsp ground cinnamon, for coating

METHOD

1. To a large saucepan, add the apple cider and the apple cider vinegar and bring to a boil over high heat, uncovered. This mixture must boil down to a volume of 1 cup (235ml) and will take 25 to 30 minutes. As it approaches 20 minutes, monitor the saucepan for scorching and lower the heat if necessary. Once reduced, allow the reduction to cool to room temperature before proceeding.

2. Transfer the cider reduction to a large bowl and whisk in the sugar and the eggs until uniform. Whisk in the butter, followed by the vanilla extract.

3. In a separate bowl, combine the 4 cups (560g) of flour, the yeast, baking powder, baking soda, nutmeg, and salt. Add to the wet ingredients and mix until a cohesive, workable dough begins to form, switching to your hands when using a spoon presents too difficult. Gather the dough into a ball within the bowl, cover with foil or plastic wrap, and let stand for 1 hour.

4. Punch down the dough and briefly knead again. If the dough is too sticky to work with, more flour may be kneaded in, up to 1 cup (140g).

5. Dust a work surface liberally with flour and turn out the dough. Divide the dough to be rolled into smaller portions if you have a small worktop. Roll evenly to ½-inch (1.3cm) thick and cut with a floured doughnut cutter. Leave the cut rings to rise on the counter while you heat the oil.

6. In a large pot or Dutch oven, add the oil to a depth of at least 2 inches (5cm) and heat to 375°F (190°C).

7. Free the cut doughnuts from the work surface using a turner or offset spatula. Carefully lower them into the oil and fry 2 or 3 at a time until golden brown on each side, about 2 minutes per side. Briefly set the fried doughnuts on a wire rack lined with paper towels before coating in cinnamon sugar while still warm.

MAPLE CREEMEE PIE

ICEBOX PIE • 9-INCH PIE
PREP: 25 MINUTES • BAKE: 12 MINUTES • CHILL: 6 HOURS

I have a soft spot for Vermont. It's made of maple and cream, which can be eaten via cone, spoon, or through a garden hose piped directly to the tanks of this state's dairies and maple farms. The Vermonter's maple creemee is the ruling ice cream in these parts, and through its soft churning and melding with pure, local maple syrup, it's risen to become the coolest object of affection from Jericho to East Montpelier.

Vermont is a state renowned for its sugarbushes, sugar shacks, and sugar works that tap trees and take no prisoners of sweet tooths. When the sap runs in the early spring, the locals and tourists flock to get a taste of what makes Vermont famous. "Sugar on Snow" is the purest method to enjoy this liquid gold, where heated maple syrup is poured over fresh snow and enjoyed in a candylike fashion, but I don't think it comes close to the creemee. This pie is a 9-inch ode to sugaring in the Green Mountain State, with the flavors of the maple creemee skiing perfectly over a graham cracker crust and coming to rest in a soft icebox filling. It's a green run in simplicity, but a double black diamond in thrills.

CRUST
1½ cups (165g) graham cracker crumbs

¼ cup (50g) granulated sugar
½ cup (115g) butter, melted

FILLING
2 (8oz/226g) packages cream cheese, softened
¼ cup (85g) pure maple syrup (not table syrup)
3 tbsp brown sugar
¼ tsp salt

1 tsp vanilla extract
1 tsp maple extract
1 cup (235ml) heavy cream
½ cup (60g) powdered sugar

CRUST METHOD

1. Preheat the oven to 375°F (190°C).

2. In a medium bowl, combine all the crust ingredients and mix until the mixture is a uniform consistency, like that of wet sand.

3. Evenly press the crumb mixture into a 9-inch (23cm) pie dish, ensuring the sides are well covered.

4. Bake for 12 minutes. Remove from the oven and place on a wire rack to cool completely. The crust must be cool prior to filling.

FILLING METHOD

5. In the bowl of a stand mixer fitted with a paddle attachment, or in a large bowl in tandem with a hand mixer, beat the cream cheese until smooth and uniform, about 2 minutes. Beat in the maple syrup, brown sugar, salt, and vanilla and maple extracts. Scrape down the sides of the bowl as needed.

6. In a clean bowl, again with a mixer (this time with a whisk attachment), beat the heavy cream and powdered sugar until stiff. Beat slightly stiffer than you would want for whipped cream, but not to the point of becoming clumpy.

7. Fold the whipped cream into the cream-cheese mixture until smooth and uniform. Transfer to the cooled pie shell. Refrigerate overnight, or for a minimum of 6 hours. Keep refrigerated. The pie is well suited to freezing and may be served frozen.

Tip

If you don't wish to make your own crust, you can use a store-bought graham cracker pie crust

SNICKERDOODLES

COOKIE • 3 DOZEN
PREP: 25 MINUTES • BAKE: 10 MINUTES

Although Connecticut is known as the Nutmeg State, it's the cinnamon snickerdoodle that comes in as a Connecticut favorite. If one flips through enough church and community cookbooks from the Constitution State, one might start to believe there's a secret underground cinnamon conspiracy, as Connecticut pens a disproportionately large amount of snickerdoodle recipes to what their population would suggest.

The only judicious conclusion is that Connecticuters are trapped. They've boxed themselves in as nutmeggers and are forced to hide their adoration for the Amish-born, cakey, and fluffy cookies in hushed tones. I'm not one to blow their cover, but this recipe deserves praise. It's a blend of Connecticut's best and proves that though nutmeggers may love their spice, *Snickerdoodles* are the cookies that capture their hearts, whether they realize it, or not.

INGREDIENTS

¾ cup (135g) vegetable shortening, or lard

¼ cup (55g) butter, softened

¾ tsp salt

1½ cups (300g) granulated sugar

2 eggs

3 cups (420g) all-purpose flour

1 tsp baking soda

3 tsp cream of tartar

½ cup (100g) granulated sugar, mixed with 3 tbsp ground cinnamon

METHOD

1. Preheat the oven to 350°F (180°C) and line a baking sheet with parchment paper.

2. In a large bowl, beat together the shortening and the butter until uniform. Cream in the salt and the sugar until light and fluffy before beating in the eggs.

3. In a separate large bowl, combine the flour, baking soda, and cream of tartar. Mix into the creamed mixture, switching to your hands when needed to knead into a cohesive ball of dough.

4. Pinch off heaping tablespoons of the dough or scoop by cookie scoop (#50), and roll the portioned dough in the cinnamon-sugar mixture before placing them on the prepared baking sheet, allowing 2 inches (5cm) between each. Do not flatten them.

5. Bake for 10 minutes. Allow the cookies to cool briefly on the baking sheet before transferring to a wire rack to cool completely to room temperature.

6. Optionally, to amplify the classic cinnamon-sugar flavor, make two separate batches of cinnamon sugar: one for rolling the raw dough in and one for rolling the baked cookies in.

ALMOND JOY BARS

CONFECTION · 24 BARS
PREP: 30 MINUTES · CHILL: 1 HOUR · COOK: 5 MINUTES

Like the second *c* in its name, Connecticut is easily overlooked by those out west. To them, it could be any of the itty-bitty states within the squashed lines of the Northeast. But to New Englanders and East Coasters alike, Connecticut sits conspicuously as a fashionable, if not uppity, docksider-wearing member of the Atlantic family.

Though the babies born here shoot out pre-accoutred in Vineyard Vines and Lacoste, not everything in Connecticut is Ivy League. North of New Haven in a town called Naugatuck, the confectionery company Peter Paul humbly churned out the first ever Almond Joy in 1946. This spawned not only a nationwide hankering for milk chocolate and coconut, but also forever cemented Almond Joys as the proud export of this state. Hershey's may have closed the Peter Paul Naugatuck plant in 2008, ending a sixty-year legacy, but you can carry the torch with this copycat recipe. It's unusually fun to prep, entrancing to veil in chocolate, and stunningly close in taste to Connecticut's icon from '46.

Tip

For easier coating, this recipe calls for more chocolate than is needed to cover all the candies. The remaining chocolate may be poured into a thin layer on a sheet of parchment or wax paper to set and be used later for melting purposes.

INGREDIENTS

1 (14oz/396g) can sweetened condensed milk

2 tbsp imitation vanilla flavoring

2 cups (240g) powdered sugar

4 cups (340g) desiccated coconut, or unsweetened coconut flakes pulsed fine in a food processor

48 whole salted almonds, toasted (roughly 1 cup/140g)

4 cups (680g) semisweet chocolate chips

2 tsp vegetable shortening, or solid coconut oil

METHOD

1. Line a 9×13-inch (23×33cm) pan or casserole dish with a parchment sling.

2. In a large bowl, combine the sweetened condensed milk and imitation vanilla. Mix in the powdered sugar.

3. Mix in the coconut, ensuring all coconut is coated and no dry spots remain. Knead together with wetted hands if necessary.

4. Transfer the mixture to the prepared pan and thoroughly press into an even layer. Compact further using a flat-bottomed implement, like a heavy glass. Ensure the coconut mixture is of an even thickness throughout.

5. Press the almonds into the coconut in the fashion of a grid: 8 almonds across the pan's longer side and 6 up the shorter, making 48 in total. Envision each rectangular bar to be cut to include two nuts. If the almonds do not firmly adhere, they may be dipped in water before pressing.

6. Freeze the pan for a minimum of 1 hour until firm. If the pan does not fit in the freezer, refrigerate for 2 hours.

7. In the top of a double boiler filled with simmering water, add the chocolate chips and the shortening. Once melted, stir until uniform. Reduce the burner to its lowest setting to keep warm.

8. Remove the pan from the freezer or fridge, free any stuck sides with a sharp knife, and lift the sheet by the parchment sling onto a cutting board. Remove the parchment, and cut into even, rectangular bars, with each bar including 2 almonds, for a total of 24 bars.

9. Holding a fork in your nondominant hand, place a bar on it and dip into the chocolate. Using a knife in the other hand, coat the top and sides of the bar. Lift, and scrape the bottom of the fork with the knife to remove any excess chocolate. Use the knife to slide the bar off the fork and onto a sheet of parchment or wax paper. Repeat with the remaining bars and chocolate. Let the bars sit at room temperature for the chocolate to set.

10. If your kitchen is too warm or if the chocolate fails to set after 90 minutes, the bars may be refrigerated. In either case, store refrigerated in an airtight container once set.

COFFEE MILK CHEESECAKE

CHEESECAKE • 9-INCH SPRINGFORM
PREP: 30 MINUTES • BAKE: 40 MINUTES • CHILL: 3 HOURS

While everyone else squeezes chocolate syrup into milk to make chocolate milk, the Rhode Islander reaches for a sturdy and somewhat automotive-looking bottle of coffee syrup to make their time-honored and beloved drink: coffee milk.

Here in Lil' Rhody, these pitch-black bottles of concentrated, sweetened java keep the Rhode Islander in a constant caffeinated state of New England preparedness, ready to battle DMV clerks, wayward tourists, or the general decrepitude of their roads. No matter the clientele, coffee milk is unanimously praised, whether by the artsy Providence newbie or the old-money dandy in Newport. It is both a sipping respite and a cool refresher wherever it's made its way into the coffee cabinet: coffee milk's milkshake equivalent. For your delight, we present an equally New England–baked cheesecake imbued with all the tastes of Rhode Island. Set within a crisp and curious saltine crust, this smooth and velour-like *Coffee Milk Cheesecake* is a big win for the union's smallest state.

Tip

Autocrat, Eclipse, or Coffee Time syrups are recommended.

CRUST

50 saltine crackers, finely crushed (preferably using a food processor)

⅓ cup (65g) granulated sugar

⅔ cup (150g) butter, melted

FILLING

2 (8oz/226g) packages cream cheese, softened

3 eggs

2 tsp vanilla extract

½ cup (120ml) coffee syrup (see Tip)

¼ cup (22g) instant coffee granules

¼ cup (35g) cornstarch

¼ tsp salt

CRUST METHOD

1. Preheat the oven to 400°F (200°C) and lightly grease the sides of a 9-inch (23cm) springform pan.

2. In a medium bowl, combine the saltine crumbs, sugar, and butter. Mix until uniform and press evenly into the bottom of the pan and partway up the sides to form a crust.

3. Bake for 8 minutes. Let cool on a wire rack while you prepare the filling. Reduce the oven temperature to 375°F (190°C).

FILLING METHOD

4. In the bowl of a stand mixer fitted with a paddle attachment, or in a large bowl in tandem with a hand mixer, beat the cream cheese until smooth and uniform, about 2 minutes. Beat in the eggs one at a time, waiting until each egg has fully combined before adding the next. Beat in the vanilla extract, followed by the coffee syrup and the instant coffee granules. The instant coffee need not be fully dissolved. Finally, beat in the cornstarch and salt until the filling is smooth and uniform. Scrape down the sides as needed.

5. Transfer the filling to the crust. (It needn't be completely cool.) Bake for about 30 minutes, or until the cheesecake's center no longer wobbles when jostled.

6. Transfer the pan to a wire rack to cool completely to room temperature, then refrigerate overnight or for a minimum of 3 hours. Do not refrigerate the cheesecake while warm. Once chilled, uncouple the pan, and slice as you would a pie. Keep refrigerated.

NEW YORK

TAXI

NEW JERSEY

PENNSYLVANIA

PITTSBURGH

MARYLAND

DELAWARE

WASHINGTON, DC

Mid-Atlantic

Welcome to the heart of the East Coast's roar,
the thrumming center where commerce soars.
Ports of entry mark the nation's parentage
of Yankee gumption and baker's heritage.
In one afternoon, these states you can tour,
through parallel parking and turnpike gore.
Her concrete jungles and squeals of trains
echo the Mid-Atlantic's boldest refrains.

Culture Capital

PITTSBURGH

Riveters, smelters, blacksmiths, and metalworkers built this city in the cacophony of America's industrial past. Establishing itself as the Iron City, Pittsburgh can be thanked as the force behind the great expansion West, feeding a nation thirsty for railroads, bridges, and hulking machines of industry. Miser-turned-softy Andrew Carnegie leveraged Pittsburgh's might as the Steel City when his cornering of improved metal-working processes made him—and in many ways this city—among the richest in America's history. If Philadelphia is the brains of Pennsylvania, then Pittsburgh is assuredly the brawn. And today, that strength remains evident should you walk its broad spans of steel bridges that tame and conquer the confluence of the Allegheny, Monongahela, and Ohio Rivers with man's might. Pittsburgh is an easily overlooked city, but its inland beauty, echoes of industry, and role as a repository for some of Pennsylvania's most unique recipes make it a stunning respite from the coastal din of the Mid-Atlantic metropolises.

Strawberry Pretzel Salad photographed on Carnegie Street, Lawrenceville, Pittsburgh.

STRAWBERRY PRETZEL SALAD

BAR • 9×13-INCH PAN
PREP: 25 MINUTES • BAKE: 8 MINUTES • CHILL: 3 HOURS

Pennsylvania is a wide girly, but too often she's reduced to the metropolitan center of Philadelphia within the urban, heavily trafficked Northeast corridor. Yes, Billy Penn lords over that cheesesteak city with frightening verticality, but travel west past Lancaster and Harrisburg, and a comparatively unsung expanse waits for its time in the limelight. Quaint towns in Butler, Mercer, and Crawford Counties have long been making the curious *Strawberry Pretzel Salad* for their gatherings, and they, along with the steel capital of Pittsburgh, deserve representation.

Built upon the pretzel-centric tastes of the early German immigrants to Pennsylvania, the *Strawberry Pretzel Salad* adds the gelatin-obsessed ideals of the 1960s to the potluck-pleasing filling of Cool Whip and cream cheese. It's a soft, cool reprieve with a salty crunch that's been honed by generations to satiate those of any age, and this recipe provided by my editor's mother is among the best of them.

CRUST
2 cups (220g) pretzel crumbs, crushed moderately fine

¼ cup (50g) granulated sugar
¾ cup (170g) butter, melted

FILLING & TOPPING
1 (8oz/226g) package cream cheese, softened

1 cup (200g) granulated sugar

¼ tsp salt

1 (8oz/226g) tub Cool Whip, thawed

2 cups (470ml) boiling water

2 (3oz/85g) packages strawberry gelatin

2½ cups (425g) sliced frozen strawberries

CRUST METHOD

1. Preheat the oven to 400°F (200°C).

2. In a large bowl, combine all crust ingredients until a uniform crumb is formed. Evenly spread and pat this mixture into the bottom of a 9×13-inch (23×33cm) pan. Bake for 8 minutes. Remove the pan from the oven and let cool to room temperature on a wire rack.

FILLING & TOPPING METHOD

3. In a large bowl, beat together the cream cheese, sugar, and salt until uniform. Fold in the Cool Whip and spread evenly over the cooled crust. Refrigerate as you continue.

4. In a separate large heatproof bowl, pour the boiling water over the gelatin and stir to dissolve. Add the strawberries and refrigerate for 20 minutes, or until the gelatin thickens but has yet to fully set.

5. Remove the pan from the fridge and pour the strawberry mixture on top, evenly distributing the berries in the process. Return to the fridge for a minimum of 3 hours before slicing into bars and serving from the pan. Keep refrigerated.

Tip
It's important to use frozen strawberries for this recipe, so please don't substitute with fresh strawberries.

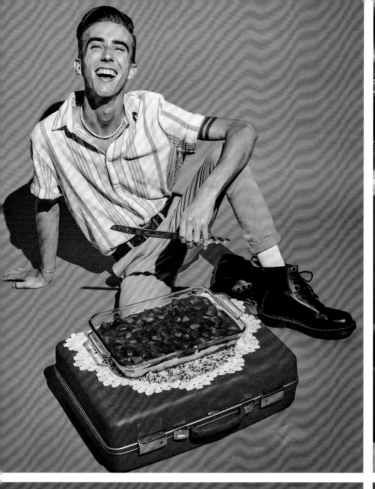
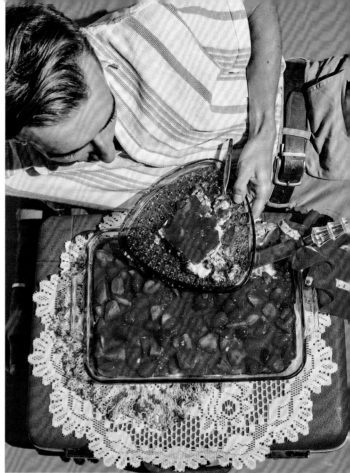

Schenley Plaza and the Cathedral of Learning, Oakland, Pittsburgh.

A Community Pa
the Renaissance of Pitts
City of Pittsburgh   Pittsbu
2003 - 2007 Majo

Pennsylvania
IRISH POTATO CANDY

CONFECTION · 3 DOZEN SMALL CANDIES
PREP: 30 MINUTES · CHILL: 1 HOUR 30 MINUTES

This recipe from Philadelphia is neither Irish, nor does it contain potato. And while it is entirely American, its origins can be traced to the Pennsylvania Germans and Pennsylvania Dutch. There is obviously a lot going on here, but to our benefit, I'm happy to report from PA that all of it is good.

Every March, the shopkeepers and confectioneries of Philadelphia put out these dusty, potato-looking morsels of coconut for the enjoyment of the City of Brotherly Love. Locals might remember a time when they haphazardly made them in school. Should they not, they'll certainly remember devouring them in their yard and the funny powdered lip that ensued. *Irish Potato Candy* may be mass-produced in these parts, but even so, it manages to retain that special type of goodwill that homemade candies exude. It's soft, it's sweet, and it's chewy.

Its exterior, most often covered with a singular dose of cinnamon, has been tweaked by Pennsylvania candymakers like Stutz to include cocoa powder, and sometimes even a powdered-coffee coating. With this recipe, I'll argue for the winning combo of cinnamon and cocoa to save you from the smoker's cough that a swift inhalation of pure cinnamon might induce.

INGREDIENTS

¼ cup (55g) butter, softened

4oz (113g) cream cheese, softened

½ tsp salt

½ tsp coconut extract (optional)

2 tsp vanilla extract

4 cups (480g) powdered sugar

2 cups (170g) desiccated coconut

1 cup (120g) walnut halves, toasted and very finely chopped

½ cup (60g) cocoa powder, for coating

3 tbsp ground cinnamon, for coating

Pine nuts, for decoration

METHOD

1. In the bowl of a stand mixer fitted with a paddle attachment, or in a large bowl in tandem with a hand mixer, beat together the butter and cream cheese until lightened, about 2 minutes. Beat in the salt and the extracts before slowly beating in the powdered sugar, ¼ cup (30g) at a time. Beat until very smooth.

2. Using a spatula, mix in the coconut and the walnuts until uniformly distributed before covering the bowl and refrigerating for a minimum of 1 hour.

3. Once chilled, line a baking sheet or tray that will fit in your fridge with parchment paper. Pinch off golf-ball-size portions of the mixture and shape with your hands into irregular oblong potato shapes. Place them on the lined sheet and return it to the fridge to cool and dry for 30 minutes.

4. In a small bowl, mix together the cocoa powder and the cinnamon. Roll and coat each "potato" thoroughly, pressing a couple of pine nuts into each one to mimic sprouts. Place them in an airtight container and store in the fridge.

Irish Potato Candy on Smithfield Street, downtown Pittsburgh.

A slice of *Shoofly Pie* in Allegheny Cemetery, Lawrenceville, Pittsburgh.

SHOOFLY PIE

PIE • 9-INCH PIE
PREP: 20 MINUTES • BAKE: 40 MINUTES • COOL: 3 HOURS

Lancaster County, Pennsylvania is a place outside of time. Things here feel definitively different. Those who grew up visiting Lancaster will recall green hills, undulating farmlands, and red, covered bridges. Whether traveling through Intercourse, Blue Ball, or the community of Fertility, this part of PA is ripe with titillating towns that are as unorthodoxly orthodox as the baked goods their Amish residents churn out. Here, everyone has their favorite PA Dutch delight, be it friendship bread or sticky buns. But, right alongside horse-drawn buggies, nothing is more unabashedly Amish than *Shoofly Pie*.

Classified as brethren to the coffee cake, this sugary crumble is a sumptuous bed of sweet, tangy molasses held neatly together by pie pastry. *Shoofly Pie* is unusual when compared to other pies, as there's no fruit, no nuts, no lattice work, and no ice cream. Instead of being eaten as a dessert, the Pennsylvania Dutch reach for this sturdy anomaly as a breakfast item alongside their coffees. This hair-on-the-chest combination makes my love of lemon tea and Pop-Tarts seem positively yuppie by comparison.

To the northeast, the folks of Lehigh County make their *Shoofly Pie* as a "dry-bottom" variant, where the crumb mixture is added to the shell alternately with the molasses, resembling more of a coffee cake. But in Lancaster, the recipe calls for a "wet-bottom" pie. It is a rich experience to slice into this tamed molasses and buttery crumb, and it's with earnestness that I thank the Anabaptist traditions for this pitch-black beauty.

INGREDIENTS

1 single-crust Pie Crust (page 17)

1 cup (140g) plus 1 tbsp all-purpose flour, divided

½ cup (110g) brown sugar

1 tsp ground cinnamon

½ cup (115g) butter, cold and cubed

¾ cup (255g) molasses

⅓ cup (80ml) water

1 egg

⅛ tsp salt

½ tsp baking soda

METHOD

1. Fit the prepared pastry into a 9-inch (23cm) pie pan and crimp the edges. Place a baking sheet or sheet of aluminum foil on the lowest rack to catch potential spillage. Preheat the oven to 375°F (190°C).

2. In a large bowl, combine the cup of flour, the brown sugar, and the cinnamon. Add the butter and rub it into the dry ingredients with your fingers or a pastry cutter until the mixture is a uniform, crumbly consistency. Set aside.

3. In a large saucepan, thoroughly whisk together the molasses, water, egg, salt, baking soda, and remaining tablespoon of flour. Cook over low heat until it foams, whisking constantly.

4. Once the molasses mixture has foamed, carefully pour it into the prepared pie shell, evenly sprinkle the crumb mixture on top, and bake on the middle rack for 40 minutes, or until the crumb and crust are golden brown. Transfer the pan to a wire rack, and allow to cool completely to room temperature, a minimum of 3 hours. The pie will not be set nor sliceable while warm.

A NEW YORK CHEESECAKE

CHEESECAKE • 9-INCH SPRINGFORM
PREP: 25 MINUTES • BAKE: 1 HOUR 40 MINUTES • COOL: 1 HOUR • CHILL: 6 HOURS

CRUST

1½ cups (165g) graham cracker crumbs

⅓ cup (65g) granulated sugar

½ cup (115g) butter, melted

CHEESECAKE

3 (8oz/226g) packages cream cheese, room temperature

1lb (454g) small-curd cottage cheese, room temperature

1¾ cups (350g) granulated sugar

3 eggs, room temperature

Yolks of 2 eggs, room temperature

3 tbsp cornstarch

1 tbsp vanilla bean paste

Zest and juice of 1 lemon

½ tsp salt

Tip

This cheesecake uses cottage cheese. If you prefer a perfectly smooth texture, purée the cottage cheese before beginning. Also, ensure your cheeses and eggs are at room temperature to help prevent cracking during baking.

CRUST METHOD

1. Create a watertight seal around a tall 9-inch (23cm) springform pan by using oven bags or temperature-safe brine bags, or by wrapping it in extra-wide aluminum foil. The cheesecake will bake and cool in a water bath, so it is imperative to prevent water ingress. Wrapping the pan with layers of regular-width foil will not work, as water will be drawn in through suction as the cheesecake cools.

2. Lightly grease the bottom and sides of the pan. In a medium bowl, combine the crust ingredients and mix until a uniform crumb is formed. Press the mixture into the bottom of the pan and partway up the sides, creating a shallow well. Set aside.

CHEESECAKE METHOD

3. In the bowl of a stand mixer fitted with a paddle attachment, or in a large bowl in tandem with a hand mixer, beat the cream cheese until smooth and uniform. Beat in the cottage cheese, followed by the granulated sugar. Beat very well, about 2 minutes.

4. Beat in the eggs and egg yolks, one at a time until well incorporated. Beat in the remaining ingredients, scraping down the bowl as necessary.

5. Turn the mixture into the prepared crust. It will rise minimally and can be filled to ½ inch (1.3cm) below the rim. Vigorously tap the pan on the counter to free any bubbles of air. Let the mixture sit in the pan as you preheat the oven to 350°F (180°C).

6. When the oven is at temperature, place the prepared, watertight pan into a larger vessel that allows water to be added to a height of 2 inches (5cm) up the sides of the springform pan, such as a roasting pan. Place the unfilled assembly in the oven, carefully fill the larger vessel with hot tap water, and bake for about 1 hour and 40 minutes, or until the cheesecake wobbles only slightly in the center when jostled and has browned thoroughly on top.

7. Turn off the oven and leave the door ajar, letting the cheesecake remain in the water bath. Let cool until the water is lukewarm, about 1 hour. Dispense with the water bath and let the cheesecake cool completely to room temperature before refrigerating overnight, or for a minimum of 6 hours. Do not refrigerate a warm cheesecake. When ready to serve, run a sharp, warm knife around the edges before uncoupling the pan and cutting the cake into slices. Keep refrigerated.

Living in New York City commands respect like the ocean demands assiduousness. Those who naively mistake it for a trendy backdrop to their thirties do not last long, and he who refuses to adapt to the city's expectations is soon left penniless, alone, or both. Conversely, those who listen intently, harbor spirit, and leer back at Gotham's prying streets with restless resolve will be rewarded with a setting that invigorates and inspires. The exception to this rule are the unhinged: eccentrics and those whose screws have loosened do rather well here.

I know I'd do great in NYC—perhaps through citing the previous point, sure—but the presence of *A New York Cheesecake* is another mighty powerful incentive. Cheesecake is older than dirt, but the New York way of dense cream cheese baked within a graham crust is thanks to Arnold Reuben in the '20s and affirmed by copious others after. The locals will offer a firm handshake to its rich, luxurious filling, and while the best can only be achieved by stout grandmothers with frilly aprons, this cheesecake holds a candle to Lady Liberty's flame.

WALDORF EN STASE

The Waldorf salad, invented at the titular New York hotel by maître d' Monsieur Oscar Tschirky in the spring of 1896, is the perfect salad, as far as I'm concerned, with its snap of celery and tart apples mixed with lightly sweetened mayonnaise. I would argue that New York's Waldorf Astoria is similarly perfect and is among the world's most important and iconic hotels. It's a bastion of America's high society where ballrooms once hummed with cha-chas, and New Year's Eve was all but defined by Guy Lombardo's big band broadcasts from its top floors. The current hotel was completed in 1931 on Park Avenue, and stands today as an echo of the Big Apple's gilded past.

This recipe is a 1950s continuation of the original Waldorf salad, featuring the now-required grapes, raisins, and walnuts. It's also encased in gelatin and sits in stasis—*en stase*: joviality defined. Though my tongue is in my cheek, you have my assurance that if you were to ever like but one gelatin mold, it would be this one. Serve it to the astonishment of your fellow tablemates, slice it cleanly, and bask in its slab-sided absurdity.

INGREDIENTS

½ cup (120ml) water

¼ tsp salt

1 (0.25oz/7g) sachet or 1 tbsp unflavored gelatin crystals

3 green apples, cored and finely chopped (about 420g)

Zest of 1 lemon

Juice of ½ lemon

2 cups (350g) small seeded grapes, quartered

½ cup (60g) minced celery

1 cup (160g) raisins

1 cup (120g) walnut halves, toasted and finely chopped

1½ cups (355ml) heavy cream

¼ cup (50g) granulated sugar

1 cup (230g) mayonnaise

METHOD

1. In a small saucepan, combine the water and the salt. Evenly sprinkle the gelatin over the water to soften. Do not heat, and set aside.

2. Place the apples in a large bowl and toss in the lemon zest and juice. Add the grapes, celery, raisins, and walnuts.

3. In the bowl of a stand mixer fitted with a whisk attachment, or in a large bowl in tandem with a hand mixer, beat the cream, slowly adding the sugar, until stiff. Set aside in the refrigerator.

4. Heat the softened gelatin mixture over low heat until steaming and simmering around the edges, stirring occasionally. Do not allow it to boil. Remove from the heat and let it cool for 5 minutes. Whisk in the mayonnaise. The mixture will be thin and may appear curdled.

5. Thoroughly mix the mayonnaise mixture into the fruit mixture before folding in the whipped cream until uniform. Grease your 10-cup Bundt pan or fluted mold with nonstick spray and fill with the salad. Refrigerate overnight, or for a minimum of 6 hours.

6. To unmold, briefly submerge the pan in a vessel of hot water up to its rim. Submerging for too long will cause weeping. Remove from the water, place a cutting board or serving tray atop, and invert. Repeat should the mold not release. Pat dry any liquid. Slice with a very sharp knife and serve chilled. Store refrigerated.

Tip

For a presentable, sliceable, and functional mold, it is imperative to cut the ingredients very finely, and to choose a nonstick mold.

RED VELVET CAKE

LAYER CAKE • TWO 9-INCH LAYERS
PREP: 1 HOUR • BAKE: 30 MINUTES • CHILL: 15 MINUTES

CAKE

½ cup boiling water

3 tbsp cocoa powder, non-dutched

½ cup (90g) vegetable shortening, or lard

1¾ cup (385g) brown sugar

2 eggs

1 tbsp white vinegar

2 tsp vanilla extract

A few drops of red gel food coloring, optional

2 cups (280g) all-purpose flour

1 tsp salt

1 tsp baking soda

¾ cup (180ml) buttermilk

ERMINE FROSTING

½ cup (70g) all-purpose flour

2 cups (400g) granulated sugar

¼ tsp salt

2 cups (470ml) whole milk

1½ cups (340g) unsalted butter, softened and cubed

1 tbsp vanilla bean paste

Tip

This frosting is roux-based, with flour and butter cooked to a paste. It's important to cook and thicken the ermine frosting's flour mixture low and slow. Cooking at higher temperatures may result in thickening before the flour has cooked completely, leaving the frosting with a raw-flour taste.

CAKE METHOD

1. Preheat the oven to 350°F (180°C) and grease two 9-inch (23cm) cake pans.

2. In a small bowl, pour the boiling water over the cocoa powder and stir to combine. Set aside.

3. In a large bowl, cream together the shortening and the brown sugar until light and fluffy. Beat in the eggs, vinegar, and vanilla extract. Beat in the food coloring, if using, to form a deep red.

4. In a separate large bowl, combine the flour, salt, and baking soda. Fold into the creamed mixture alternately with the chocolate mixture and the buttermilk.

5. Divide evenly into the two prepared cake pans and bake for 30 minutes, or until toothpicks inserted into the cakes' centers can be removed cleanly. Allow the cakes to cool in their pans for 20 minutes before turning out onto a wire rack to cool completely to room temperature before frosting.

ERMINE FROSTING METHOD

6. In a large saucepan over medium-low heat, combine the flour, sugar, and salt and slowly whisk in the milk. Whisk constantly until the mixture thickens to a custard-like consistency, about 12 minutes.

7. Remove from the heat and pass the mixture through a sieve into a heatproof bowl. Beat the mixture until cool using a stand mixer or a hand mixer for about 10 minutes. The mixture must be cool enough to not melt the butter, and the butter must be soft enough to incorporate without lumps. Slowly add the butter while beating, followed by the vanilla bean paste. Beat until smooth and fluffy.

8. Prepare a suitable place to assemble the cake, keeping in mind how it will be served. Ideally, use a cake stand with a cake board.

9. Using an offset spatula, spread a generous layer of the frosting evenly atop the first cake. Place and center the second cake atop the first. Apply a scant base layer of frosting over the whole cake, smoothing out the sides and filling any gaps. It is expected that this layer will have a few crumbs, but avoid returning any cake crumbs to the bowl of frosting. Once covered, refrigerate both the cake and the remaining frosting for 15 minutes.

10. Once chilled, frost the entire cake in earnest. This frosting benefits from broad, decorative strokes of the offset spatula, but you may choose to transfer the filling to a piping bag and frost as desired.

Food historians have long languished over who invented *Red Velvet Cake*. Without dated written records of every baked good from every kitchen, the task becomes more an issue of anthropology than mere pinpointing. From Southern roots to Depression-era recipe advertisements, this cake has many viable origins. History often cites those who first published or popularized a dish as its progenitor in lieu of a concrete inventor. This is the case with the famous Waldorf Astoria hotel in New York City that put *Red Velvet Cake* on the menu in the late 1920s, quickly cementing it as one of America's standout cakes. You'll notice this isn't the only recipe in this book from our gilded Waldorf.

This early *Red Velvet Cake* was a novel variation of chocolate cake that used non-dutch cocoa powder in scant proportions instead of the more common melted-chocolate method. By also controlling the acidity of the batter, bakers noticed that these cocoa-powder cakes took on ruddy hues and were quick to market the fact. Without food coloring, these early cakes were never truly red, but their mere hint of color was enough to enamor and inspire. This recipe boasts a magnificent ermine roux frosting that firmly holds the vintage mahogany crumb with 1920s sophistication.

BLACK & WHITE COOKIES

COOKIE • 1 DOZEN
PREP: 40 MINUTES • BAKE: 15 MINUTES

A black and white, or less commonly a half and half, is a genial, two-tone frosted cookie that has graced the hands of New Yorkers for more than a century. They're large to begin with, but whenever they go by the name half-moons, it's very likely they'll need to be held by both hands. These cookies are cakey, sweet, and delightful. Importantly, there isn't a singular recipe or method that defines them, but rather their coloration alone.

Black & White Cookies are a bonafide curious fixture of this city and state. Native New Yorkers will happily nod to its association with their home—speaking to its ubiquity in city bakeries and bagelries— but nobody has much else to say about it. The cookie has become so common and expected that it's been rendered nearly invisible.

It isn't that they aren't enjoyed. Underwriters and MTA operators chow down on them just as schoolchildren and the city's traffic officers do. Yes, *Black & White Cookies* are a fixture of NYC that easily go unnoticed, but should they ever disappear from this marvelous metropolis, their absence would be painfully evident.

COOKIES

½ cup (115g) butter, softened

1 cup (200g) granulated sugar

2 eggs

2 tsp vanilla extract

2½ cups (350g) all-purpose flour

½ tsp baking powder

½ tsp baking soda

¾ tsp salt

1 cup (250g) sour cream, room temperature

ICING

3 cups (360g) powdered sugar

2 tbsp corn syrup

3 tbsp warm water

½ cup (60g) cocoa powder

COOKIES METHOD

1. Preheat the oven to 350°F (180°C) and line a baking sheet with parchment paper.

2. In a large bowl, cream together the butter and the sugar until light and fluffy. Beat in the eggs and the vanilla extract.

3. In a separate large bowl, combine the flour, baking powder, baking soda, and salt. Fold into the creamed mixture alternately with the sour cream.

4. Using a trigger-release ice cream scoop or jumbo cookie scoop (#20), drop the batter in portions of 3 tablespoons each onto the prepared baking sheet, allowing at least 2 inches (5cm) between cookies. Bake for about 15 minutes, or until the cookies' edges are defined and their tops have colored. Allow to cool briefly on the baking sheet before transferring to a wire rack to cool completely.

ICING METHOD

5. Once the cookies have completely cooled, combine the powdered sugar, corn syrup, and warm water in a large bowl and mix to a uniform consistency. The icing should be thick yet spreadable.

6. Divide the icing in half and transfer one half to a separate bowl. To one of the bowls, sift in the cocoa powder and mix until uniform, before slowly adding water to match the consistency of the white icing.

7. Using a thin butter knife or a small spatula, apply the white icing to one half of each cookie's flat bottom, trying your best to keep a straight midline. The icing may have to be stirred periodically if it develops a skin.

8. After all cookies have had their white icings applied, stir the chocolate icing, checking if it may benefit from additional water. Apply in the same manner to the other half of each cookie. Allow the icing to harden before serving. Keep in an airtight container in a cool place.

New Jersey

BLACK MAGIC TOMATO CAKE

CAKE • 9×13-INCH PAN
PREP: 15 MINUTES • BAKE: 35 MINUTES

If you ever find yourself in New Jersey, you can't pump your own gas, you can't escape the turnpike, and you probably can't afford New York. New Jersey lives in the shadow of the Big Apple, and the state's reputation, marked by industry and mild seediness, certainly precedes it. While you might have an easier time navigating a bowl of spaghetti than this state's roadways, many locals are smitten with their home—they're just hiding the fact. Many of the jokes about New Jersey's reputation are just a ruse fabricated by the state's own citizens.

Campbell Soup is the vaunted product of this state, founded and operating here since 1896. Their red-and-white cans have indelibly colored Americana and fed generations of people just the same. Their recipes from yesteryear have attracted attention for their eccentric inclusion of soup, particularly the 1950s tomato soup cake. This cake is a lesser-known version from Camden. Named so for its mysterious ability to amplify the taste of chocolate to heretofore unknown heights, this soft and moist chocolate cake's secret is condensed tomato soup. It may be black magic, but it's 100 percent New Jersey.

INGREDIENTS

3 eggs

2 cups (400g) granulated sugar

½ cup (120ml) vegetable oil

1 tsp vanilla extract

1 (10.75oz/305g) can condensed tomato soup

1¾ cups (245g) all-purpose flour

¾ cup (75g) cocoa powder

1 tsp salt

2 tsp baking soda (use 1 tsp if baking at or above 5,000 feet)

1 tsp baking powder

1 cup (235ml) buttermilk

Powdered sugar, for dusting

METHOD

1. Preheat the oven to 350°F (180°C) and grease a 9×13-inch (23×33cm) pan.

2. In a large bowl, combine the eggs, sugar, oil, vanilla extract, and tomato soup. Whisk vigorously until uniform and no longer grainy. Set aside.

3. In a separate large bowl, combine the flour, cocoa powder, salt, baking soda, and baking powder. Working quickly, fold this dry mixture into the tomato-soup mixture, alternately with the buttermilk.

4. Turn into the prepared cake pan and bake for 30 to 35 minutes, or until a toothpick inserted into the cake's center can be removed cleanly. Let the cake cool in the pan for 10 minutes before transferring to a wire rack to cool completely. Serve liberally dusted with powdered sugar.

AUNT SALLIE'S FROZEN CREAM

ICE CREAM • 1½ QUARTS
PREP: 30 MINUTES • COOK: 25 MINUTES • CHILL: 3 HOURS

Delaware has crowned the peach pie the state dessert, but this designation seems surprising given Georgia's claim to the fruit. Instead, the answer for which recipe to feature for this state lay in Delaware's deep history, and after much digging, the story of Aunt Sallie Shadd came to light.

Sallie Shadd was living as a freed slave in Wilmington in the 1810s, and though little was kept of African-American history during these times, what *is* known is that she set up a catering business and began scooping a new creation of frozen sweetened cream with fruit—one of the first people to do so. First Lady Dolley Madison traveled to Wilmington after hearing of Shadd's dessert and took it upon herself to serve this fanciful strawberry cream at the president's inaugural ball in 1813.

Today, Delaware retains much of its appreciation for ice cream with its many local farm creameries. The University of Delaware even operates its own nonprofit, student-run creamery, UDairy, selling ice cream from university cows and operating the university ice cream truck, the MooMobile. For our sweet treat, we return to the methods of Aunt Sallie Shad and combine milk, cream, and sugar with mashed strawberries the Delaware way, just like it was done two hundred years ago.

INGREDIENTS

¾ cup (150g) granulated sugar, divided

½ tsp salt

1½ cups (470ml) heavy cream

1 cup (235ml) whole milk

8oz (227g) hulled whole strawberries

Yolks of 4 eggs

1 tsp vanilla extract

METHOD

1. Place a long and shallow dish, such as a casserole dish, in the freezer to chill.

2. In the top of a double boiler filled with simmering water, add ½ cup (100g) of the sugar and the salt. Whisk in the heavy cream and the milk. Cook for 12 minutes, stirring occasionally.

3. While the cream scalds, add the remaining ¼ cup (50g) sugar to a large bowl with the hulled strawberries. Mash them to a pulp using a fork or potato masher and set aside.

4. In a small bowl, thoroughly beat the egg yolks. Using a ladle or a suitably large spoon, take roughly ¼ cup (60ml) of the hot cream mixture and slowly add it to the beaten yolks while whisking to temper them. Whisk the tempered yolks into the cream mixture in the double boiler. Continue to cook for 10 minutes longer.

5. Remove the bowl from the double boiler and mix in the strawberries and the vanilla extract.

6. Pour the mixture into the chilled dish. Place in the freezer. Agitate the mixture every 45 minutes by stirring and pulling the freezing edges of the mixture inward. Repeat three to four times before serving.

Tip

If you possess and wish to use an ice cream maker that will accommodate 1½ quarts (1.4L), you may use it for this recipe.

BERGER COOKIES

COOKIE • 2 DOZEN
PREP: 40 MINUTES • BAKE: 15 MINUTES • COOL: 1 HOUR

Baltimore's Berger Cookie has a face made for radio; it's certainly no looker. Upon Maryland's platters, the Berger sits portly and tottering, sporting a layer of chocolate that appears to be applied via trowel. But, it's hard not to swoon when the weight of its icing exceeds that of the cookie itself. This cookie has the gonads to disobey protocol and appropriate serving suggestions. The result is a beloved, recognizable, and outright-tasty pillar of Maryland. Its fame is thanks to DeBaufre Bakeries, which traces its roots back to German immigrant Henry Berger, who opened his first shop in East Baltimore soon after he arrived in America in 1835.

I was served my first Berger in Westminster, MD, in the summer of 2023. Hearing the name without seeing the spelling was a rather nail-biting ordeal, as I wasn't sure whether to expect a cookie of ground beef or a cookie set between two buns. Thankfully I bit into neither but rather a grin-inducing dose of milk chocolate with a cheery crumble beneath. I was sold right then and there. If Britain's modestly coated digestive biscuit is customary, then Baltimore's Berger is heresy, and you're sure to be a converted heretic whenever you enjoy this vanilla cookie with enough chocolate to sink a ship.

COOKIES

½ cup (90g) vegetable shortening
½ cup (100g) granulated sugar
1 egg
1 tbsp imitation vanilla flavoring

2 cups (280g) all-purpose flour
1½ tsp baking powder
¾ tsp salt
¾ cup (180ml) buttermilk

ICING

2 cups (340g) semisweet
    chocolate chips
1 cup (235ml) heavy cream

1 tbsp corn syrup
¼ tsp salt
1½ cups (180g) powdered sugar

COOKIES METHOD

1. Preheat the oven to 350°F (180°C) and line a baking sheet with parchment paper.

2. In a large bowl, cream together the shortening and the sugar until light and fluffy. Beat in the egg and the imitation vanilla.

3. In a separate large bowl, combine the flour, baking powder, and salt. Mix into the creamed mixture alternately with the buttermilk.

4. Drop by rounded tablespoon or cookie scoop (#50) onto the prepared baking sheet, allowing 3 inches between each, and bake for 15 minutes, or until the edges of the cookies are golden and defined. Allow to cool briefly on the baking sheet before transferring to a wire rack to cool completely. Once all cookies have been baked and have cooled to room temperature, prepare the icing.

ICING METHOD

5. In the top of a double boiler filled with simmering water, combine the chocolate chips, heavy cream, corn syrup, and salt. Once melted, stir until uniform before sifting in the powdered sugar. Whisk thoroughly until all lumps have been incorporated.

6. Remove the chocolate from the double boiler, place the bowl in an ice bath, and beat until the chocolate thickens to a heavy, spreadable consistency that holds a peak, like that of peanut butter.

7. Using a butter knife or offset spatula, roughly pile chocolate onto each cookie's flat side, covering it to the edge, and forming a mound. Each cookie should have a rather absurd layer, and all chocolate should be used. Allow them to set in a cool place for a minimum of 1 hour before enjoying.

Berger Cookies on North Market Street, Frederick.

Culture Capital

WASHINGTON, DC

From here are telegraphed the movements of this great nation. You've seen television coverage of this place from newscasts, addresses, and other assorted drivel, but to see it in person is surprisingly grounding. Manicured and planned with the mall, monoliths, and monuments, America's capital seems curiously European in the shocking ease with which one can walk around. Its harmony is thanks to the Frenchman and city planner Charles L'Enfant, but don't tell the Americans that. Amid the palatial views, artsy metros, traffic circles, and neat public squares, the utter crapshoot of political drama feels all the more absurd. The regal hand of Abraham Lincoln, the sloppy stains of Nixon's Watergate, the starched lapels of Congress, and the dirty business of lobbyists all make this place a real-life show with endless seasons. Don't misconstrue my cynicism: this town is a helluva character, and one that offers many reasons to crack a smile.

The Watergate complex, Rock Creek and Potomac Parkway, Washington, DC.

WATERGATE CUPCAKES

CUPCAKE • 1 DOZEN
PREP: 40 MINUTES • BAKE: 22 MINUTES • COOL: 10 MINUTES

In a saucy bid to undermine the presidential election of 1972, President Richard Nixon sent a secretive group known as the "plumbers" to blatantly burgle the Democratic National Committee headquarters in Washington, DC in the dead of night. Presumably masked with ladies' pantyhose and festooned in black-and-white stripes, these oafs broke into the sixth floor of the Watergate building with the stealth and grace of stuck pigs. Despite the paper trails and tapes, Tricky Dicky spent the rest of the decade claiming his innocence, resigning from office in 1974 before managing to pull a full pardon from his successor, Gerald Ford. I often wonder how Nixon must have felt about his nation plastering the name of his darkest hour upon the cakes and salads of the seventies. How about a Watergate salad for your starter, Mr. President?

I love the Watergate scandal because it underlines just how fevered the climate of DC can get. From the dizzying studies of Georgetown law students to sprinting correspondents and coffee-juggling interns, this open-air museum of a city keeps watch o'er the buzz with its multitude of bronze plinths and marbled heads of politicians past. Here, the storied Watergate complex still looms large as the physical eponym for both the Watergate cake and the salad, dishes which carry the Watergate flavor profile of kitschy, imitation pistachio. In place of a cake or salad, this recipe is a holdable cupcake of political peculiarity. Seldom are we ever afforded such a queer crossroads of politics, Americana, seventies garishness, and cuisine. So here in DC, may your cupcakes ever be pistachio green.

CUPCAKE
½ cup (90g) vegetable shortening, or lard
½ cup (100g) granulated sugar
4 eggs
1½ cups (210g) all-purpose flour

1 (3.4oz/96g) package pistachio-flavored instant pudding mix
1½ tsp baking powder (use 1 tsp if baking at or above 5,000 feet)
½ tsp salt
¾ cup (180ml) milk

FROSTING
1 cup (180g) vegetable shortening
2 tsp vanilla extract
¾ tsp butter extract

Few drops of green food coloring
5½ cups (660g) powdered sugar
¼ cup (60ml) water

CUPCAKE METHOD

1. Preheat the oven to 350°F (180°C) and line a muffin pan with paper liners.

2. In a large bowl, cream together the shortening and the sugar until light and fluffy. Beat in the eggs, one at a time, until smooth and uniform.

3. In a separate large bowl, combine the flour, pudding mix, baking powder, and salt. Add to the creamed mixture alternately with the milk.

4. Turn the batter into the liners, filling them three-quarters full. Bake for 22 minutes, or until a toothpick inserted into a cupcake's center can be removed cleanly. Allow the cupcakes to cool in the pan for 10 minutes before transferring to a wire rack to cool completely to room temperature before frosting.

RECIPE CONTINUES . . .

Watergate Cupcakes at the Watergate complex, Washington, DC.

FROSTING METHOD

5. In the bowl of a stand mixer fitted with a paddle attachment, or in a large bowl in tandem with a hand mixer, beat the shortening until it lightens. Beat in the vanilla and butter extracts, followed by the green food coloring.

6. Beat in the powdered sugar and the water in alternate additions, 1 cup and 1 tablespoon, respectively. Once all the sugar and water are incorporated, beat on high speed for 2 minutes until fluffy, scraping down the bowl intermittently.

7. Transfer the frosting to a piping bag fitted with a star tip of your choosing. Decoratively apply a hefty amount of frosting atop each cupcake, either in one large piped star, or in a spiral fashion if using a small star. Keep covered in a cool place. These need not be refrigerated.

South

SOUTH ATLANTIC · SOUTH GULF
SOUTHERN INTERIOR

VIRGINIA

NORTH CAROLINA

SOUTH CAROLINA

GEORGIA

FLORIDA

SAVANNAH

South Atlantic

Get jolly, get limber, we're headed southbound
to a balmy land of butter by the pound.
Good food, good folks, and genteel's the day
they welcome you all, but "y'all's" their way.
On islands, on coasts, it's all quite plain.
They're in no hurry, and just who can blame?
Verandas on which Southern charms convey
their smiles like that of a magnolia bouquet.

PUERTO RICO

Culture Capital

SAVANNAH

Should you ever want to pretend your name is Lila Mae and your only responsibilities are to rock on your porch, drink sweet tea, and prepare a pecan pie before nightfall, then Savannah, Georgia, is the place for you. This honorable town sits nearly hidden beneath canopies of old-growth trees and Spanish moss, which creep over its squares and cobblestoned alleys with the same ease and languidness with which the locals conduct their daily business. Savannah feels as if you've been transported into a novel, and the only indication that you're not in a literary setting is the lack of frilly hats and double-breasted day coats upon those who stroll by in Forsyth Park. During our visit here, we stayed in a historic three-story manor. To fry hush puppies and bake pie—all for which the South sings—in such a befitting place was as close to perfection as any baker could wish. Should you visit Savannah, you won't need wishes. Southern hospitality will grant whatever desire their hearty meals and rich desserts can't. This town is the belle of the South, and one whose pace can slow even the most persistent nagging of life's many trifles.

A slice of *Sorghum & Honey Pecan Pie* inside a manor house, Whitaker Street, Savannah.

Georgia

SORGHUM & HONEY PECAN PIE

PIE • 9-INCH PIE
PREP: 20 MINUTES • BAKE: 1 HOUR • COOL: 3 HOURS

Potluck law in the US decrees that one shall not desecrate any of the holiday mainstays. And in Georgia, the pecan pie should especially remain untouched. With risk, however, comes the potential for high reward. I stumbled upon this curious recipe while sorting through a collection of handwritten index cards, cookbooks, and periodicals purchased on eBay in 2019. The box was shipped from Savannah and had the usual mix of things often cleared from basements, most dated between 1972 and 1983. The periodicals included were directed to a PO box in Milledgeville, Georgia. But it was an ingredients-only recipe for this pie that caught my eye in a metal tin filled mostly with blank index cards. Handwritten by an unknown author and titled "Georgia Pecan," it met only my curiosity at first.

I later filled in the gaps and made the pie, only to find that it unlocked a depth to the filling that was both bold and perfectly sweet: silky pecan richness, with honey and Southern sorghum enrobing and elevating the candied slices to pecan paradise. It was clear this wasn't just a twist on tradition—but a revelation.

Perhaps the original owner, famous for bringing this pie to her Thanksgiving potlucks, guarded its secrets from her praising parishioners. Or perhaps it was dictated over the phone to a curious granddaughter, eager to preserve a good thing. Regardless of its origins, it stands as a stellar idea that delivers pecan pie in a most Southern, charming way.

INGREDIENTS

1 single-crust Pie Crust (page 17)
1½ cups (180g) pecan halves, chopped
3 large eggs
½ cup (100g) granulated sugar
½ cup (120ml) sorghum syrup
½ cup (120ml) honey
1 tsp vanilla extract
2 tbsp all-purpose flour
¼ cup (55g) butter, melted
¼ tsp salt

METHOD

1. Place a baking sheet or a folded sheet of aluminum foil on the middle oven rack (so as to catch potential spillage) and preheat the oven to 400°F (200°C).

2. Fit the prepared bottom pie crust in a standard 9-inch (23cm) pan and evenly place the chopped pecans within.

3. In a large bowl, vigorously whisk together the eggs and the granulated sugar until combined.

4. Whisk in the remainder of the ingredients in the order listed, and pour atop the pecans in the pastry.

5. Bake for 10 minutes, before reducing the heat to 350°F (180°C), and continue to bake for another 40 to 50 minutes, or until the center of the pie has noticeably puffed and browned. Place on a cooling rack and allow to cool for a minimum of 3 hours before slicing. The pie will neither set nor be sliceable while warm.

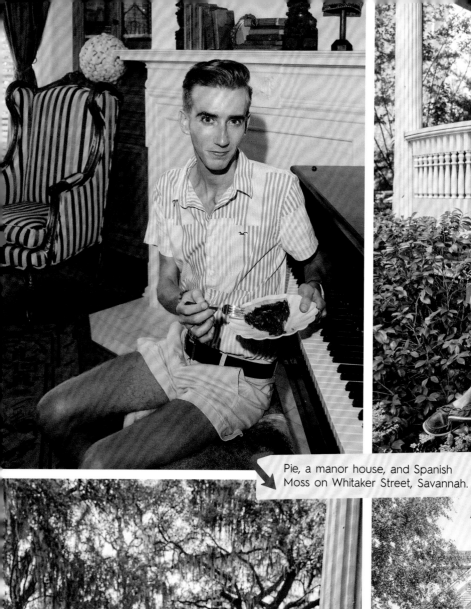

Pie, a manor house, and Spanish Moss on Whitaker Street, Savannah.

Peach Cobbler under magnolias, Forsyth Park, Savannah.

PEACH COBBLER

BAKED DESSERT • 9×13-INCH CASSEROLE
PREP: 25 MINUTES • BAKE: 50 MINUTES • COOL: 10 MINUTES

Prior to my visit to Georgia, I expected that while there I'd unearth juicy secrets or guarded insider information as to what makes this famed dish of the Peach State special. Surely the native sons, daughters, and kinfolk of towns like Peachtree Corners or Peachtree City would pass down complex and spellbinding tomes on the most righteous way to cobble one's peaches. However, when one Savannah lady began her answer to my prodding questions on the matter with "Oh, darlin' . . ." I knew I would get no further.

So, what did I find? I found that almost every cobbler recipe in Georgia is identical. Sure, there were some that blurred the lines between crumbles and crisps with additions like streusel and oats. Cinnamon was, of course, commonly cited. A wonderful Miss Patrice in Lithonia wrote to inform me that brown sugar *must* be sprinkled atop, and I even found a recipe to serve fifty. But I found no illustrious Georgia recipe to trump the rest. The reasoning here was not veneration of the basics, but rather that all the work, effort, and complexity of what makes the *Peach Cobbler* good is done not by the cook but by the tree. The secret is not to interfere with that which nature has made scrum-diddily-umptious on its own. And so we have the following for your delight: a cobbler made with fresh peaches, brought to confiture only by way of heat and sugar, and melded effortlessly with a lightly spiced batter. Downright peachy.

FILLING

5 medium Georgia peaches
1 cup (200g) granulated sugar
½ tsp baking soda

1 tsp ground cinnamon
½ tsp salt

BATTER

⅔ cup (150g) butter
2 cups (280g) all-purpose flour
1 cup (200g) granulated sugar
1 tsp baking powder

1⅓ cups (315ml) milk, room temperature
⅓ cup (60g) coarse-grained cane or demerara sugar (substitute with brown sugar)

FILLING METHOD

1. Preheat the oven to 350°F (180°C).

2. Wash, pit, and cut the peaches into slices, like an apple. You do not need to peel the peaches, but may do so if you wish.

3. Combine the peaches with the rest of the filling ingredients in a medium saucepan, and cook over medium heat for 10 minutes, stirring often. Set aside.

BATTER METHOD

4. Add the butter to a 9×13-inch (23×33cm) casserole or baking dish and place in the oven until melted. Take care when removing from the oven.

5. In a large bowl, combine the flour, granulated sugar, and baking powder, before mixing in the milk to make the batter.

6. Without mixing the two, spoon the batter over the melted butter, followed by evenly spooning the peach-filling mixture and juices atop this. Sprinkle with coarse-grained sugar and bake for 45 minutes, until the batter has risen and the top has browned. If using a metal baking dish, check at 40 minutes.

7. Remove from the oven and place on a wire rack to cool for 10 minutes. Serve warm, ideally with a fat scoop of vanilla ice cream.

A slice of *Peach Cobbler* among daisies, Forsyth Park, Savannah.

Hush Puppies and the docked riverboat *Georgia Queen* on River Street, Savannah.

Georgia
HUSH PUPPIES

FRITTER · 1½ DOZEN
PREP: 20 MINUTES · COOK: 25 MINUTES

Like much of the South, a fish fry in Georgia can only be considered sufficiently accoutred if it sports the hush puppy on its docket. Like remedial liquor to a hangover, there is nothing better suited to fried fish than a fried side dish, and in these parts *Hush Puppies* reign proudly.

To define precisely the birth of these fritters remains nonviable. Various stories allege that soldiers mid–Civil War, in an attempt to quiet dogs by throwing them fried batter, would scold, *"Hush, puppies!"* But you've my assurance these tales are pure claptrap. What *is* true is that they first appeared circa 1900 in the area surrounding the final stretch of the Savannah River.

Newspapers—most notably the *Augusta Chronicle* in 1903—took note of one Romy Govan, an emancipated slave who would fry his famed "red horse bread" (named so to accompany red horse, a river fish) along the South Fork banks of the neighboring Edisto River in Bamberg County, SC, to much acclaim. This creation was a simple unleavened fried cornmeal batter, and its popularity soon spread from the Lowcountry. On the Georgia side of the Savannah River, folks soon came to add leavening and began calling red horse bread "Hush Puppies." And, considering this is the name that remains and that *Hush Puppies* are now exclusively leavened, I'd say Georgia rightfully champions them.

The definitive hush puppy contains more cornmeal than it does flour, is fried to an unmistakable brown, and is cooked in the same oil used to fry one's fish.

INGREDIENTS

1 cup (150g) cornmeal

½ cup (70g) all-purpose flour

½ tsp salt

1½ tsp baking powder

¼ tsp baking soda

1 medium Vidalia, or other sweet onion, finely chopped

1 egg

¾ cup (180ml) milk

Canola, corn, or peanut oil, or lard, for frying

METHOD

1. In a large bowl, mix together the cornmeal, flour, salt, baking powder, and baking soda. Then add the onion and mix to coat.

2. In a separate bowl, beat together the egg and the milk before adding to the dry ingredients. Beat until smooth.

3. Let the batter rest for 10 minutes while you prepare the oil.

4. Add the oil or lard to a large pot or Dutch oven to a depth of 3 inches (7.5cm) and heat to 365°F (185°C).

5. Using a trigger-release ice cream scoop or large cookie scoop (#40), drop rounds of batter into the hot fat, no more than 4 fritters at a time.

6. Fry until well browned and crisped on both sides, about 3 minutes per side. Transfer to a wire rack or other surface topped with paper towels to absorb excess fat. Allow them to dry briefly before serving.

KEY LIME PIE

PIE • 9-INCH PIE
PREP: 20 MINUTES • BAKE: 20 MINUTES • CHILL: 3 HOURS

Florida is a special land where you can share golf courses with gators, fend off Disney devotees, and have your choice of getting lost in either the paranormal Everglades or its endlessly liminal retirement communities. Head south on I-95, and the coastal counties begin to smell of sunscreen and cream of coconut, while the northern woods along I-10 offer deep Southern scenes of rusty pickups and pilsners upon porches. Of the things you'll find most abundant here—right behind clapped-out golf carts and sensational "Florida Man" headlines—is the *Key Lime Pie*.

First appearing in the 1930s, the pie's origins are debated. Some say it was created by Key West fishermen seeking a creamy dessert without refrigeration, while others believe it was inspired by Borden's "Magic Lemon Cream Pie," a pioneering recipe that thickened condensed milk and "cooked" the egg yolks using only the acid of lemons. The early uncooked *Key Lime Pie* used the leftover egg whites to finish the pie with a meringue, but Florida now prefers its state pie baked and topped with whipped cream. The key to this refreshingly tart beauty is to use proper key limes. They're tiny and practically yellow when ripe, elevating the flavor of this pie to the stratosphere.

CRUST

1½ cups (165g) graham cracker crumbs

⅓ cup (65g) granulated sugar

½ cup (115g) butter, melted

FILLING

2 tbsp key lime zest

½ cup (120ml) key lime juice, from about 14 key limes

1 (14oz/396g) can sweetened condensed milk

Yolks of 4 eggs

¼ tsp salt

TOPPING

½ cup (120ml) heavy cream

Zest of 1 key lime, for garnish

Lime wedges, for garnish

CRUST METHOD

1. Preheat the oven to 350°F (180°C).

2. In a medium bowl, combine the crust ingredients and mix until a uniform crumb is formed. Press the mixture evenly into the bottom and up the sides of a 9-inch (23cm) pie pan.

FILLING METHOD

3. In a separate large bowl, combine the filling ingredients and whisk until uniform. Pour into the prepared crust and bake for 20 minutes. Place the pan on a wire rack to cool completely to room temperature before refrigerating for a minimum of 3 hours. The pie will neither set nor be sliceable while warm.

TOPPING METHOD

4. Once the pie has chilled, beat the heavy cream stiff in a clean bowl using a stand mixer or hand mixer. Dollop or pipe decoratively around the pie's edge, garnish the entire pie with the lime zest, and position the lime wedges at its circumference for each serving to be sliced. Serve chilled and keep refrigerated.

As an islander, I can get behind all things Puerto Rico. Whether speaking of its plentiful beaches, yesteryear's danza music, or the colorful streets and rugged fortifications of old San Juan, newcomers are never left wanting for vibrant sights. The cuisine is equally colorful: the proud birthplace of the spice mixture sofrito, and the land that gave us cream of coconut and the piña colada, the preferred drink of sunburn-dazed tourists.

Among its many dishes to offer, like mofongo and pasteles, is this baked *Piñon*: a splendid combination of robust culantro (or recao, an herbaceous cousin to cilantro), sweet plantains, tangy peppers, and roasted flavors layered precisely for your enjoyment. As I possess no Puerto Rican flair whatsoever, this *Piñon* was constructed with help from a 1979 recipe generously provided by Dr. Hernán Padilla, a former mayor of San Juan (1977–1985). Thanks to him, *Piñon* has become one of my new favorite comfort foods. Should you be in need for a taste of the islands, I think you'll feel the same.

PIÑÓN
- PLANTAIN MINCEMEAT PIE -

CASSEROLE • DEEP 9-INCH SQUARE BAKING DISH
PREP: 45 MINUTES • BAKE: 40 MINUTES • COOL: 10 MINUTES

INGREDIENTS

5 plantains

4 cups (950ml) hot water mixed
   with 1 tbsp salt

1 green bell pepper, minced

4 banana peppers, minced

1 medium white onion, chopped

2 tbsp minced culantro, or cilantro

1 tbsp minced garlic

¼ cup (45g) minced pimiento-stuffed olives

1½ tsp salt

1lb (454g) ground beef or pork,
   or a mixture of both

¾ cup (180ml) vegetable oil, divided

⅓ cup (75g) canned tomato sauce

1 (14.5oz/411g) can green beans, drained

Whites of 6 eggs

Yolks of 6 eggs, beaten

METHOD

1. Peel the plantains and quarter them lengthwise, creating long slices. Place the cut slices in a large bowl with the 4 cups of salted hot water.

2. In a separate large bowl, thoroughly mix together the bell pepper, banana peppers, onion, culantro, garlic, olives, and salt. Mix in the ground meat. Alternatively, all ingredients in this step may be minced together in a food processor.

3. In a large frying pan or iron skillet, heat ¼ cup (60ml) vegetable oil over high heat until it shimmers. Add the minced vegetable and meat mixture and cook uncovered for 5 minutes, stirring often to avoid scorching. Reduce to low heat, stir in the tomato sauce and the green beans, and cook uncovered for 15 minutes, stirring occasionally, then cover and keep warm.

4. Meanwhile, remove the soaked plantains from the water and pat dry. Over medium-high heat, heat the remaining ½ cup (120ml) vegetable oil in a separate deep-frying pan or skillet until shimmering, and fry the plantains until well browned. Once browned, remove from the heat and carefully set them on a plate or wire rack lined with paper towels to dry.

5. Preheat the oven to 300°F (150°C).

6. In the bowl of a stand mixer fitted with a whisk attachment, or in a large bowl in tandem with a hand mixer, beat the egg whites until stiff. Fold in the beaten egg yolks until uniform. The mixture will deflate slightly.

7. Into a deep ovenproof dish, layer the *Piñon* as follows: ½ egg mixture, ⅓ plantains, ½ meat mixture, ⅓ plantains, ½ meat mixture, ⅓ plantains, ½ egg mixture.

8. Bake the assembled *Piñon* for 30 minutes. Increase the oven temperature to 350°F (180°C) and bake 10 minutes more. Let cool for 10 minutes before cutting into squares to serve as a side dish or alongside rice and beans.

South Atlantic   **97**

SPOON BREAD

PUDDING • 2 QUART BAKING DISH
PREP: 20 MINUTES • BAKE: 35 MINUTES

The air in Virginia is as thick with old, Southern languor as it is with humidity. It's a state that's been around the block more than once. In addition to its Appalachian folk heritage and Southern chronicles, Virginia's proximity to Washington, DC, enshrines it further as a cornerstone of the founding colonial past. Even without mentioning Jamestown, Virginia's history is so rich that it threatens to render disinterested middle schoolers catatonic if delivered all at once.

One of the true Southern delicacies from this state is *Spoon Bread*. Neither a bread made of spoons nor a spoon made of bread, this dish is best described as cornbread in pudding form. With a texture similar to polenta yet firm enough to hold its fluffy shape, *Spoon Bread* is arguably the quirkiest and least-encountered entry in our cornbread lexicon. Though its name derives from its necessity to be served via spoon, you might just choose to eat it caveman-style once you discover the homestyle wonder of its soft, Southern charm.

INGREDIENTS

1½ cups (200g) white cornmeal, medium grind

3 tbsp granulated sugar

1¼ tsp salt

1½ cups (355ml) water

¼ cup (55g) butter, plus more for serving

1 cup (235ml) whole milk

5 eggs

1 cup (235ml) buttermilk

3 tsp baking powder (use 2 tsp if baking at 5,000 feet or above)

½ tsp baking soda

METHOD

1. Preheat the oven to 400°F (200°C) and liberally butter a 2 quart or similar 8 cup (1.9L) baking dish.

2. In a large saucepan or pot, combine the cornmeal, sugar, and salt. Begin cooking over medium heat while mixing in the water. Cook, stirring often, until the mixture thickens and leaves distinct trails when a spoon is scraped across the bottom, about 3 minutes.

3. Reduce the heat to low and mix in the butter, followed by the whole milk. Cook for 10 minutes, stirring occasionally to prevent clumping at the bottom. Remove from the heat and set aside to cool slightly.

4. In a large bowl, beat together the eggs and the buttermilk. Slowly whisk in the cornmeal mixture, before vigorously whisking in the baking powder and baking soda.

5. Turn into the prepared casserole dish, place in the oven, and immediately lower the temperature to 350°F (180°C). Bake for 30 to 35 minutes, or until the edges are well browned. The finished bread will deflate slightly when cooled. Portion by spoon and serve hot with pats of butter.

Spoon Bread on the steps of the William Ramsay House, King Street, Old Town, Alexandria.

Chess Pie on an 18th century cannon near the Potomac River, Old Town, Alexandria.

Virginia
CHESS PIE

PIE • 9-INCH PIE
PREP: 20 MINUTES • BAKE: 50 MINUTES • COOL: 2 HOURS

Spend time with old cookbooks from the South, and you'll notice there is no pie as prevalent as *Chess Pie*. Beneath the Mason-Dixon Line, this pie reigned supreme for years, and despite its meager nature, it continues to hold office as a defining dessert of old Virginia. You will find nothing special in its ingredients: its building blocks of butter, flour (sometimes cornmeal), sugar, and eggs could amount to practically any baked good across time. *Chess Pie* is simplicity sliced, so it's understandable that the anecdote (pronounced in a Southern drawl) "It's just pie!" could easily be vernacularized to "*Chess Pie*." However, as with other recipe monikers from the past, a consensus on the origins of the name is as conflicting as its methods of preparation are varied.

In today's South, you'll find coconut, buttermilk, lemon, or chocolate variations of the *Chess Pie*. There's even the spiced and meringue-topped Jeff Davis Pie. A great take if it weren't named after a git. But, here in Virginia, they like it just the way they've been making it for more than a century: silky, buttery, and custardy.

INGREDIENTS

1 single-crust Pie Crust (page 17)
½ cup (115g) butter, melted and slightly cooled
4 eggs
Yolks of 2 eggs

1 ¾ (350g) cups granulated sugar
2 tbsp white vinegar
1 tbsp vanilla extract
3 tbsp all-purpose flour
½ tsp salt

METHOD

1. Preheat the oven to 350°F (180°C) and fit the prepared pastry into a 9-inch (23cm) pie pan.

2. In a large bowl, thoroughly whisk together the rest of the ingredients in the order listed until smooth and uniform. Ensure your melted butter is not too hot so as not to cook the eggs.

3. Pour into the prepared pie crust and bake for 45 to 50 minutes, or until the top of the pie has browned substantially and only wobbles slightly in the center when jostled. Place on a cooling rack and allow to cool for a minimum of 2 hours before slicing. The pie will neither set nor be sliceable while warm.

MORAVIAN SPICE COOKIES

ROLLED COOKIES • 4 DOZEN
PREP: 10 MINUTESS • CHILL: 30 MINUTES • BAKE: 10 MINUTES

What do Moravian Protestants, underwear, cigarettes, and doughnuts have in common? It isn't the order of operations for a cabaret of debauchery, but rather the anchoring forces of the double-barreled city of Winston-Salem. Founded by immigrant Moravians in 1766, the town of Salem at first stood alone. In 1870, the arrival of the North Carolina Railway spurred massive development of its northern neighbor Winston, and the two towns' proximal chemistry led to their marrying in 1913. Its ideal proximity to the railway and the coast quickly saw P.H. Hanes Knitting Company and Reynolds Tobacco churn out undergarments and Camel cigarettes respectively from what was North Carolina's largest city by 1920. Main Street in Winston-Salem even hosted the grand opening for a little doughnut shop called Krispy Kreme in 1937, and by all accounts, they've done pretty well.

Old Salem, with its deep-rooted Moravian influences, is the place to find our recipe for "the world's thinnest cookie." This centuries-old treat was brought from overseas and became tightly woven into local culture. These cookies are beloved by North Carolina, and just as they were rolled by Protestants past, no holiday gathering today is complete without the paper-thin snap of the spicy molasses and ginger wonders of Tar Heel's twin city.

INGREDIENTS

½ cup (115g) butter
½ cup (110g) brown sugar
½ cup (170g) molasses
2 cups (280g) all-purpose flour
¼ tsp salt
½ tsp baking soda

1 tsp ground cinnamon
1 tsp ground ginger
½ tsp ground cloves
½ tsp ground allspice
½ tsp ground mustard
½ tsp white pepper

METHOD

1. To a large saucepan, add the butter, brown sugar, and molasses. Cook over medium heat, stirring occasionally, until the mixture reaches a light simmer. Remove from the heat and set aside.

2. In a large bowl, combine the flour, salt, baking soda, and spices. Pour the hot molasses mixture over the top, and mix until a stiff dough begins to form. Switch to kneading in the bowl with your hands to form a uniform ball. Gather the dough, form a rough disk, cover, and refrigerate for a minimum of 30 minutes. Then, preheat the oven to 375°F (190°C) and line a baking sheet with parchment paper.

3. Once the dough is chilled, take roughly a quarter of it, dust the counter or work surface liberally with flour, and begin rolling out to as thin a sheet as possible. Only initially, be sure to periodically rotate and shift the dough over the floured surface to ensure it doesn't stick.

4. Once paper-thin, cut out disks with a 2-inch (5cm) fluted cookie cutter. Using a thin turner or offset spatula, carefully free the disks from the counter and transfer to the prepared baking sheet. Bake for 6 minutes, allow to cool briefly on the baking sheet, and transfer to a wire rack to cool completely. Repeat with the remaining dough.

Foreigners often say America has little in the way of culture or traditions. This is nonsense. One homegrown tradition for Americans is the permanent borrowing of other people's things and celebrating it as their own. As far as cake is concerned, this applies to the proliferation of this island favorite, a pineapple and banana-filled beauty.

The Doctor Bird Cake is a cake of 1960s Jamaica, which is also when the country's tourism board began promoting the cake across the Gulf. A Mrs. Higgins who lived in Greensboro, North Carolina, submitted a recipe to *Southern Living* in February of 1978 for the Doctor Bird, altering it by covering the cake in a tangy cream cheese frosting and sporting a new name: *Hummingbird Cake*. A tactful rebranding, given Americans know not of Jamaica's national Doctor Bird but are well-acquainted with the avian family's more common name of the hummingbird. Thanks to North Carolina's Mrs. Higgins, the cake instantly became a Southern staple. With or without cream cheese frosting, its long-standing gravity is testament to a darn-good idea. The cake, for one, certainly doesn't care who claims it as their own.

HUMMINGBIRD CAKE

LAYER CAKE • THREE 9-INCH LAYERS
PREP: 45 MINUTES • BAKE: 35 MINUTES • COOL: 1 HOUR • CHILL: 1 HOUR

CAKE

3 eggs

2 cups (400g) granulated sugar

1 cup (240ml) vegetable oil

½ cup (120ml) buttermilk

2 tsp vanilla extract

1½ cups (375g) mashed ripe bananas
(about 3 large bananas)

1 (8oz/227g) can crushed pineapple
in juice, undrained

3 cups (420g) all-purpose flour

¾ tsp salt

1½ tsp baking soda (use 1 tsp if baking
at or above 5,000 feet)

2 tsp ground cinnamon

1 cup (120g) pecan halves,
toasted and very finely chopped

CREAM CHEESE FROSTING

2 (8oz/226g) packages cream cheese, softened

1½ cups (340g) unsalted butter, softened

3 tbsp cornstarch

1 tsp vanilla extract

7 cups (840g) powdered sugar

1½ cups (180g) pecan halves,
toasted and chopped

CAKE METHOD

1. Preheat the oven to 350°F (180°C) and grease three 9-inch (23cm) cake pans.

2. In a large bowl, vigorously whisk together the eggs, sugar, oil, buttermilk, and vanilla extract until smooth and uniform. Whisk in the bananas, then switch to a spatula and mix in the pineapple and its juice.

3. In a separate large bowl, combine the flour, salt, baking soda, and cinnamon. Add in the wet mixture, and fold until barely combined. Fold in the pecans.

4. Divide the batter evenly into three parts (this is best done with a scale) and pour into the prepared cake pans. Bake for 30 to 35 minutes, or until a toothpick inserted into the cakes' centers can be removed cleanly. Transfer the pans to a wire rack and allow the cakes to cool in their pans for 1 hour, before transferring directly to the wire rack to cool completely to room temperature.

CREAM CHEESE FROSTING METHOD

5. In the bowl of a stand mixer fitted with a paddle attachment, or in a large bowl in tandem with a hand mixer, beat together the cream cheese, butter, cornstarch, and vanilla extract until lightened and uniform, about 5 minutes. Add the powdered sugar ¼ cup (30g) at a time while beating. Beat on the highest speed for 3 minutes. Set aside.

6. Prepare a suitable place to assemble the cake, keeping in mind how it will be served and that it will need to be refrigerated during the frosting process. Ideally, use a cake stand with a cake board.

7. Place down the first cake and generously cover with frosting. Place and center the second cake atop and cover its top with frosting. Place and center the final cake, without frosting its top. Refrigerate the cake for a minimum of 30 minutes.

8. After chilling, liberally frost the entire assembled cake before smoothing with a bench scraper. Alternatively, the frosting can be transferred to a piping bag and frosted in this manner. Once frosted, take handfuls of the chopped pecans and press them onto the sides of the cake, reusing any which do not adhere. Refrigerate the cake for a further 30 minutes, before slicing and serving. This cake must be kept refrigerated.

BENNE WAFERS

WAFER • 4 DOZEN SMALL WAFERS
PREP: 25 MINUTES • BAKE: 10 MINUTES

Charleston, South Carolina, is a veritable Southern belle. Warm, grand, and easygoing, its comforting temperament is reflected in its beloved *Benne Wafer* (pronounced benny), which you'll find packaged by the pound throughout Charleston County. Occupying a peculiar position somewhere between a savory cracker and a sweet cookie, these thin, crispy creations can seemingly only be consumed in multiples of ten. Attempting any less is a sweat-inducing exercise in self-control I don't recommend. What sets *Benne Wafers* apart from the rest of the country's cookie creations is their exotic primary constituent: benne seeds.

"Benne" is the Gullah word for the sesame seed, and much of South Carolina's distinct cuisine, including utilization of the sesame seed, is thanks to the Gullah people, descendants of West Africa brought to the United States' shores during the very dark 18th century. Here in the Lowcountry, you'll hear about Gullah-Geechee, a combined heritage of African peoples surrounding the states of South Carolina and Georgia who trace themselves back from across the Atlantic. To read about them from the source, I highly recommend the book *Gullah Geechee Home Cooking* by the Mother of Edisto Island, Miss Emily Meggett, my personal hero of South Carolina. But, for now, consider these delightful crisps your introduction to the charms of Charleston, suited both to snacking with cheeses or eating as standalone pick-me-ups. *Benne Wafers* are a real treat.

INGREDIENTS

1 cup (150g) benne seeds,
   or white sesame seeds

½ cup (115g) butter, softened

1¼ cups (275g) brown sugar

1 egg

1 tsp vanilla extract

Zest of ½ lemon

1 cup (140g) all-purpose flour

¼ tsp salt

¼ tsp baking soda

METHOD

1. Preheat the oven to 375°F (190°C) and line a baking sheet with parchment paper.

2. In a large nonstick frying pan or skillet, toast the benne seeds over medium heat until fragrant and golden, about 2 to 3 minutes. Shake the pan often or move the seeds around with a turner to ensure even toasting. Remove from the heat and set aside.

3. In a large bowl, cream together the butter and the brown sugar until light and fluffy. Beat in the egg, vanilla extract, and lemon zest.

4. In a separate small bowl, combine the flour, salt, and baking soda. Mix this into the creamed mixture. Add the toasted benne seeds and mix, switching to your hands to knead in the bowl until a uniform dough is formed.

5. Pinch off teaspoon-size portions or use a very small cookie scoop (#100) and place them on the prepared baking sheet, allowing at least 2 inches (5cm) between each.

6. Bake for 8 to 10 minutes or until golden. Allow the wafers to cool briefly on the baking sheet before transferring to a wire rack to cool completely. Repeat with the remaining dough.

CHARLESTON CHEWIES

BAR • 9×9-INCH PAN
PREP: 20 MINUTES • BAKE: 40 MINUTES • COOL: 2 HOURS

I'm dogmatic and possess very strong opinions on baked goods, which I have no right to hold considering my minimal training in the field. One of these opinions is that a brownie should only ever be chocolate. That is to say, the proliferation of modern recipes like blondies—brownies without chocolate—are a daft affront to the kitchen and fly in the face of etymological logic. If this trend continues, I fear we'll soon have fruitless fruitcakes and sugarless sugar cookies. So, imagine my conflicted horror when I found myself delighted by *Charleston Chewies* . . . which are blondies.

The Palmetto State's largest city of Charleston forced me to rethink my worldview with their chewie: a crispy, brownie-like exterior that gives way to a fudgy, buttery center, richly flavored with brown sugar and bursting with pecans. These could not be improved, not even with chocolate. *Charleston Chewies* are what you want when you crave a sumptuous dessert without complication, and I'd happily place them among other heavy hitters like sticky-toffee pudding and pecan pie. South Carolinians know good eating, and heavens, you're only an hour away from knowing their secret too.

INGREDIENTS

1 cup (225g) butter,
   melted and slightly cooled

2 cups (440g) brown sugar

2 eggs

2 cups (280g) all-purpose flour

½ tsp salt

½ tsp baking powder

2 cups (240g) pecan halves,
   toasted and finely chopped

METHOD

1. Preheat the oven to 350°F (180°C) and line a 9-inch (23cm) square pan with a parchment sling.

2. In a large bowl, thoroughly mix together all ingredients in the order listed. Turn into the prepared pan and bake for 35 to 40 minutes, until a toothpick inserted into the center can be removed with only a few crumbs.

3. Place the pan on a wire rack and let cool completely to room temperature, about 2 hours. Gently lift the square out by the sling, transfer to a cutting board, and cut into bars with a sharp knife.

MISSISSIPPI

ALABAMA

LOUISIANA

WE MARCH WITH SELMA!

HORSE SHOE

NEW ORLEANS

Enter the frying pan of these Deep South states,
over humid bayous and Mississippi straits.
This Gulf sets a tempo hot and bold
for Louisiana jazz and Alabama soul.
But full-bosomed Texas seems rather unsure
of its place in the union and its role on the shore.
Still neighborly sit these foundational few,
the southernmost desserts, their sweetest purview.

NEW ORLEANS

Nowhere beats a more flamboyant and lively pace than the cultural jamboree that is New Orleans, Louisiana. It takes only seconds walking its streets to realize just how special this town is. Whispers and tales of a cryptic and occult past writhe just below perception, while above, waistcoated maître d's with polished buttons serve the renowned fare these bayous forged long ago from their Cajun and Creole lifelines. In this city, the streets roar with music and baubles, the masked dance, and the dead are honored. The veil between reality and the paranormal feels thin here, as I could not pin from where this town's energy and dynamism flows. But know that it is palpable, and it is encompassing. New Orleans, with its epicurean devotion and its jazzed command over rhythms savory and sweet, offers a sensory experience of excellence.

BEIGNETS

FRITTER • 2 DOZEN
PREP: 3 HOURS • COOK: 20 MINUTES

It's hard to fathom it, but the loud and proud thrumming of the Louisiana we walk today is but a fraction of what came before. Beneath her present surface lies a vast, intricate tapestry of intertwined histories that would physically overwhelm if unraveled at once. Those uncareful might use the term "melting pot," but I think Louisiana, and New Orleans in particular, is more suited to a "powder keg" of Acadian, Creole, African, and Francophone cultures. To give a bit of context as to why there's so much Frenchness in this town: the state of Louisiana was but a smidgen of the land claimed in the name of King Louis XIV, who reigned over it as part of New France, a French-controlled district that extended from the Gulf of Mexico to the Great Lakes from 1682 to 1762. I'll leave the rest to the historians.

Even further back than that, however, lies the simple truth: humans the world over have long loved to deep-fry dough, and fried dough is precisely what *beignet* means in French. Name a shape, filling, size, composition, and method—it has universally been done before. To risk being thrown into the bayou, I'll say that the beignet is nothing too unique in this matter. But oh how it sings when done the New Orleans way.

The beignet's existence in town is thanks to the Creoles, and it's inextricably tied to coffee and how the Acadians like to drink it: married with chicory and scalded milk, the *café au lait*. Both coffee and beignets are the specialty of one Café Du Monde on Decatur Street, the de facto authority on these fritters. The café fries them up with fervor, shrouds them in a cloud of powdered sugar, and doles them out in threes. They can barely keep pace with the demand.

INGREDIENTS

2 (¼ oz/7g) packets or
   4½ tsp active dry yeast
½ cup (120ml) lukewarm tap water
1 egg
⅓ cup (65g) granulated sugar
½ tsp salt

¾ cup (180ml) evaporated milk
4 cups (560g) all-purpose flour
Canola, corn, or peanut oil,
   or lard, for frying
Powdered sugar, for serving

METHOD

1. In a large bowl, sprinkle the yeast over the warm water and whisk together. Let stand for 10 minutes.

2. Whisk in the egg, sugar, salt, and evaporated milk until well combined.

3. Using a spoon, mix in half of the flour. Continue to mix in the remaining half until it becomes workable with the hands. Knead the last of the flour into the dough in the bowl. Continue until you are able to form a smooth, round ball of dough. Alternatively, you may use a stand mixer with a dough hook.

4. Transfer the dough to a clean, lightly greased bowl, cover with plastic wrap or aluminum foil, and allow to rise in a warm place for a minimum of 2 hours. Dough should typically double in size.

5. Once risen, add the oil or lard to a large pot or Dutch oven to a depth of 3 inches (7.5cm) and heat to 365°F (185°C).

6. Transfer the dough to a well-floured workspace and roll out to a thickness of ½ inch (1.3cm). Using a knife or pizza wheel, cut the dough into large, 2½-inch (6.4cm) squares.

7. Carefully drop the pieces into the hot fat, no more than 3 at a time. Flip after about a minute or so, and repeat the process until the beignets are a deep golden brown. Transfer to a wire rack or other surface topped with paper towels to absorb excess fat. Allow them to cool and dry briefly.

8. Prepare in batch sizes that allow you to serve the beignets warm and dusted liberally with powdered sugar.

Beignets at Café du Monde,
French Quarter, New Orleans.

Powdered sugar everywhere at Café du Monde, French Quarter, New Orleans.

Bananas Foster served at Brennan's restaurant, Royal Street, New Orleans.

BANANAS FOSTER

SUNDAE • 4 SERVINGS
PREP: 10 MINUTES • COOK: 10 MINUTES

In 1951, a Dutchman named Paulus Lodivicus Blange was working at Owen Brennan's Vieux Carré restaurant on Bourbon Street and was instructed by Mr. Brennan to come up with a dish featuring the much-hyped banana. There were plenty of bananas in New Orleans since the city served as the operations center for the lucrative fruit trade, processing inbound produce from the islands. The result was the *Bananas Foster*, named after longtime customer and chairman of the New Orleans Crime Commission, Richard Foster.

Owen croaked in 1955, just months before his restaurant initiated its big move to its current location on Royal Street. Paul Blange continued his devotion to making Brennan's the institution it is today, with *Bananas Foster* remaining the restaurant's most-ordered item. Blange passed away in 1977, allegedly buried with a Brennan's menu, but you'll still find his work leaving the kitchen at a blistering pace each day, with his recipe serving as a New Orleans fixture.

Bananas Foster is most easily described as sumptuous: the realization of the most natural harmony between sugary bananas, cinnamon, and rum, in tandem with the dissimilitude of warm tenderness and cool, creamy vanilla. It's one of those things I wish I could experience again for the first time.

Despite its assumed rarity in your cabinet, I recommend you source the banana liqueur, though the dish *will* still shine without it. However, you must not substitute the dark rum. I forbid it, as does Paul's ghost. To note, *Bananas Foster* includes ignition à la flambé, but do not fear it, nor feel you are beholden to it. Its primary purpose is one of showmanship in the dining room and on film, and skipping it will not impact the end result of your dish very much.

INGREDIENTS

¼ cup (55g) butter

2 tsp ground cinnamon

1 cup (220g) packed dark brown sugar

¼ cup (60ml) crème de banane liqueur

4 medium bananas, halved crosswise, then lengthwise

1 tsp coarse-grained or kosher salt, plus more if needed

⅓ cup (80ml) dark rum

Vanilla ice cream, for serving

METHOD

1. In a large skillet or frying pan over low heat, melt the butter before stirring in the cinnamon and brown sugar. Once the sugar has thoroughly dissolved and the mixture has thickened slightly, stir in the crème de banane liqueur.

2. Carefully add the bananas, cut side down, to the pan and evenly sprinkle the salt overtop. Bring the heat to medium and allow the bananas to slightly brown, coating them with sauce and periodically shaking the pan, about 2 minutes.

3. Carefully add the dark rum to the pan, and with a lighter, ignite it. Shake the pan periodically until the flames dissipate. If you do not wish to flambé, simply continue to cook and shake the pan for another minute, then remove from the heat.

4. Using tongs, equally portion the bananas, cut side up, into small rimmed bowls or plates, then spoon the sauce over them. Add a scoop or two of vanilla ice cream and serve at once.

Waiter Darryl C. expertly flambés and plates *Bananas Foster* at Brennan's, Royal Street, New Orleans.

Brandon Pellerin, owner of the Calas Café, taught us all about *Calas* in the Tremé neighborhood of New Orleans.

THE HISTORY OF CALAS

Finding oneself in Louisiana, surrounded by snoballs and cakes of Doberge, King, and Chantilly, it's an immensely difficult task to pick just a few of these dishes to develop for the purposes of a travel-centric cookbook. The fact that these unique dishes are so prevalent in the bayou state, however, is an indication that they need little help being remembered. That isn't so much the case with calas, a breakfast staple of New Orleans' yesteryear, which can be considered critically endangered compared to its past popularity.

It's argued that calas cropped up as a breakfast item in New Orleans during the third term of French Louisiana's Montreal-born colonial administrator Jean-Baptiste Le Moyne de Bienville (a name as succinct as it is humble) around 1723, when Bienville christened La Nouvelle-Orleans the capital of French Louisiana. In the surrounding years, you wouldn't find calas in the home, but rather shouted and carried about by Creole street vendors after church with cries of "Calas, belle calas! Tout chaud!" This was during rice's infancy as a crop in America, the knowledge of which was forcibly and cruelly brought into New Orleans from West Africa. Thus, calas are tied to the African side of Creole heritage in New Orleans, and with so much colonial French influence going around, I decided to look further into the recipe's history so I could feature it.

My oldest and most valuable cookbook, given to me by a kindly fan, gave me the start I needed. In this first-edition *Picayune Creole Cookbook*, there was a surefire calas story and recipe. Even at its publication in 1900, the book spoke nostalgically of Calas as a dying fixture of "Old Creole Days," with only a few Black Creole ladies remaining who walked the streets with filled towels in the early morn, selling servants a warm bounty of nuggets for their household's breakfasts. It is supposedly from one of these old guards that the Picayune obtained the recipe, and for you, dear reader, I have only minorly altered it to fit today's measures and kitchens.

However, the story of calas reaches beyond the scope of mere history and this recipe. Calas are inextricably woven into the cultural tapestry of New Orleans. It is a food that emancipated, enriched, and enlivened those who lived under very cruel circumstances. While I may provide a recipe and some historical context, I fully recognize that this is not my story to tell, and I defer to those whose heritage it belongs to. To fully appreciate the weight of calas, I urge you to visit Mr. Brandon Pellerin at Calas Café in the Tremé neighborhood. He is a passionate calas expert who humbled me, and his passion for this dish is evident in both his words and his skillful recreation, which honors its place in the legacy of this vibrant city.

Louisiana
CALAS

FRITTER · 1½ DOZEN
PREP: 1 HOUR 30 MINUTES · COOK: 30 MINUTES

INGREDIENTS

1 (¼oz/7g) packet or 2¼ tsp active
   dry yeast

1 cup (235ml) lukewarm water

2 cups (400g) cooked white rice

3 eggs

½ cup (100g) granulated sugar

½ tsp salt

1 tsp ground nutmeg

2 tsp baking powder

1 cup (190g) rice flour (or substitute
   with all-purpose), plus more
   if needed

Canola, corn, or peanut oil,
   or lard, for frying

Powdered sugar, for serving (optional)

METHOD

1. In a large bowl, sprinkle the yeast over the warm water and mix together. Add the cooked rice and briefly combine. Cover and let sit for at least 1 hour. Traditionally, let sit at room temperature overnight.

2. Beat the eggs into the rice mixture thoroughly, followed by the sugar. Add in the salt, nutmeg, and baking powder, and mix very well.

3. Slowly begin mixing in the flour until a thick, droppable consistency is achieved. The amount needed will vary depending upon the type of rice used. Let sit while you heat the oil.

4. Add the oil or lard to a large pot or Dutch oven to a depth of 3 inches (7.5cm) and heat to 370°F (190°C).

5. Using a trigger-release ice cream scoop or large cookie scoop (#40), drop rounds of batter into the hot oil, no more than 4 fritters at a time

6. Allow to fry for about 1½ minutes on each side, flipping with a spider or suitable spoon.

7. When golden brown, transfer to a wire rack or other surface covered with paper towels to absorb excess oil. Allow to cool and dry briefly, before optionally dusting with powdered sugar and serving warm.

Calas at the Calas Café on Treme Street in the Tremé neighborhood, New Orleans.

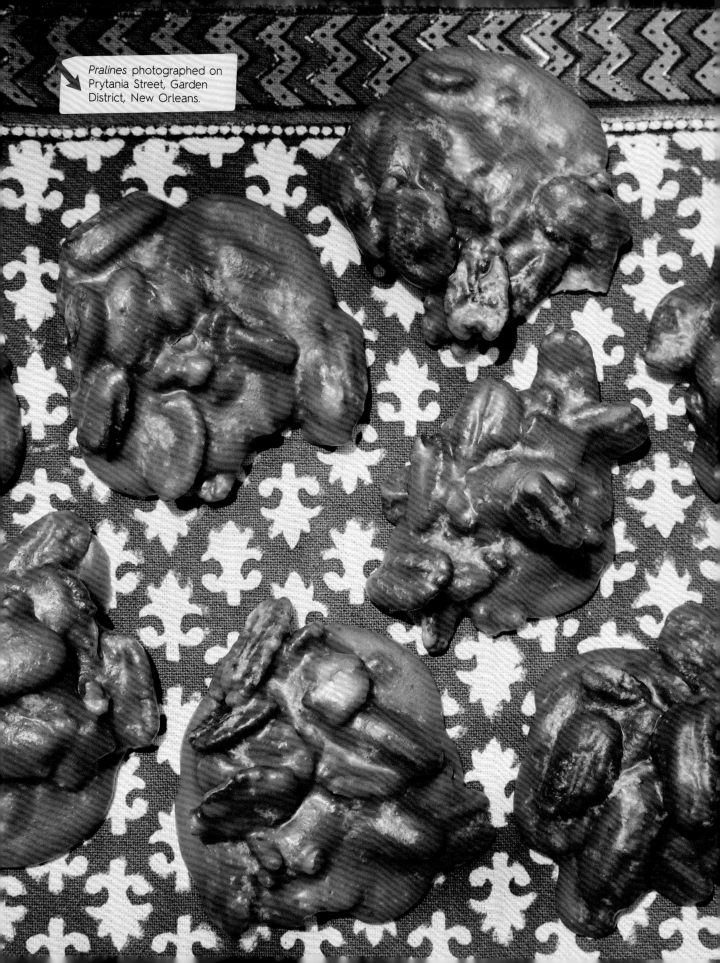

Pralines photographed on Prytania Street, Garden District, New Orleans.

PRALINES
- PRALINES AUX PACANES -

CONFECTION • 1 DOZEN
PREP: 30 MINUTES • COOK: 25 MINUTES • COOL: 1 HOUR

Praline has become one of those befuddling words in cookery. Ask five people what a praline is and you're sure to get five different answers. In Belgium, a praline is any type of chocolate-filled truffle, whereas in the rest of Europe, a praline can denote a specific filling for truffles: that of a ground paste of caramelized nuts. It's confusing, but understandable when you consider that the word was coined in 17th-century France as the name for any nut coated with caramelized sugar.

French settlers brought this love of sugar and nuts to Louisiana, and in tandem with the rapid cultivation of pecan trees, it set the stage for today's Southern praline: a singular object of affection in the South that denotes a softish, round confection of sugar and pecans. The beating heart of Dixie's praline obsession is no doubt New Orleans, where to my surprise, it is pronounced as the British do: "prah-line" and "prah-lun." As a consequence of my time in this city, I pronounce pralines as "mmmmHMM" now, as this is the only noise I can manage when scarfing them down. Here you'll find them by the pound in most any store, or the specialty of institutions like Aunt Sally's Creole Pralines, where the ingredients used still resemble those pralines of yore: sugar, cream, and pecans.

Our recipe for *Pralines* will be familiar to those who possess any old rural Southern cookbook and is well suited to making a batch for a family rather than an entire parish. It will unlock a door that leads to a little taste of Decatur or Rampart Street from your kitchen, and as the soft caramel melts away, so will the commotions of your day.

INGREDIENTS

1 cup (200g) granulated sugar
1 cup (220g) packed dark brown sugar
2 tbsp corn syrup
½ cup (120ml) evaporated milk
3 tbsp butter, softened
2 cups (240g) pecan halves or large pieces, toasted

PREPARATION

1. Ensure the ingredients are prepped and ready before beginning. Lay out a sizable sheet of parchment paper on a heatproof surface, such as a baking sheet, near the stovetop.

2. Place two soup spoons or dinner spoons nearby. Also, ready a suitable place to quickly divest of your candy thermometer and stirring spoon when the time comes, such as an empty sink.

METHOD

3. In a large heavy-bottomed saucepan, combine the sugars, corn syrup, and evaporated milk. Cook over medium heat until the mixture reaches 210°F (100°C), stirring only occasionally.

4. Add the butter and the pecans. Cook until the mixture reaches 230°F (110°C), stirring constantly. This should take about 7 to 8 minutes.

5. Once the mixture reaches 230°F (110°C), work quickly to dispatch the candy thermometer, remove the pot from the heat, and vigorously beat it until it noticeably begins to thicken. This occurs almost instantly or within a few seconds.

6. Using the soup spoons, quickly drop spoonfuls of the mixture onto the parchment paper to cool, allowing some room for them to spread. Work quickly to drop the pralines, as the mixture will set fast in the pot and become grainy.

7. Allow at least 1 hour for the pralines to fully set. Store in an airtight container at room temperature. Your pralines may bloom as they cool, this is normal.

Texas Sheet Cake in the Crestview neighborhood of Austin.

The state most suited to exist as its own nation would certainly be Texas. It is far too large. In fact, driving from New York City to Louisville, Kentucky, is a shorter drive than from El Paso to Houston. They don't lament this in Texas, they're proud of it, along with all the other large things they're partial to. You'd of course expect their cakes to be large as well, and this is very much the case with the *Texas Sheet Cake*.

With the help of my friend JJ Harbster at the Library of Congress in DC, it's safe to say we have no bloody clue from whom this cake originates. It's just how it goes sometimes. From what we can glean, its fanciful (and nonstandard) size gives primary credence to its name, as does the Texan love of buttermilk and pecans—all fixtures of our chocolate slab in question. Most, if not all, recipes you'll find call for a 1:1 ratio of flour to sugar, to mix these two ingredients together first (instead of the typical creaming method), and to bake the creation in the curious 10×15-inch (25×38cm) jelly roll pan.

It's a dense, frosted, and rich 1-inch-tall slice of decadence that shares more similarities with a brownie than it does any other cake, and I find myself thinking about a second piece long before I even bite into my first. It's a shame then that in Texas, your best luck encountering this dessert is when someone kicks the bucket. It is a well-established fixture at wakes, where it dutifully serves its purpose to lift the spirits of the bereaved. You may even want to consider moving yourself and your friends to Texas upon retirement, so that you can secure a steady and free supply of this chocolaty unit well into old age.

TEXAS SHEET CAKE

CAKE • 10×15-INCH CAKE
PREP: 40 MINUTES • BAKE: 20 MINUTES • COOL: 1 HOUR

CAKE

2 cups (280g) all-purpose flour

2 cups (400g) granulated sugar

¼ tsp salt

¾ cup (180ml) water

1 cup (180g) vegetable shortening, or lard (butter may be used, but shortening is preferred)

⅓ cup (40g) cocoa powder

½ cup (120ml) buttermilk

2 eggs, beaten

1 tsp baking soda (use ½ tsp if baking at 5,000 feet or above)

ICING

½ cup (115g) butter

⅓ cup (80ml) buttermilk

6 tbsp (30g) cocoa powder

4 cups (1lb/480g) powdered sugar

2 tsp vanilla extract

1 cup (120g) pecan halves, toasted and finely chopped

CAKE METHOD

1. To prevent spills, though unlikely, place a larger baking sheet or a folded sheet of aluminum foil on your middle oven rack. Preheat the oven to 400°F (200°C) and lightly grease a 10×15-inch (25x38cm) pan.

2. In a large bowl, combine the flour, sugar, and salt.

3. In a medium saucepan, add the water, shortening, and cocoa powder, and bring to a boil over medium heat. Once boiling, pour over the flour and sugar mixture and stir well.

4. Mix in the buttermilk, followed by the eggs, and finally the baking soda, until a batter is formed.

5. Quickly pour the batter into the prepared pan and bake for 20 to 25 minutes, or until the edges begin to pull away from the pan.

ICING METHOD

6. While the cake is baking, in a large saucepan, combine the butter, buttermilk, and cocoa powder, and bring to a boil over medium heat. Once boiled, remove from the heat and whisk in the powdered sugar, followed by the vanilla extract. Using a spatula, stir in the pecans. The icing will thicken substantially.

7. When the cake is finished baking, place the pan on a heatproof surface and evenly pour the icing on top of the warm cake. If the icing is too thick to pour, it may be reheated to a more workable consistency. Gently spread the icing to the edges of the cake with the spatula.

8. Allow the cake to cool and the frosting to set before serving, at least 1 hour. Cut into squares and serve from the pan.

BUTTERMILK PIE

PIE • 9-INCH PIE
PREP: 10 MINUTES • BAKE: 60 MINUTES • COOL: 1 HOUR

Here in Texas, the land of cattle and roughly 130 million acres of ranchland, buttermilk flows thick and heavy—not from their livestock (Texans are in the beef business), but rather into their mixing bowls. Perhaps through veins too, as every recipe from this state includes it. According to community cookbooks, Texas homemakers have long preferred buttermilk over regular milk when making their pancakes, biscuits, cakes, and even dressings. I'm almost tempted to ask if any Texans take their coffee with the stuff.

The *Buttermilk Pie* is an old mainstay and shares many similarities with the southland's *Chess Pie* and other Great Depression pies like the sugar cream, the vinegar, and the poor man's. The distinction is of course in the details, and with our pie of concern, I promise you the details are very good. A tangy, smooth vanilla custard awaits you atop a flaky crust, the elixir to melt away the troubles of a hot day. The *Buttermilk Pie* has a complexity in flavor that belies its simplistic preparation. It emanates the vibes of a grandmother's love.

It was such a favorite of former first lady of Texas Laura Bush that she developed her own recipe for the pie, to which she added coconut and a healthy topping of whipped cream. In Hays County, a ways north of San Antonio, the town of Kyle has developed a reputation as "The Pie Capital of Texas." Julie Albertson, "The Pie Queen," runs the Texas Pie Company there, where *Buttermilk Pie* is a favorite on the menu. Julie supposedly wields the magical power to imbue her custom pies with incantations meant to aid lonesome souls in finding lovers. She in fact found her husband by baking one of these "love pies."

Though I've yet to master spell craft and other matters of the occult, I feel confident that you, and indeed Texans, will find love within this recipe. Feel free to omit the coconut if you aren't partial, but I do think Miss Laura had a pretty good point with its inclusion.

INGREDIENTS

4 eggs

1⅓ cups (265g) granulated sugar

1 cup (235ml) buttermilk

1 tbsp vanilla extract

Zest and juice of ½ lemon

2 tbsp all-purpose flour

¼ tsp salt

½ tsp freshly grated nutmeg

1 cup (110g) sweetened, shredded coconut (optional)

1 single-crust Pie Crust (page 17)

1 egg, beaten together with 3 tbsp water, for egg wash

Whipped cream or whipped topping, for serving

METHOD

1. In a large bowl, whisk together thoroughly the eggs, sugar, buttermilk, vanilla extract, lemon zest and juice, flour, salt, and nutmeg, in this order, until well combined. Add the coconut, if desired, and let the mixture stand for 15 minutes while preparing the crust.

2. Preheat the oven to 325°F (165°C).

3. Roll out and fit your prepared pie crust into a deep 9-inch (23cm) pie dish. Brush the crimped edges and the bottom of the crust with the egg wash.

4. Pour the filling into the crust and bake for 50 to 60 minutes, or until the top has lightly browned and only wobbles slightly in the center when jostled. Remove and place on a wire rack for at least 1 hour to cool before serving. Serve garnished with whipped cream or whipped topping.

Buttermilk Pie on the photographer's kitchen table at her home in Austin.

A slice of *German's Chocolate Cake* in Zilker Metropolitan Park, Barton Springs Road, Austin.

What in tarnation does a German chocolate cake have to do with Texas? Well, absolutely nothing. But it's less *nothing* than you might think. The common misconception is that German refers to the nationality, or the country of origin of this cake, but in fact it's simply referring the surname of Mr. Samuel German, a food engineer who was working for the Baker Chocolate Company (now Baker's Chocolate) in the 1850s. One day he got up and decided the prototypical chocolate for baking, a semisweet product with a cacao content of around 56 percent, needed a less bitter brethren, so he threw in more sugar and created the sweeter German's chocolate, with a cacao content of just under 50 percent.

Nearly a century later, in June 1957, a Mrs. Clay from Dallas submitted her recipe for a cake that used an entire bar of this chocolate to *The Dallas Morning News'* "Recipe of the Day Column," which she titled *German's Chocolate Cake*. General Foods (which owned Baker's Chocolate) saw the newspaper recipe and in a self-indulgent tizzy, published their own take on Clay's recipe as "German Chocolate Cake," with the full power of their marketing millions.

The German chocolate cake became a household name, and advertisements featuring the recipe were plastered throughout magazines well into the 1980s. Later recipes paired the coconut filling with a common buttercream chocolate frosting on the sides of the cake, but our recipe here deals with the Texas OG.

It was customary in midcentury America to bestow recipes with exotic titles to stimulate the well-traveled desires of many an armchair adventurer, so General Foods might've dropped the apostrophe to capitalize on this. Or perhaps they just didn't like the idea of dear Samuel holding on to his cake from the grave.

Truth be told, I think the possessive version should make a return, just as Mrs. Clay intended. It'd sure ease up on the assumed Germanic origins. Indeed, you'll find that Baker's Chocolate itself correctly markets the bar as German's on store shelves, and you might as well go and pick one up because you'll need it for this Texas-born-turned-national-obsession.

GERMAN'S CHOCOLATE CAKE

LAYER CAKE • THREE 9-INCH LAYERS
PREP: 1 HOUR • BAKE: 40 MINUTES

CAKE

2 ⅔ cups (345g) cake flour

1 tsp baking soda (use ½ tsp
   if baking at 5,000 feet or above)

¼ tsp salt

½ cup (120ml) boiling water

1 (4oz/113g) package Baker's German's
   Sweet Chocolate, broken into pieces

½ cup (115g) butter, softened

½ cup (90g) vegetable shortening,
   lard, or solid coconut oil

2 cups (400g) granulated sugar

4 eggs, separated into yolks and whites

1 tsp vanilla extract

1 cup (235ml) buttermilk

FROSTING & FILLING

1 cup (235ml) evaporated milk

1½ cups (180g) powdered sugar

Yolks of 3 eggs, beaten

½ cup (115g) butter

2 tsp vanilla extract

1½ cups (165g) sweetened,
   shredded coconut

1½ cups (180g) pecan halves,
   toasted and finely chopped

Additional whole pecan halves,
   for decoration

CAKE METHOD

1. Preheat the oven to 350°F (180°C) and grease three 9-inch (23cm) pans.

2. In a medium bowl, sift together the cake flour, baking soda, and salt. Set aside.

3. In a small bowl, carefully pour the boiling water over the chocolate. Stir to melt. Set aside to cool.

4. In a large bowl, cream together the butter, shortening, and sugar until light and fluffy. Beat in the egg yolks and the vanilla extract until thoroughly combined.

5. Beat the chocolate mixture into the creamed mixture. Then fold in the dry ingredients alternately with the buttermilk.

6. In the bowl of a stand mixer fitted with a whisk attachment, or in another large bowl in tandem with a hand mixer, beat the egg whites stiff.

7. Add roughly ⅓ of the beaten whites to the batter and mix well. Use a spatula to gently fold in the remaining ⅔.

8. With care, divide the batter equally and turn it into the three prepared cake pans. A scale is helpful for portioning even amounts of batter. Bake for 35 to 40 minutes, or until a toothpick inserted in the center of a cake can be removed cleanly. Allow cakes to cool in their pans for 10 minutes before turning out to cool completely on a wire rack.

FROSTING & FILLING METHOD

9. In a large saucepan, mix together the evaporated milk, powdered sugar, and egg yolks. Add the butter and cook over low heat until the butter has melted, stirring constantly. Once the butter has melted, increase the heat to medium while continuing to stir. After 12 minutes, the mixture will be noticeably thickened and should coat the back of your spoon.

10. Remove from the heat and stir in the vanilla extract, coconut, and chopped pecans. Keep in the saucepan during the filling process.

11. Prepare a suitable place to assemble your cake, keeping in mind how it will be served. Ideally, use a cake stand with a cake board. Use a leveling knife to remove any pronounced doming for perfectly symmetrical and even cake layers.

12. With completely cool cakes, place ⅓ of the filling atop the center of the first layer and spread smooth. Stack the second layer atop and repeat the process. Stack the third cake on top. The last of the filling is spread across the top layer, and the walls of the cake remain nude.

13. Clean up any unsightly seams and decorate the border of the cake's top with pecan halves.

MISSISSIPPI MUD

BAR • 9×13-INCH PAN
PREP: 30 MINUTES • BAKE: 50 MINUTES • COOL: 2 HOURS

CRUST
40 Oreo sandwich cookies (460g),
   finely chopped to make about
   4 cups crumbs (do not remove filling)
¾ cup (170g) butter, melted

FILLING
½ cup (60g) cocoa powder
1 cup (225g) butter, melted
4 eggs, beaten
1¾ cups (350g) granulated sugar
½ tsp salt
2 tsp vanilla extract
1½ cups (210g) all-purpose flour
2 cups (240g) pecan halves,
   toasted and finely chopped
3 cups (150g) mini marshmallows

TOPPING
4 cups (1lb/480g) powdered sugar
⅓ cup (40g) cocoa powder
1 tsp vanilla extract
⅔ cup (160ml) evaporated milk
½ cup (115g) butter, melted

CRUST METHOD
1. Preheat the oven to 350°F (180°C).

2. Fine Oreo crumbs are best made using a food processor. In a medium bowl, combine the crumbs and the butter and mix until a uniform crumb is formed.

3. Press the mixture into the bottom of a 9×13-inch (23×33cm) baking pan and bake for 8 minutes. Remove and allow to cool slightly while preparing the filling. Leave the oven at 350°F (180°C).

FILLING METHOD
4. In a large bowl, add the cocoa powder before pouring the melted butter atop. This is best done while the butter is hot. Whisk together and allow to cool to lukewarm.

5. Ensuring the mixture is lukewarm, thoroughly whisk in the eggs. The mixture will thicken substantially.

6. Add the sugar, salt, and vanilla extract. Whisk until smooth and not grainy.

7. Gently fold in the flour and the chopped pecans. Do not overmix; it is okay if some streaks of flour remain.

8. Evenly spoon the batter over the prepared crust and smooth the top flat.

9. Bake for 35 minutes, or until a toothpick can be removed with minimal crumbs.

10. Remove from the oven and carefully sprinkle the mini marshmallows on top. Return to the oven and bake 5 minutes longer.

11. Remove from the oven and place the pan on a cooling rack.

TOPPING METHOD
12. In a medium bowl, combine the powdered sugar and cocoa powder before adding the vanilla extract.

13. Whisk in the evaporated milk.

14. Whisk in the butter until the mixture is uniform. This is best done while the butter is hot.

15. Evenly pour over the cooled pie, spreading gently if desired. For best results, allow to cool completely before slicing into bars and serving, at least 2 hours.

Taking a bite of *Mississippi Mud* alongside the Mississippi River, Warfield Point Park, Greenville.

One of the first songs I picked up through my 1963 Cadillac's AM radio was the 1963 country hit "Roll Muddy River" by the Wilburn Brothers: a nudie-suit wearing duo with a penchant for Brylcreem and posing near disembodied wagon wheels. Their song sang of the rolling Mississippi River, whose thick, muddy banks were the very inspiration for this chocolaty slab of delight.

Mississippi Mud is not just the name of a singular dessert in Mississippi and her surrounding states. Instead, it has become an ethereal idea for a recipe, similar to that of the Minnesotan Hotdish, and likewise has no concrete origin to speak of. In Jackson, you might find it takes the form of a chocolate silk pie topped with whipped cream; in Biloxi, a cake sporting layers of alternating pudding. One recipe from Pascagoula was simply a chocolate-imbued whipped topping christened with cookie crumbs and marshmallows. *Mississippi Mud* is all of these things and, according to one hard-of-hearing old-timer from Bolivar County, "a river soil wholly unsuitable for farming."

This recipe is a crowd-pleaser. For heaven's sake, it's a brownie, a cookie, and a chocolate pie in one! Mississippi shoots straight when it comes to dessert, and there will be no playing around. Thus I present to you *Mississippi Mud* in its form most prevalent from the '70s to the '00s, featuring the mud's most common elements: a gooey brownie baked atop a chewy crumb crust, wearing a rocky-road-esque topping that'll have you singing "Roll Muddy River" just like the Wilburn Brothers.

A road trip pit stop at Warfield Point Park in Greenville to enjoy some *Mississippi Mud*.

Topping the *Mobile Bay Peanut Butter & Chocolate Chip Pie* with whipped cream beside the Pass Picada Channel, Mobile Bay.

The Original Oyster House on Battleship Parkway, Spanish Fort.

Envision, for a moment, that you're fast asleep on a hot summer night. The open windows gently ebb the curtains, ocean sprays punctuate the dark, and the last hour before morning light builds on the bay is lending itself to a most restful sleep. Just then, sharp cracks pierce the morn as bells, at first distant and echoing then numerous and surrounding, peel and herald the resultant call of excited neighbors: "Jubilee! Jubilee!"

And so a flurry of activity begins in Mobile Bay, Alabama. The temperatures are off the charts, and the water is calm with only a gentle wind from the east. All key to the sudden influx of crab, shrimp, and fish that swarm the shallows, practically clambering to get out of the water.

It isn't known why sea life throngs America's fourth-largest estuary in droves like this, but it's a celebrated event for Baldwin and Mobile County residents, occurring only a few times each summer. In a matter of minutes, one can fill bathtubs and pickup beds with shrimp and crab. Flounder crowd the coast so abundantly that one could blindly gig the water in the dark and spear a fish with each strike.

I learned of this phenomenon at the Oyster House on the causeway that spans Mobile Bay, an Alabamian favorite first established down the road in Gulf Shores in the eighties. As a Bermudian, I could've talked shop about fish for hours, but my interest was diverted to dessert when the Oyster House boasted of a summertime favorite of locals and passersby.

This icebox pie recipe was coined by the Baldwin County business, featuring their surefire combination of cool, silky peanut butter, chocolate, and Kahlúa nestled concretely within a cookies-and-cream crust. It's a certified, jubilee dessert, sure to avail those Alabama sun-beaten beads upon your forehead.

MOBILE BAY PEANUT BUTTER & CHOCOLATE CHIP PIE

ICEBOX PIE • 9-INCH PIE
PREP: 30 MINUTES • CHILL: 3 HOURS

INGREDIENTS

20 Oreo sandwich cookies (230g), finely crushed to make about 2 cups crumbs (do not remove filling), plus 3–4 extra, roughly broken (to garnish)

5 tbsp butter, melted

1 (8oz/226g) package cream cheese, room temperature and cut into pieces

1 cup (270g) peanut butter

3 cups (360g) powdered sugar

3 tbsp Kahlúa or other coffee liqueur

2 cups (470ml) heavy cream

1 cup (170g) miniature semisweet or milk chocolate chips

METHOD

1. In a medium bowl, combine the cookie crumbs and the butter and mix until a uniform crumb is formed. Press the mixture into the bottom and up the sides of a 9-inch (23cm) pie plate and place in the freezer while making the filling.

2. In the bowl of a stand mixer fitted with a whisk attachment, or in a large bowl in tandem with a hand mixer, beat together the cream cheese, peanut butter, powdered sugar, and Kahlúa until light and fluffy, about 3 minutes.

3. In a clean bowl, and again with a mixer, beat the heavy cream to stiff peaks, slightly beyond what is typical.

4. Fold the whipped cream and the chocolate chips into the cream cheese mixture until uniform.

5. Turn the mixture into the prepared crust, piling it in the center to form a mounded pie. Sprinkle the broken sandwich cookies over the top for a tasty garnish. Allow to chill in the fridge for a minimum of 3 hours. Serve cold and keep refrigerated.

Tip
Use a food processor to make fine cookie crumbs.

Posing with *The Prized Lane Cake* at the Alabama state capitol, Montgomery.

Ask any Southerner to measure the "Southern-ness" of the southland states, and we'll find that Alabama is consistently first in rank. It isn't the depth of the drawl that lands her on the podium nor any particular product of geography. It is quite simply: pride. Alabamians are the warm Southern folk who will "bless your heart" both as a kind gesture or in response to something profoundly daft you've done.

The Heart of Dixie offers *The Prized Lane Cake* for our discerning palates. It is the 1890s creation of one Emma Rylander Lane of Clayton in Barbour County. Between 1890 and 1897, she entered the Muscogee County Fair in nearby Columbus, Georgia, and brought home the blue ribbon with this recipe, aptly naming it the "Prize Cake." As it began to attract local admiration, she later attached her name to it, calling the recipe the "Lane Cake" in her cookbook *Some Good Things To Eat*, published in 1898.

Like the famed Lady Baltimore, this cake is a true, noble fruit-filled cake that buzzes with the type of Southern wonder Al Jolson would've sung about. But like admiration for Jolson, there aren't many unburied Alabamians who admire, let alone are aware of this cake. Perhaps its boiled frosting and raisin delights no longer appeal to the living, or its comparatively complex, four-tiered assembly stammers the would-be-curious. I, however, choose to believe that it's simply been unremembered, and like the laughs brought forth from a dusty photo album, is just waiting for its turn to once more be served as your next gathering's dessert.

This recipe is mostly unchanged from Mrs. Lane's version. The original's filling was solely that of raisin, but here you'll find coconut and pecans added—something Alabamians have come to know as the de facto version. I've also clarified the amount of hooch to be used, as the original's nonstandard measuring convention of "1 to 3 cups whiskey" occasionally led to entire bottles of bourbon disappearing into the cakes and sufficiently plastering guests. (Mrs. Lane intended ⅓ cup, not 1 to 3!) This may be why the cake has become most remembered as appearing in *To Kill A Mockingbird* as one of spirited renown. Gentles and ladymen: *The Prized Lane Cake*.

THE PRIZED LANE CAKE

LAYER CAKE • FOUR 9-INCH LAYERS
PREP: 1 HOUR • BAKE: 20 MINUTES • CHILL: 2 HOURS

CAKE

3½ cups (455g) cake flour

2 tsp baking powder (use 1½ tsp if
  baking at or above 5,000 feet)

½ tsp salt

1 cup (225g) butter, softened

2 cups (400g) granulated sugar

1 whole egg, beaten

2 tsp vanilla extract

Whites of 8 eggs (reserve yolks for filling)

1 cup (235ml) whole milk, room temperature

FILLING

Yolks of 11 eggs (8 reserved from cake,
  plus 3 additional [reserve whites for frosting])

1 cup (200g) granulated sugar

½ cup (115g) butter

⅓ cup (80ml) bourbon whiskey

1½ cups (240g) raisins, finely chopped

1½ cups (130g) unsweetened toasted coconut
  (chopped if in large flakes)

1½ cups (180g) pecan halves,
  toasted and finely chopped

FROSTING

2 cups (400g) granulated sugar

⅓ cup (80ml) water

Whites of 3 eggs (reserved from filling)

1 tsp corn syrup

1 tsp vanilla extract

CAKE METHOD

1. Preheat the oven to 350°F (180°C) and line the bottoms of four 9-inch (23cm) cake pans with parchment paper, greasing both the sides and parchment with butter or shortening. Should you have fewer pans, the cake may be prepared in batches, but replicating even layers may be challenging.

2. In a medium bowl, sift together the cake flour, baking powder, and salt. Set aside.

3. In a large bowl, cream together the butter and the sugar. Mix in the beaten egg and the vanilla extract.

4. Gently fold in the dry ingredients into the creamed mixture alternately with the milk.

5. In the bowl of a stand mixer fitted with a whisk attachment, or in another large bowl in tandem with a hand mixer, beat the egg whites stiff.

6. Add roughly ⅓ of the beaten egg whites to the batter and mix well. Then gently fold the remaining ⅔ by way of a spatula.

7. With care, divide the batter equally and turn it into the cake pans. A scale is helpful for portioning even amounts of batter. Bake for 16 to 20 minutes, or until a toothpick inserted in the center can be removed cleanly. Allow cakes to cool in their pans for 10 minutes before turning out to cool completely on a wire rack. If baking in batches, the pans must be cool enough to handle before introducing batter.

FILLING METHOD

8. In a large saucepan, mix together the egg yolks and the sugar. Add the butter and cook over low heat until the butter has melted, stirring constantly. Once the butter has melted, increase the heat to medium while continuing to stir. After 12 minutes, the mixture will be noticeably thickened and should coat the back of the spoon.

9. Remove from the heat and stir in the remaining filling ingredients. Allow to cool slightly.

RECIPE CONTINUES . . .

10. Prepare a suitable place to assemble the cake, keeping in mind how it will be served. Ideally, use a cake stand with a cake board. Use a leveling knife to remove any pronounced doming for perfectly symmetrical and even cake layers.

11. With completely cool cakes, place ¼ of the filling atop the center of the first layer and spread level. Leave a small border without filling at the outer edge of the cakes to not interfere with the frosting.

12. Place the second cake on top of the first and spread another ¼ of the filling atop. Place the third cake and spread another ¼ of the filling in the same manner. Place the final fourth cake, but do not apply any filling. Reserve the remaining ¼ for later. If presenting crumbly or difficult to work with at this point, the stacked and filled cake may benefit from two hours of refrigeration before frosting.

FROSTING METHOD

13. With the stacked and filled cake prepared, and noting that the frosting will harden with time, proceed with vigor and dexterity.

14. In a medium saucepan, combine the granulated sugar and water. Heat over medium-high heat, stirring occasionally, until a bubbling syrup is formed and the mixture has lost its graininess. Reduce the heat to low and keep barely simmering.

15. Fill a separate saucepan with water and bring to a simmer. This will be the bottom of your double boiler. In a large, heat-proof bowl that will become the top bowl of your double boiler, beat the egg whites stiff using an electric hand mixer. Once stiff, move the bowl to rest above the simmering water and beat in the corn syrup and vanilla. Then, very slowly and carefully, begin pouring in the hot, liquid sugar mixture into the egg whites while beating. Once incorporated, beat on high speed until stiff peaks form and a spreadable consistency is achieved. This will take time, a minimum of 7 minutes. If the frosting has not thickened substantially, continue to cook and beat for longer.

16. Using an offset spatula, roughly apply frosting to the wall of the cake, focusing on filling the gaps between the layers, as if you were plastering. Next, coat the wall of the cake again and frost in earnest.

17. Leaving a roughly 5-inch (12cm) circle in the center of the top layer without frosting, frost the outer top surface of the cake. Place the reserved ¼ of the filling within this bare well. Decorate the frosted portion of the top with pecan halves. Keep the cake uncovered at room temperature until the frosting sets hard to the touch, after which, store covered at room temperature for up to 3 days.

The stately lane cake on the steps of the Alabama state capitol, Montgomery.

Country life abounds from these Blue Ridge Mountains,
over Oklahoma plains and Hot Springs' fountains.
The songs of the South, as sweet as their bakes,
reach to Appalachian peaks and Ozark lakes.
The homestyle ways of these humble few
make the city folk sigh, and wish they knew—
of these fields as vast as the skies are wide,
where dessert tells the story of country pride.

ROUTE 66

BATH HOUSE

OKLAHOMA

HOT SPRINGS

ARKANSAS

HOT SPRINGS

More than anywhere else in America, the place most feared by cats is the bathing capital of Hot Springs, Arkansas. Built upon hallowed waters at the turn of the 20th century, the medical maniacs of yesteryear tried their damnedest to use the boiling springs of these mountains to cure patients of their syphilis, tuberculosis, and innumerable disparate ailments. Along Bathhouse Row stand stately, gleaming edifices of ornate institutions filled with bathtubs, saunas, and swaths of outdated and horrifying medical devices to submerge people in scalding water in fun and inventive ways. The last prescription written for this thermal regimen was filled and undertaken in 1950—impressive it took that long to realize that a bath wouldn't fix a missing leg. These otherworldly ghosts survive today in what has become Hot Springs National Park, and their tiled halls play host to petrified children and us grateful subjects of modern medicine. I owe thanks to Arkansas for showing me a place I had little reason to even think existed. Hot Springs is a beautiful—if not powerful—reminder of forward progress, and it sits within one of the most picturesque townscapes of the Southern Interior.

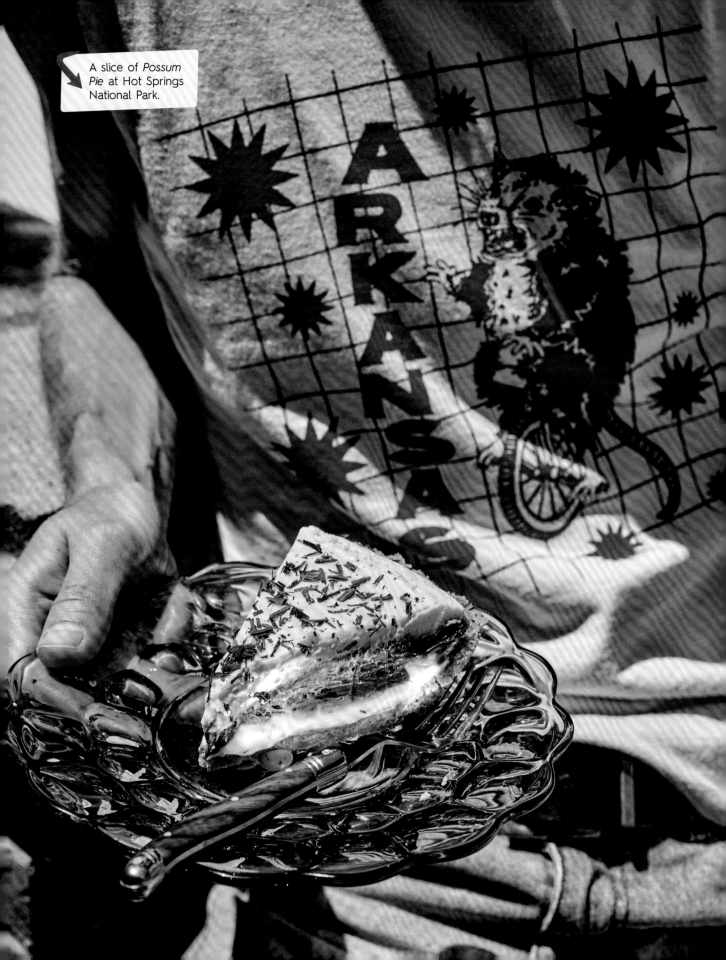

A slice of *Possum Pie* at Hot Springs National Park.

POSSUM PIE

ICEBOX PIE • DEEP 9-INCH PIE
PREP: 40 MINUTES • BAKE: 10 MINUTES • CHILL: 4 HOURS

There is nothing good to say about the possum. This marsupial shivers my timbers, and no sooner do I see one than I feel the need to physically part with my lunch. Captivatingly, they spend their days being generally foul, needing dentistry, and getting hit by cars. This latter pastime, however, spices up those monotonous eastbound I-40 journeys between Fort Smith and the Memphis-Arkansas Bridge.

Truth be told, I'm playing possum by talking possums, as none are found in the *Possum Pie*. Instead, the Arkies have been keeping a stellar example of an icebox pie hidden from us within their state lines. Somewhere between a Robert Redford and a silk pie, this creation accordions sweet clouds of alternating chocolate and vanilla atop a butternut cookie crust.

Though today's blogging bakers might offer you "scratch," "natural," or "homemade" fillings, the true *Possum Pie* is a simplistic gem born of 1980s economical and time-saving temperaments. Premade pudding mixes are its birthright, and I recommend those wary of such to dismount from their horses. We will all die one day. You might as well die having tasted this Arkansas heavyweight.

CRUST

1 cup (140g) all-purpose flour

⅓ cup (75g) packed dark brown sugar

½ cup (115g) butter, cold and cubed

1 cup (130g) finely chopped pecans

½ tsp salt

1 egg, beaten together with 3 tbsp water, for egg wash

FILLING LAYER 1

1 (8oz/226g) package cream cheese, softened

1½ cup (180g) powdered sugar

¼ cup (60ml) heavy cream

Juice of ½ lemon

FILLING LAYER 2

1 (3.9oz/110g) package chocolate instant pudding mix

1 (3.9oz/110g) package chocolate fudge instant pudding mix

2 cups (470ml) whole milk, cold

FILLING LAYER 3

1 cup (235ml) heavy cream

⅓ cup (40g) powdered sugar

½ tsp cream of tartar

1 tsp vanilla extract

1oz (28g) bittersweet chocolate, for garnish

CRUST METHOD

1. Preheat the oven to 375°F (190°C).

2. In a large bowl, combine the flour, brown sugar, butter, pecans, and salt. Rub the dry mixture into the butter with your fingers until the mixture is a uniform consistency, like that of wet sand and no large lumps of butter remain.

3. Firmly press the mixture into the bottom and up the sides of a lightly greased deep 9-inch (23cm) pie dish. Brush the egg wash as best you can over the crust, trying not to displace crumbs.

4. Bake the crust for 10 minutes. Remove and let cool completely on a wire rack.

RECIPE CONTINUES . . .

Possum Pie on the mosaicked stoop of Lamar Bathhouse, Hot Springs National Park.

FILLING METHOD

5. Prepare layer 1 in the bowl of a stand mixer fitted with a whisk attachment, or in a large bowl in tandem with a hand mixer, by whipping the cream cheese and powdered sugar until fully uniform, about 3 minutes. While still beating, add the heavy cream and lemon juice and beat for 3 minutes longer. Spread this layer atop the cooled crust and chill.

6. Prepare layer 2 in a separate bowl, by whisking together both pudding mixes and the milk. This should thicken very quickly. Spoon this atop layer 1, taking care not to unseat the bottom layer or mix the two.

7. Prepare layer 3 by again using a mixer, combining the heavy cream, powdered sugar, cream of tartar, and vanilla extract. Begin whisking slowly, before increasing to high speed. Whisk until smooth, stiff peaks are formed.

8. Spread the whipped cream evenly atop layer 2, piling excess in the center to form a mounded pie. Use a sharp knife or grater to shave chocolate over the pie for the garnish.

9. Allow a minimum of 4 hours to set firm before serving. Keep covered and refrigerated.

Searcy County Chocolate Rolls in the woods along the Peak Trail, Hot Springs National Park.

Bundled chocolate rolls on Hot Springs Mountain, Hot Springs National Park.

In Ozark-locked Searcy County (pronounced suhr-see), the dessert du jour is thy humble chocolate roll. You won't find it presented with silverware or on china, but instead bound unassumingly in plastic wrap and stacked on convenience store shelves right in line with the cigarettes, ready and willing to be thrown into the rucksack on your adventures outdoors. To those partial to pastries, it might be mistaken for a hand pie, a fried pie, a doorstop, or a large dog treat. Instead, *Searcy County Chocolate Rolls* are distinctly uncylindrical, not-rolled-but-folded, baked and blessed burrito confections.

The county seat of Marshall, its southerly neighbor Leslie, and the stretch of US Route 65 betwixt will offer you the most authentic chocolate rolls. They are crusty, they are golden, and they'll plaster a smile on your face while the Ozarks beam right back at you. They're so appreciated in Searcy County, in fact, that Marshall High School (on the imaginatively named School Street) hosts the Annual Chocolate Roll Contest and Festival each spring, where recipes are judged, rolls are eaten, and walks and races are held to help offset this beauty of a caloric disaster.

SEARCY COUNTY CHOCOLATE ROLLS

PASTRY • ½ DOZEN HAND PIES
PREP: 30 MINUTES • BAKE: 15 MINUTES

PASTRY

2 cups (280g) all-purpose flour

½ tsp salt

1 cup (180g) vegetable shortening, or lard, cubed

2 tsp white vinegar

1 egg, beaten

1 egg, beaten together with 3 tbsp water,
 for egg wash

FILLING

1 cup (225g) butter

½ cup (120g) cocoa powder

⅔ cup (135g) granulated sugar

PASTRY METHOD

1. In a large bowl, combine the flour, salt, and shortening. Rub the dry mixture into the shortening with your fingers until the mixture is a uniform consistency, like that of wet sand, and no large lumps remain.

2. Add the vinegar and the beaten egg. Using your hands, gather and knead the mixture until it becomes a workable dough.

3. Divide the dough by pinching it into six equal balls. The use of a scale will make this more precise.

4. If you have the counter space, roll out all six pastry squares before preparing the filling. If that's not an option, prepare the filling and keep it warm while you work in batches.

5. On a lightly floured surface, roll each ball into a roughly 8-inch (20cm) square, using a knife to remove excess.

FILLING METHOD

6. To prepare the filling, melt the butter in a small saucepan over low heat before whisking in the cocoa powder and the sugar. Whisk well until uniform. If the mixture begins to set while you are filling and folding the pastry, warm over low heat.

7. Preheat the oven to 425°F (220°C), and line a baking sheet with parchment paper.

8. Spoon the filling to cover each prepared pastry square, about 3 tablespoons per square.

9. To make the rectangular pastry, fold the leftmost side to the center of the square, then fold the rightmost to barely overlap the left. Fold the top and bottom of each about 1 inch (2.5cm) inward toward the center, applying slight pressure to each seam to crimp the pastry.

10. Using a brush, apply the egg wash on top of the rolls.

11. Bake for 12 to 14 minutes, or until golden brown. Cool briefly on the baking sheet, before transferring to a wire rack to cool completely.

THE VANILLA WAFERS OF NORTH LITTLE ROCK

COOKIES • 3 DOZEN SMALL COOKIES
PREP: 30 MINUTES • BAKE: 30 MINUTES

Picture a dark, heavy December night. Pulaski County's thoroughfares are glisteningly lit by taillights, windows are fogging up, storm drains are gurgling, and the hollow intersections are playing host to the familiar sibilance of tires moving down wet pavement. Inside the warm glow and quiet aisle of a sleepy Kroger in North Little Rock, the last bag of Jackson's old fashioned vanilla wafers lies unceremoniously discounted amid the 120hz hum of nearby freezer bins, and for the first time in 90 years, never to be restocked again.

Since 1933, the Jackson Cookie company had been churning out spades of beloved morsels for Arkansans young and old, with the company quickly becoming a fixture of the city. Legend has it that if the winds allowed, the Jackson plant on South Olive Street would waft scents of scrumptious splendor throughout downtown, filling the air with such a sweetness that young'uns couldn't help but pull the arms of their parents like dinner bells, suggesting it might be time for a lemon Jumble, or any other of the venerable Jackson creations.

But in 2004, all quieted when sales and acquisitions shuttered the North Little Rock plant. Slowly, their lineup of adored cookies dominoed to a single entrant. Now, tucked between the shade of shelves, this single entrant becomes the sole survivor. The last bags of Jackson's vanilla wafers were produced with an expiry date of July 2023. Here, we pay homage to the fallen North Little Rock wafer and attempt to capture that which made Jackson's special. This recipe is proud of its simple, crispy, banana pudding ready Arkansas demeanor.

INGREDIENTS

Whites of 3 eggs,
 room temperature
½ cup (120ml) vegetable or
 liquid coconut oil
3 tbsp imitation vanilla flavoring

1 cup (120g) powdered sugar
½ tsp salt
1½ cups (210g) bread flour
¼ tsp baking soda

METHOD

1. Preheat the oven to 350°F (180°C) and line a baking sheet with parchment paper.

2. In a large bowl, thoroughly whisk together the egg whites, oil, vanilla flavoring, powdered sugar, and salt, about 3 minutes.

3. In a separate small bowl, sift together the bread flour and the baking soda to combine, then sift again, slowly, into the first mixture while continuing to whisk.

4. Whisk until the mixture is uniform, then let sit undisturbed for 10 minutes.

5. Using a spatula, transfer the mixture to a piping bag and pipe quarter-size rounds onto the prepared baking sheet, leaving 1½ inches (3.8cm) between them.

6. It is important that these piped rounds have no appreciable peaks. In such a case, smooth their tops with a wetted finger.

7. Bake for 12 minutes. Remove from the oven and lower the oven temperature to 300°F (150°C). Let the cookies remain on the sheet for 10 minutes.

8. Return to the oven and bake the wafers for 5 minutes longer. Remove and let cool completely on the baking sheet.

A tin of vanilla wafers on the front porch of a house, Cumberland Street, Little Rock.

FRIED PIES

PASTRY • 6 HAND PIES
PREP: 20 MINUTES • CHILL: 30 MINUTES • COOK: 20 MINUTES

Pies are not recipes so much as they are credo; they're nearly a stand-alone cuisine. I'd go so far as to say that every remaining meal in your life could take the form of a pie and you'd never once feel bored. This would be especially true if you were near death. Expiration aside, the regrettably shaped state of Oklahoma has been carving its initials into the art of pie-making for quite some time with their handheld, deep-fried pies.

Amid the swaths of crusts, galettes, tarts, and lattices, Oklahomans prefer a standard dough cut into cutesy circles, filled and folded over sweetened fruit, before subjecting it to the time-honored tradition of boiling hot oil. Within the state's Arbuckle Mountains, set between the Chickasaw National Recreation Area and Turner Falls, Arbuckle Mountain Fried Pies on US 77 has been the engine driving this Oklahoma force since 1954. Berries, apples, and cherries have long filled these golden half-moons, but fillings of pecan, cream, and chocolate make for standout options. Our recipe from 1980s Murray County keeps things sweet and simple via the thrills of canned pie filling: an unlikely hero when warmed beneath the crispy, flaky shell of Oklahoma's handheld heroes.

INGREDIENTS

3 cups (420g) all-purpose flour

¼ cup (50g) granulated sugar

1 tsp salt

½ cup (90g) vegetable shortening, or lard, cubed

¾ cup (180ml) buttermilk

1 (21oz/595g) can of pie filling

Corn, canola, or peanut oil, for frying

Powdered sugar, for coating

METHOD

1. In a large bowl, combine the flour, sugar, and salt. Using a pastry cutter or two knives, add the shortening and cut it into the dry ingredients until the largest pieces are the size of peppercorns. Add the buttermilk and mix until the dough forms a ball. Gather the dough, wrap it in plastic wrap, and refrigerate for a minimum of 30 minutes.

2. On a lightly floured work surface, roll out the chilled dough to a ¼-inch (0.6cm) thickness. If you have a small work surface, divide the dough and roll it out in batches.

3. Using a salad plate or an equally sized circular implement as a guide, cut the dough into circles of 6 to 7 inches (15 to 18cm) in diameter. Spoon about ¼ cup (250g) fruit filling onto the center of each circle, wet the circumference with a finger dipped in water, and fold the circle in half. Crimp the seam shut with a fork. Repeat with the remaining dough.

4. To a large pot or Dutch oven, add frying oil to a depth of at least 3 inches (7.5cm). Heat to 365°F (180°C).

5. Using a spider or tongs, gently add 1 formed pie to the hot oil and fry until well golden on both sides, about 90 seconds on each side. Carefully spoon hot oil over exposed parts while frying. Depending on the size of your vessel, you may be able to fry 2 pies at once, though frying only 1 at a time is recommended. Place fried pies on a wire rack lined with paper towels and serve at once, dusted with powdered sugar.

NASHVILLE GOO CLUSTERS

CONFECTION • 2 DOZEN
PREP: 45 MINUTES • COOK: 5 MINUTES • CHILL: 1 HOUR

INGREDIENTS

1 (7oz/198g) jar marshmallow fluff/creme

½ cup (135g) chunky peanut butter

¼ tsp salt

1 cup (120g) powdered sugar, plus more if needed

⅔ cup (85g) salted peanuts

3 tbsp honey

3 ½ cups (600g) semisweet chocolate chips

2 tsp vegetable shortening or solid coconut oil

METHOD

1. In a large bowl, mix together the marshmallow fluff, peanut butter, and salt with a butter knife. Add the powdered sugar and mix in the same fashion until a raggedy fondant begins to form. Switch to using your hands to knead in the bowl until uniform and pliable. It should not be sticky in any way. If so, add powdered sugar 2 tablespoons at a time while kneading.

2. Gather and flatten the fondant into a rough disk. Place on a clean work surface and roll out to a circle about ½ inch (1.3cm) thick. Using a 1-inch (2.5cm) cookie cutter or a small glass (like a shot glass or champagne flute), punch disks into the fondant and carefully transfer to a parchment- or wax paper–lined baking sheet or plate that will fit in the freezer. Gather the scraps and repeat until all the fondant is used.

3. In a small bowl, mix together the salted peanuts and the honey until the nuts are evenly coated. Using your fingers, adhere and gently press several peanuts into the top of each disk of fondant. Transfer to the freezer and freeze for a minimum of 1 hour.

4. In the top of a double boiler filled with simmering water, add the chocolate chips and the shortening. Once melted, stir until uniform. Reduce the burner heat to its lowest setting to keep warm.

5. Holding a fork in your nondominant hand, place a cold disk on it and dip into the chocolate. Using a knife in the other hand, coat the top and sides of the candy. Lift, and scrape the bottom of the fork with the knife to remove any excess chocolate. Use the knife to slide the candy off the fork and onto a sheet of parchment or wax paper. Repeat with the remaining ingredients. Let sit at room temperature for the chocolate to set.

6. If the kitchen is too warm, or if the chocolate fails to set after 90 minutes, the clusters may be refrigerated to do so. Store refrigerated in an airtight container once set.

Tip

For easier coating, this recipe calls for more chocolate than is needed to cover all candies. The remaining chocolate may be poured into a thin layer on a sheet of parchment or wax paper to set and be used later for melting purposes.

Tennessee is easy to love and even easier to misspell. Here, the capital city of Nashville reverberates over the rolling Cumberland River with yesterday's honky-tonks and today's twangs. Gator-skin boots, multicolored sequin suits, and silver-dollar-studded Cadillacs were once the norm here when charting a hit meant cutting a record. And while I won't disparage modern country with its tales of unfaithful trucks and diesel women, much of what I love about Nashville is thanks to its ever-present charm of yesteryear.

Just a few blocks from the Grand Ole Opry's Ryman Auditorium, where Webb Pierce and Hank Snow once bowed to audiences of cigarette smoke and Brylcreem, you'll find another Nashville institution older than the hills on 3rd Avenue South: goo goo clusters. These curiously named morsels of nougat, caramel, chocolate, and peanuts have gripped the snacking attentions of Tennesseans since 1912, and there's no hint that the goo goo will go go anytime soon. They're upsettingly desirable and among the things I feel the need to hoard just in case they vanish on a whim. In such a case, this recipe will prove useful, as it offers a delicious homemade equivalent to Nashville's celebrated clusters. With its peanut-butter-marshmallow filling and a salty crunch 'neath a chocolate veil, it's a country cheers to music city.

Bourbon's story starts in Bourbon County, Kentucky, and often ends up passed out on the front lawn. Yes, Kentucky might as well be named Bourbon. There's bourbon honey, bourbon balls, bourbon festivals, and bourbon toothpaste. I was once told at a Jamey Aebersold Jazz Camp in Louisville that half the lawnmowers in the state run on bourbon, and I'm still not certain that was a lie. While other whiskeys can be made from any grain, bourbon must be at least 51 percent corn, its barrels must be oak, and it can only carry the name when made in the US. That's why the big hogs like Jim Beam, Woodford, and Maker's are all here in Kentucky.

Compared to the smoky and peaty whiskey of Ireland or Scotland, Kentucky bourbon whiskey is sweet, smooth, and vanillin. An easy pairing for a baker, and an even easier partner for warm, rich desserts like this bread pudding. Cream, cinnamon, bourbon, and butter waltz effortlessly together to make this dangerously good dessert. You'd think it's meticulously crafted from the ground up, but it's rather like throwing things into a dish. Expect requests for more should you share this, and be sure to serve yourself first.

Kentucky
BOURBON BREAD PUDDING

PUDDING • 9×9-INCH PAN
PREP: 45 MINUTES • BAKE: 45 MINUTES

PUDDING

1 cup (160g) raisins

¾ cup (180ml) Kentucky bourbon whiskey

4 eggs

1 cup (200g) granulated sugar

2 tsp vanilla extract

1 tbsp ground cinnamon

½ tsp ground allspice

1 cup (235ml) milk

1 cup (235ml) heavy cream

8 cups (360g) torn crusty bread, like a baguette
   or boule, torn in 1-inch (2.5cm) chunks

SAUCE

½ cup Kentucky bourbon,
   reserved from soaking the raisins above

½ cup (115g) butter

1 egg

1 cup (200g) granulated sugar

PUDDING METHOD

1. In a small bowl, combine the raisins and the bourbon to cover. Set aside to let soak for a minimum of 30 minutes. After which, preheat the oven to 350°F (180°C) and liberally butter a 9-inch (23cm) square pan.

2. In a large bowl, thoroughly whisk together the eggs, sugar, vanilla extract, cinnamon, and allspice. Whisk in the milk and heavy cream. Set aside.

3. Drain the raisins, reserving the bourbon for making the sauce later, and begin spreading the bread into the pan while distributing the raisins throughout. Slowly pour the whisked mixture over the bread, pressing down as the bread shrinks.

4. Bake uncovered for 40 to 45 minutes, or until the top of the pudding is golden and begins to pull away from the sides of the pan. As the pudding nears completion, prepare the sauce. When the pudding is done, set the pan on a wire rack to cool as you continue.

SAUCE METHOD

5. If you don't have ½ cup (120ml) bourbon leftover from the soaked raisins, add more to equal. In a medium saucepan, thoroughly whisk together all the sauce ingredients. Place over low heat, whisking constantly until the mixture begins to thicken. Then, increase the heat to medium and continue whisking until noticeably thick, about 5 minutes.

6. Pour the sauce over the baked and slightly cooled pudding and serve warm from the pan. Alternatively, cut squares from the pan and serve the sauce alongside.

Kentucky
JAM CAKE

CAKE • 9×9-INCH PAN
PREP: 25 MINUTES • BAKE: 30 MINUTES • COOL: 1 HOUR

CAKE

¼ cup (55g) butter, softened

¼ cup (50g) granulated sugar

2 eggs

1½ cups (210g) all-purpose flour

1 tsp baking powder (use ¼ tsp if baking at or above 5,000 feet)

¾ tsp baking soda

2 tsp ground cinnamon

1 tsp ground nutmeg

1 tsp ground ginger

½ tsp ground allspice

½ tsp salt

¾ cup (255g) blackberry jam, room temperature

1 cup (235ml) buttermilk

FROSTING

¼ cup (55g) butter

½ cup (120ml) heavy cream

½ cup (110g) brown sugar

1 tsp vanilla extract

2 cups (240g) powdered sugar

CAKE METHOD

1. Preheat the oven to 400°F (200°C) and line the bottom of a 9-inch (23cm) straight-sided square pan with a square of parchment paper. Do not grease the pan.

2. In a large bowl, cream together the butter and the sugar until light and fluffy. Beat in the eggs. Set aside.

3. In a separate large bowl, combine the flour, baking powder, baking soda, cinnamon, nutmeg, ginger, allspice, and salt. Set aside.

4. In another large bowl, whisk smooth the jam, before whisking in the buttermilk.

5. Beat the dry ingredients into the creamed mixture alternately with the jam mixture, ensuring the batter gets neither too dry nor too liquid. Beat well until uniform.

6. Turn into the lined pan and bake for about 30 minutes, checking after 25 minutes, until a toothpick inserted into the cake's center can be removed cleanly. Place the pan on a wire rack to cool for 10 minutes. Run a thin knife down the cake's edges and transfer to a cooling rack, remove the parchment paper, and cool completely to room temperature before proceeding, at least 1 hour.

FROSTING METHOD

7. In a medium saucepan, combine the butter, heavy cream, and brown sugar. Heat over medium heat until it boils, stirring often. Once boiled, remove from the heat and stir in the vanilla extract.

8. Mix in the powdered sugar until uniform and thick. Pile and spread frosting on top of the cooled cake. Allow 30 minutes for the frosting to harden before slicing with a clean, sharp knife.

Tip

With high temperatures and sugary jam, it is preferable to use a lighter metal sheet pan such as aluminum as opposed to a darker one. This prevents sticking or burnt flavors on the cake's bottom and sides, especially if your cake needs a little longer to bake.

The sun shines bright on old Kentucky. The folks here are kind and hardworking, and the older ladies consistently have good taste in perfume. From bustling Louisville and Lexington to the secluded Appalachian outpost of Harlan, I'd call this state an outlier for being southernly northern yet modernly old fashioned. When it comes to food, Kentucky prides itself on preserving traditions. Colonel Sanders, the patron saint of *oh god, I need more napkins*, concocted his mystical mix of eleven herbs and spices just north of Corbin. At Churchill Downs, the famous Derby pie reigns as the sweet of Kentucky, but its humorless proprietor Kern's Kitchen will litigiously bite off the limbs of those who dare whisper its name or attempt its recreation.

Southern gumption and Appalachian self-sufficiency mean the canning and preserving of seasonal abundances here remains a happy pastime. Even more so when early 20th-century bakers began to define a cake of Kentucky that was sweetened by their stockpiled jams, warmed by allspice, and mingled with caramel icings and glazes. Through years of cookbooks and marred index cards, it's obvious that this brown-sugar-topped beauty—dense yet soft as Kentucky bluegrass—has waned in popularity since the 1980s. But like dust upon an old garaged car, take a moment to investigate and you'll find an astounding gem beneath.

Basking in the magic of Berkeley Springs with *Black Walnut Bread*, featuring James Rumsey's Mill-Stone.

BLACK WALNUT BREAD

QUICK BREAD • 9×5-INCH LOAF
PREP: 20 MINUTES • BAKE: 1 HOUR

There exist a number of things that are worthy of our focused harassment: those who willingly neglect to shovel their sidewalks, birds, leaf blowers, and the needlessly unclean-able venetian blind. What is not worthy of this harrying is the black walnut, a misunderstood tree lambasted as a scourge upon backyards and subjected to public prejudice for centuries. It's all slander, and it is high time we reconcile with one of America's native and truly unique nuts.

The black walnut is much the same as the ubiquitous English walnut, albeit harder to open, but its flavor is nuttier and twice as intense. Though many think they dislike the taste, it's probable this judgment stems from mishandling. If care is taken to expose and dry out the husk promptly when the tree produces, America's diamond of baking lies within. Conversely, leave the tannin-rich fruit to blacken over the nut, and acrid tastes quickly develop.

West Virginia leads the black walnut refor-mation. The people here can see beyond the pungent fruit to the veritable treasure inside, raking in and seizing the bounty of free deli-ciousness that drops from the sky. When the trees begin to produce in October, the town of Spencer in Roane County hosts the annual Black Walnut Festival, a romance of parades, baking competitions, and all things nut. They praise this Appalachian delicacy just as their forebears did in mountain cookbooks and on index cards, filled with cookie and cake recipes that take advantage of its exceptional flavor—with recipes like this wholesome nut bread of yesteryear. Cut into its tender crumb, savor the black walnut, and know that you have a slice of Appalachia upon your plate.

INGREDIENTS

¼ cup (60ml) vegetable oil or melted coconut oil, cooled

½ cup (100g) granulated sugar

½ cup (110g) brown sugar

2 eggs

1 cup (250g) unsweetened applesauce

½ tsp vanilla extract

2½ cups (270g) chopped black walnuts, divided

1 cup (140g) all-purpose flour

1 tbsp cocoa powder

½ tsp ground cinnamon

½ tsp salt

1 tsp baking powder

½ tsp baking soda

METHOD

1. Preheat the oven to 350°F (180°C) and grease the bottom of a 9×5-inch (23×13cm) loaf pan.

2. In a large bowl, thoroughly whisk together the oil, sugars, eggs, applesauce, and vanilla extract.

3. Using a food processor or food grinder, process 1 cup (120g) of the chopped black walnuts into a very fine meal. Thoroughly mix this into the wet mixture.

4. In a separate large bowl, combine the flour, cocoa powder, cinnamon, salt, baking powder, and baking soda. Fold into the wet mixture until uniform. Fold in the remaining chopped black walnuts.

5. Turn into the prepared loaf pan and bake for about 1 hour, or until a toothpick inserted into the loaf's center can be removed cleanly. Allow the loaf to cool in the pan for 10 minutes, before turning out onto a wire rack to cool completely to room temperature before slicing. Store in an airtight container at room temperature.

Midwest

GREAT LAKES · GREAT PLAINS

Great Lakes

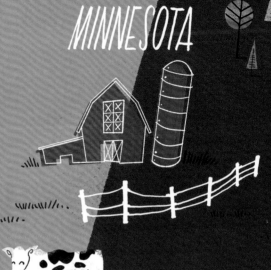

MINNESOTA

WISCONSIN

MICHIGAN

CHICAGO

CHICAGO
CHICAGO
THEATRE

1

OHIO

INDIANA

ILLINOIS

These Great Lake states, peculiar and grand,
whose cities rise from bare flatland,
tame the shivering waters with nautical pride,
and set the pace of the Midwest's stride.
From dairy lands' moos and Minnesota bakers
to Chicago's and Detroit's movers and shakers,
there's much to admire by this freshwater tide,
and oh yes, Ohio is also here, off to the side.

CHICAGO

I knew little about Chicago before I was thrown into its deep end. I understood Illinois to be a quiet and sleepy farming state, well regarded for its flatness and its propensity for growing corn. So my driver was rather confused as I begged him to confirm we weren't in fact in New York City the moment I gazed up at the passing skyscrapers that towered overhead. Morning light revealed massive bridges, elevated railcars, and all the hustle and bustle of any frenetic metropolis, yet it appeared to have materialized within Illinois like a gleaming Ferrari in a cornfield. Amazingly, what soars over the Magnificent Mile is the reprise of a city once burned to its foundations in 1871, and as I learned further of Chicagoland, its people, and its foods, its soul became clear as one of Midwestern values powering modern innovation. To me, Chicago is the industrious sibling who has earned their fortune, while New York and Los Angeles possess the prestige of those long accustomed to wealth. This town is a busy and fast-paced reminder that greatness isn't inherited—it is cultivated, much like those Illinois cornfields.

Atomic Cake on the sculpture
Loop Da Loop by John Adduci,
North State Street, Chicago.

Across my travels of these United States, the gold-medal winner for the most absurd recipe goes unanimously to Chicago's *Atomic Cake*. Here in the glinting Great Lake metropolis of the Midwest, I could scarcely carry the heft and might of this triple-layer, multi-filled beast across its streets. Concocted during the forward-facing optimism of the 1950s atomic age, Chicago's southside bakeries like Wolf's and Weber's felt it prudent to apply every conceivable space-age hope, prayer, and dream to a single dessert. Three discrete cakes of banana, chocolate, and vanilla trisect fillings of fruits, preserves, and puddings, with its sides left bare in a bid to beg astonishment from dapper Dans and ditzy Daisies.

Over the years, the order and nature of the Atomic's construction have varied depending on which unhinged Chicagoan prepares it. While some use Bavarian cream, others use custard or pipe ganache. This cake wasn't created for any need, but simply for ballsy Chicago to answer the question as to whether it could be done.

Like man's dawning conquest into space, the *Atomic Cake* stands as a pillar of human accomplishment: worthy of praise for its ludicrousness just as it is for its utility—because if you don't fancy one part, you've got a few more tries to change your mind.

ATOMIC CAKE

LAYER CAKE • THREE 9-INCH LAYERS
PREP: 2 HOURS 30 MINUTES • BAKE: 1 HOUR 30 MINUTES

BANANA CAKE

½ cup (115g) butter, softened

¾ cup (150g) granulated sugar

1 egg

1 cup (250g) mashed ripe bananas
(about 2 bananas)

1½ cups (210g) all-purpose flour

¼ tsp salt

1 tsp baking powder

½ tsp baking soda

½ cup (120ml) buttermilk

CHOCOLATE CAKE

½ cup (115g) butter, softened

¾ cup (150g) granulated sugar

2 eggs

1½ cups (210g) all-purpose flour

¾ cup (90g) cocoa powder

¼ tsp salt

1 tsp baking powder

½ tsp baking soda

¾ cup (180ml) buttermilk

YELLOW CAKE

½ cup (115g) butter, softened

1 cup (200g) granulated sugar

3 eggs, well beaten

1 tsp vanilla extract

2 cups (280g) all-purpose flour

¼ tsp salt

2 tsp baking powder

1 cup (235ml) milk

BANANA CAKE METHOD

1. Preheat the oven to 350°F (180°C). Grease a 9-inch (23cm) cake pan.

2. In a large bowl, cream together the butter and sugar until light and fluffy. Beat in the egg, followed by the mashed bananas.

3. In a separate large bowl, combine the flour, salt, baking powder, and baking soda. Fold into the creamed mixture. Add the buttermilk and mix until combined.

4. Turn the mixture into the prepared cake pan and bake for 35 minutes, or until a toothpick inserted into the center can be removed cleanly. Cool in the pan for 10 minutes before transferring to a wire rack to cool completely.

CHOCOLATE CAKE METHOD

5. Preheat the oven to 350°F (180°C). Grease a 9-inch (23cm) cake pan.

6. In a large bowl, cream together the butter and sugar until light and fluffy. Beat in the eggs.

7. In a separate large bowl, combine the flour, cocoa powder, salt, baking powder, and baking soda. Add to the creamed mixture alternately with the buttermilk, folding until the mixture is uniform.

8. Turn the mixture into the prepared cake pan and bake for 30 minutes, or until a toothpick inserted into the center can be removed cleanly. Cool in the pan for 10 minutes before transferring to a wire rack to cool completely.

YELLOW CAKE METHOD

9. Preheat the oven to 350°F (180°C). Grease a 9-inch (23cm) cake pan.

10. In a large bowl, cream together the butter and sugar until light and fluffy. Beat in the beaten eggs and the vanilla extract.

11. In a separate large bowl, combine the flour, salt, and baking powder. Add to the creamed mixture alternately with the milk, folding until the mixture is uniform.

12. Turn the mixture into the prepared cake pan and bake for 30 to 35 minutes, or until a toothpick inserted into the center can be removed cleanly. Cool in the pan for 10 minutes before transferring to a wire rack to cool completely.

RECIPE CONTINUES . . .

WHIPPED CREAM

1½ cups (355ml) heavy cream

1 cup (120g) powdered sugar

1 tsp cream of tartar

FILLING 1

1¼ cups (300ml) cold milk

1 (3.4oz/96g) package vanilla instant pudding mix

1 banana

FILLING 2

1 cup (320g) strawberry jam

1 cup (140g) hulled whole strawberries, sliced thin (about 8 large strawberries)

WHIPPED CREAM, FILLING & ASSEMBLY METHOD

13. Once all cakes are completely cool, prepare a suitable place to assemble the cake, keeping in mind how it will be served. Ideally, use a cake stand with a cake board. Use a leveling knife to remove any pronounced doming. The first cake placed will be the banana cake.

14. In the bowl of a stand mixer fitted with a whisk attachment, or in a large bowl in tandem with a hand mixer, beat together the heavy cream, powdered sugar, and cream of tartar until stiff peaks form. Transfer the whipped cream into piping bags (snipped or fitted with a ½-inch [1.3cm] or larger tip), keeping them cool.

15. Prepare Filling #1 by whisking the cold milk into the instant pudding until uniform and thick. Pipe a thick ring of whipped cream around the circumference of the banana cake, dollop the prepared vanilla pudding inside this ring, cut the banana into slices, and evenly distribute atop.

16. Gently place the chocolate cake on top of the banana filling. Pipe a thick ring of whipped cream around its circumference. Prepare Filling #2 by dolloping the strawberry jam inside this ring before evenly distributing the sliced strawberries atop.

17. Place the yellow cake on top of the strawberry filling and decoratively pipe the remaining whipped cream over the entire top of the assembled cake. The sides will remain bare. Keep refrigerated until time to serve.

Standing outside the Chicago Theatre with the *Atomic Cake*, North State Street, Chicago.

The Brownie and an old fashioned in the lobby of the Palmer House, East Monroe Street, Chicago.

THE BROWNIE

BAR • 9×13-INCH PAN
PREP: 30 MINUTES • BAKE: 40 MINUTES • COOL: 1 HOUR • CHILL: 5 HOURS

For many people, chocolate is their greatest weakness. For Chicago, it was a cow and a lantern. While the creaking husk of the city smoldered for weeks after the great conflagration of 1871, its embers were outmatched by the fiery resilience of a Chicago poised to rebuild. The Palmer House on Monroe Street welcomed guests a mere fortnight before it was razed, rebuilt, then burned again in 1874, but you would never know it today when ascending to its lobby of marble, stone, and polished torchieres. Just two decades after the city was leveled, it hosted guests for the 1893 Chicago World's Fair. Among the exhibits of electric light, industrial prowess, and the newfangled Ferris wheel, a neat little morsel of chocolate called a brownie first made its debut.

The Palmer House brownie I inhaled in this very lobby was baked from the same recipe born here more than 130 years ago. Though not the first to print, it *can* be called the first ever brownie. Devised by the hotel's chef at the request of Bertha Palmer, who sought something new for her World's Fair ladies' luncheon, this brownie is a solid brick of pure, fudgy indulgence. With minimal flour and maximum chocolate, it remains soft and velvety beneath its apricot-glazed cobbling of walnuts. Like cappuccino to Rome and caviar to St. Petersburg, a brownie in Chicago is an epicurean coupling to the highest, fiery degree.

BROWNIES

14oz (400g) semisweet chocolate bar (3½ [4oz] Baker's bars)
1¾ cups (350g) granulated sugar
2 cups (450g) butter
6 eggs
2 tsp vanilla extract

1⅓ cups (185g) all-purpose flour
½ tsp baking powder
½ tsp salt
2 cups (240g) walnuts, finely chopped

APRICOT GLAZE

¼ cup (235ml) water
1 tsp unflavored gelatin

½ cup (160g) apricot preserves

BROWNIES METHOD

1. Preheat the oven to 300°F (150°C) and line the bottom of a 9×13-inch (23×33cm) pan with parchment paper.

2. Place a large heatproof bowl over a pot of simmering water and melt the chocolate, stirring occasionally. Once melted, whisk in the granulated sugar, followed by the butter. The mixture may appear grainy until the butter melts.

3. Turn off the burner and whisk in the eggs one at a time, followed by the vanilla extract. Remove the bowl from the pot and set aside.

4. In a separate large bowl, mix together the flour, baking powder, and salt. Add to the chocolate mixture and whisk until no streaks of flour remain. Pour into the prepared pan, evenly distribute the walnuts on top, and bake for about 40 minutes, or until the edges appear firm. Place the pan on a wire rack to cool as you prepare the glaze.

APRICOT GLAZE METHOD

5. Add the water to a small saucepan and evenly sprinkle the gelatin atop. Let sit for 3 minutes. Whisk in the apricot preserves, and over medium heat, bring the mixture to a simmer, then remove from the heat. Use a brush to gently apply the glaze over the entire surface of the baked brownie. Use a dabbing motion so as to not unseat the nuts.

6. Allow the brownie to cool to room temperature before refrigerating overnight, or for a minimum of 5 hours. Once chilled, free the sides with a knife, carefully transfer to a cutting board, and cut the brownies into rectangular fingers, or squares. These brownies are very fudgy, and always require refrigeration.

A slice of *Lemon Fluff* reflected on the North State and East Wacker Street bus stop, Chicago.

Oh, how humanity yearns for lemons. From candies, teas, and cans of furniture polish, mankind has a lemon-flavored, lemon-scented alternative for everything beneath the sun. I've always found it queer considering the citrus itself cannot be bitten into without a cockeyed screwing of the features. Just as pure grain alcohol cannot be imbibed without punishing miscalculations of staircases and social cues, the lemon alone commands respect. Perhaps the moral here is that all good things possess a challenge that requires our masterful tempering to savor.

Chicago's bakers have certainly mastered and harnessed the mighty lemon where the layer cake is concerned. An airy chiffon sponge with a whipped custard filling is how Illinois prefers its lemon cake, and from its origins at Wolf's Bakery in the suburbs of Evergreen Park, it has become a certified dessert of the Land of Lincoln. Though the original is left bare-sided, our *Lemon Fluff* is enrobed in a cream-cheese frosting that amps up the sweet, tart, and bright palate of this Illinois luxury.

LEMON FLUFF

CAKE

2⅓ cups (350g) all-purpose flour

½ tsp salt

3 tsp baking powder (use 2 tsp if baking above 5,000 feet)

9 eggs, yolks and whites separated

⅔ cup (160ml) vegetable oil

2 tsp vanilla extract

1½ cups (300g) granulated sugar

Zest and juice of 2 lemons

½ tsp cream of tartar

LEMON FILLING

1 (3.4oz/96g) package lemon-flavored instant pudding mix

1½ cups (355ml) cold milk

Zest of 1 lemon

CREAM-CHEESE FROSTING

2 (8oz/226g) packages cream cheese, softened

¾ cup (170g) unsalted butter, softened

1 tsp vanilla extract

6 cups (720g) powdered sugar

CAKE METHOD

1. Preheat the oven to 325°F (165°C) and line the bottom of 2 tall (with a sidewall of at least 4 inches [10cm]) 9-inch (23cm) cake pans with parchment rounds. Do not grease. It is imperative that the rounds be cut exactly to size. Any exposed bottom will cause irreparable adhesion.

2. In a medium bowl, combine the flour, salt, and baking powder. Set aside.

3. In a large bowl, vigorously whisk the egg yolks, oil, vanilla extract, and sugar until uniform. Whisk in the lemon zest and juice. Fold in the dry mixture until combined. Set aside.

4. In the bowl of a stand mixer fitted with a whisk attachment, or in a large bowl in tandem with a hand mixer, beat together the egg whites and cream of tartar to stiff peaks.

5. Thoroughly mix ⅓ of the egg whites into the batter, before gently folding in the remaining ⅔.

6. Divide the batter in half (this is best done with a scale) and turn into the 2 prepared cake pans. Bake for 40 to 45 minutes, or until the cakes have fully domed and their edges appear to curl at the wall of the pans.

7. Turn off the oven, crack the oven door to its first detent, and leave the cakes within for a full 60 minutes. Then, remove.

8. Using a thin, narrow knife, like a boning or fillet knife, free the adhered cakes from the wall of the cake pans by running the knife along their circumferences. Keep it flush and parallel to the walls to avoid marring the cakes. Once freed, gently transfer them to a wire rack, peel off the parchment bottoms, and allow to cool completely before filling and topping.

LEMON FILLING METHOD

9. In a separate bowl, vigorously whisk together the lemon pudding mix, cold milk, and lemon zest. It should thicken substantially. Set aside at room temperature as you prepare the frosting.

RECIPE CONTINUES . . .

CREAM-CHEESE FROSTING METHOD

10. In the bowl of a stand mixer fitted with a paddle attachment, or in a large bowl in tandem with a hand mixer, beat together the cream cheese, butter, and vanilla extract until lightened and uniform, about 5 minutes. Add the powdered sugar ¼ cup (30g) at a time while beating. Beat on the highest speed for a further 3 minutes. Set aside.

11. Prepare a suitable place to assemble the cake, keeping in mind how it will be served and that it will need to be refrigerated during the frosting process. Ideally, use a cake stand with a cake board.

12. Place down the first cake and generously cover with the thickened pudding, leaving at least a 1-inch (2.5cm) border unfilled at the edges. Place and center the second cake atop the filling.

13. Using a bench scraper or an offset spatula, apply a crumb coat by placing enough frosting to thinly coat the entire wall of the cake, focusing only on filling gaps and trapping most of the cake's crumbliness. Refrigerate the cake for a minimum of 30 minutes.

14. After chilling, frost the entire cake in earnest. Alternatively, the frosting can be transferred to a piping bag and frosted in this manner.

Savoring *Lemon Fluff* beneath the Wrigley Building and Tribune Tower along the Chicago River, Chicago.

HOOSIER PIE

PIE • DEEP 9-INCH PIE
PREP: 15 MINUTES • BAKE: 1 HOUR • COOL: 3 HOURS

Indianans are Hoosiers, and the Indiana state pie is the *Hoosier Pie*, but you'll be grateful to know that the *Hoosier Pie* contains no Hoosiers, as that would be macabre and illegal. Brought to Indiana from out east in the early 1800s by Amish and Shaker settlers, this sugar cream pie is just as it sounds: a sweet and soft vanilla crème atop a buttery crust. This winning combination was ordained by the Indiana General Assembly in 2009 to be the official state pie for this busy little Midwestern state. The epicenter for *Hoosier Pie* is not Indianapolis, but rather the little town of Winchester in Randolph County along State Road 32. Here they have their priorities straight: what's good in life is all sugar and cream, and the famous Wick's Pie Company has built a legacy making and packaging up the *Hoosier Pie* for Indiana potlucks, Thanksgivings, and dinner parties for generations.

The pie endures as a lovably humble treat. Much like the Chess Pie of the South, it glimmers not from arduous prep or epicurean pizzazz, but from confidence in simplicity from homestyle hearts. The decadence of *Hoosier Pie* is proof that Indiana has no need to prove itself through flashy means, and just like the old song goes, "Hang out the stars in Indiana," and let *Hoosier Pie* shine the brightest.

PIE
1 single-crust Pie Crust (page 17)
1½ cups (300g) granulated sugar
⅓ cup (45g) cornstarch
½ tsp salt
1 cup (235ml) whole milk
2 cups (470ml) heavy cream
1 tbsp vanilla extract

TOPPING
1 tbsp ground cinnamon
½ tsp ground nutmeg
¼ cup (50g) coarse-grained sugar

METHOD

1. Preheat the oven to 375°F (190°C).

2. Fit the prepared pie crust in a deep 9-inch (23cm) pie pan, line with parchment paper, and fill with pie weights or dry beans. Bake for 15 minutes. Place the pan on a wire rack to cool and remove the pie weights and paper. Set aside.

3. To a large saucepan, add the sugar, cornstarch, and salt. Whisk in the milk.

4. Cook over medium-high heat while slowly whisking in the heavy cream.

5. Bring the mixture to a light boil. Once boiling, reduce the heat to low and cook for 10 minutes, stirring frequently to avoid burning. The filling should be thick and custard-like. Remove from the heat, stir in the vanilla extract, and pour the mixture into the baked pie shell.

6. Bake for 25 minutes, or until the crust has browned and the filling is bubbling. Meanwhile, combine all the topping ingredients in a small bowl.

7. Reduce the temperature to 300°F (150°C), carefully distribute the topping over the baking pie, and bake for a further 15 minutes.

8. Let the pie cool to room temperature and solidify on a wire rack for a minimum of 3 hours before serving. The pie will neither set nor be sliceable while warm. The pie may be refrigerated after this point and served cold.

BUCKEYES

CONFECTION • 3 DOZEN • 2½LB
PREP: 30 MINS • CHILL: 1 HOUR

"Welcome to Ohio, we're halfway to every-where else." This was the slogan given to me by my friend Stephen Klum, who grew up in Dayton. The most anybody seems to say about Ohio is that it's the most average of states imaginable. The middest of the Midwest—the regional equivalent of a Toyota Corolla. After arduous research, I can firmly say that Ohio is definitely a state.

But from within this averageness emerges the shining gem of homemade candies: a Midwestern tincture of peanut butter fudge and chocolate, rumored to be so good that it's probably not even from Ohio. *Buckeyes* are the beloved confection of these lands, named after and crafted to resemble the state tree's inedible and toxic nut—logic which has yet to be decoded by man. Yet one doesn't need logic to appreciate that *Buckeyes* are the pearls within Ohio's crusty oysters. It is a critical invention that helps set the state apart as the very best of average places. Risk the thrill of forming an opinion with this easy and playful recipe, and you might be left just as enamored with averageness as I am.

INGREDIENTS

½ cup (115g) butter, softened

1½ cups (400g) creamy peanut butter

¼ tsp salt

1 tbsp vanilla extract

3 cups (360g) powdered sugar

2 cups (12oz/370g) semisweet chocolate chips

2 tsp vegetable shortening, or solid coconut oil

METHOD

1. In a large bowl, beat together the butter, peanut butter, salt, and vanilla extract until smooth and uniform. Beat in the powdered sugar 1 cup (120g) at a time until stiff and well combined.

2. Using a small cookie scoop (#70), scoop and portion the mixture before rolling between the hands to form uniform balls. Place the balls on a parchment- or wax paper-lined baking sheet that will fit in your fridge. Chill for a minimum of 30 minutes.

3. In the top of a double boiler filled with simmering water, combine the chocolate chips and the shortening. Once melted, stir until uniform.

4. Take a toothpick or skewer, pierce the top of a chilled peanut butter ball and carefully dip and rotate to cover the surface with chocolate, leaving a small round uncoated space at the top, as if the ball has a bald spot. Let excess chocolate drip off, and replace the buckeye on the prepared baking sheet, freeing the toothpick in the process. The hole may be pinched and smoothed over with the fingers. Repeat until all are covered.

5. Chill the prepared buckeyes until the chocolate has set, about 30 minutes. Serve cold and keep refrigerated.

Time and time again, iconic names are affectionately shortened. The Mackinac Bridge becomes The Big Mac, and a Lansing-made Cadillac becomes a Caddy. To be nicknamed is an honor, and one that befell the beloved cake of Detroit: the century-old *Bumpy Cake*.

Started in downtown Detroit in 1875, the Sanders Confectionery Company became the dessert shop du jour when they unveiled the "Sanders Devil's Food Buttercream Cake" after the turn of the century. Craving a mouthful of chocolate and not a mouthful of syllables, mobs of Motown motorists stopped by the store, clamoring for "the cake with the bumps!" In short order, this chocolate sheet cake with its rich and fudgy icing that veils ribbons (the "bumps") of sweet buttercream became known as the *Bumpy Cake*. It's a facet of many Michigander's childhoods, a rosy ode to local confectionery, and the worthiest of entries to Detroit's culinary legacy.

Michigan

BUMPY CAKE

CAKE • 9×13-INCH CAKE

PREP: 1 HOUR • BAKE: 40 MINUTES • CHILL: 2 HOURS 30 MINUTES

CAKE

1 cup (235ml) boiling water

¾ cup (90g) dutch-process cocoa powder

1¾ cups (350g) granulated sugar

½ cup (120ml) vegetable oil

2 eggs

1 cup (235ml) buttermilk

2 cups (280g) all-purpose flour

¾ tsp salt

1 tsp baking soda

1 tsp baking powder

BUTTERCREAM BUMPS

⅓ cup (75g) unsalted butter, softened

2 cups (240g) powdered sugar

2 tsp vanilla extract

FUDGE ICING

½ cup (115g) butter

¼ cup (80g) corn syrup

½ cup (60g) dutch-process cocoa powder

¼ tsp salt

½ cup (120ml) buttermilk

3¾ cups (450g) powdered sugar

1 tsp vanilla extract

CAKE METHOD

1. Preheat the oven to 350°F (180°C) and grease the bottom and sides of a 9×13-inch (23×33cm) pan.

2. In a large heatproof bowl, pour the boiling water over the cocoa powder and whisk until uniform. Add the granulated sugar and the oil, followed by the eggs. Whisk thoroughly before whisking in the buttermilk.

3. Add the flour and the salt and whisk until smooth. Add the baking soda and baking powder and whisk briefly. Turn the batter into the prepared pan and bake for 35 to 40 minutes, or until a toothpick inserted into the cake's center can be removed cleanly.

4. Place the pan on a wire rack to cool completely to room temperature before placing it in the freezer for at least 1½ hours. At which point, you can prepare the buttercream.

BUTTERCREAM BUMPS METHOD

5. In the bowl of a stand mixer fitted with a paddle attachment, or in a large bowl in tandem with a hand mixer, beat the butter until it lightens, about 5 minutes. Gradually beat in the powdered sugar until pale, creamy, and uniform. Beat in the vanilla extract and continue to beat for a further 3 minutes. The buttercream should be smooth but firm.

6. Remove the cake from the freezer. Transfer the buttercream to a piping bag with a wide tip (at least ½-inch [1.3cm]) and pipe 7 equally spaced lines of frosting crosswise (parallel to the shorter dimension) over the cake. These lines of buttercream are the "bumps."

7. Return the cake to the freezer for a further 30 minutes. Then, you can prepare the fudge icing.

FUDGE ICING METHOD

8. In a large saucepan over medium heat, combine the butter, corn syrup, cocoa powder, and salt. Whisk thoroughly until the butter has melted and the mixture is uniform. Whisk in the buttermilk and bring the mixture to a boil. Let boil for 3 minutes.

9. Whisk in the powdered sugar in small additions until the mixture is smooth and silky. Remove from the heat and whisk in the vanilla extract. Let cool for 10 minutes, or until the saucepan is cool enough to touch.

10. Remove the cake from the freezer and evenly pour the fudge frosting over the top, tilting the pan as needed to cover. If the fudge develops a skin, or presents too firm to pour, it may be briefly heated and whisked to a smooth consistency before pouring.

11. Refrigerate the cake for a final 30 minutes before cutting into bars and serving from the pan. To portion, slice in between the bumps and then again lengthwise across the middle, cleaning your knife with each cut. Keep refrigerated and serve cold.

CHERRY WINKS

COOKIE • 2 DOZEN
PREP: 25 MINUTES • BAKE: 15 MINUTES

Echoing out from the spooky walls of the Battle Creek Sanitarium in Calhoun County, a professional lunatic named John Harvey Kellogg and his madcap brother W.K. Kellogg laughed to the crack of thunder as they invented cornflakes one stormy night in 1894. First intended to stymie the carnal desires of Battle Creek's patients, the pressed flakes would begin to see new life after being patented and marketed in 1896, growing more popular the farther they were distanced from the two quacks.

We have the state of Michigan to thank for the modern implementation of cereals in cookery. Besides the most famous recipes, Rice Krispies Treats and scotcheroos (both Michigander Kellogg creations), there are also the cornflake–rolled Cherry Winks of the 1950s. Your grandparents are sure to recognize the name, as these peculiar, cheery cookies graced the tables of midcentury Christmases and community cookbooks by the numbers. With dates, nuts, and maraschinos in place of modern add-ins like chocolate, they're certainly a product of their time. Nevertheless, they stand as a testament to Michigan's place as the cereal capital of the United States.

INGREDIENTS

¾ cup (170g) butter, softened

1 cup (200g) granulated sugar

2 eggs

1½ tsp vanilla extract

2¼ cups (315g) all-purpose flour

1 tsp baking soda

½ tsp salt

1 cup (120g) pecans, toasted and finely chopped

1 cup (150g) chopped dates

1 cup (170g) maraschino cherries, drained and chopped

2½ cups (75g) cornflakes, crushed

Quartered maraschino cherries, patted dry, for garnish

METHOD

1. Preheat the oven to 375°F (190°C) and line a baking sheet with parchment paper.

2. In a large bowl, cream together the butter and sugar until light and fluffy. Beat in the eggs, followed by the vanilla extract.

3. In a separate large bowl, combine the flour, baking soda, and salt. Mix into the creamed mixture. Add the pecans, dates, and cherries.

4. Drop by level tablespoon or small cookie scoop (#60) into a bowl containing the crushed cornflakes. Roll to coat, ensuring the ball of dough is covered in a hefty layer of crushed cornflakes.

5. Place rolled cookies on the prepared baking sheet, topping each with a quartered maraschino cherry. Bake for 12 to 14 minutes, or until the edges appear browned and crispy. Allow to cool briefly on the sheet before transferring to a wire rack to cool completely.

MACKINAC ISLAND FUDGE

CONFECTION • 2LB
COOK: 15 MINUTES • COOL: 1 HOUR 15 MINUTES

Arriving on Mackinac Island feels like stepping into a living amusement park. The well-manicured streets of downtown are bordered by colorful wood buildings with bright white trim that feature signage suggesting a time far older than the present. Continue touring the island and you'll notice more temporal anomalies. Despite being in the automobile mecca of Michigan, Mackinac appears to be completely unaware of the invention of the motorcar. Transportation on the island consists of the horse, the bicycle, or the power of one's feet—Henry Ford's purgatory.

Walking Mackinac might just be the best, however. Not only to take in the coastal sights of Lake Huron, but to offset the inevitable pounds of fudge you're soon to consume from any one of the retreat's many confectioneries. Here, *Mackinac Island Fudge* is the method by which you stamp your passport, earn your pin, or send your postcard. It's a beloved treat defined by simple ingredients and traditional pulling, and this smooth embodiment of the island's charm is yours to have with just a little patience and a keen eye on the thermometer.

INGREDIENTS

1 cup (235ml) heavy cream

4oz (113g) unsweetened chocolate, roughly chopped

3 tbsp corn syrup

1 cup (220g) brown sugar

¾ cup (150g) granulated sugar

¾ tsp salt

1 tsp vanilla extract

¼ cup (55g) butter, cut into pats and softened

1 cup (150g) chopped nuts or toffee bits, if desired

METHOD

1. To a large heavy-bottomed saucepan, add the cream, chocolate, corn syrup, both sugars, and salt. Cook over medium heat, stirring constantly until the mixture reaches 230°F (110°C). Remove from the heat and let stand for 5 minutes.

2. After 5 minutes, and without stirring, add the vanilla extract and evenly dot the surface of the fudge with the butter. Let stand until a probe thermometer reads 115°F (46°C) at the fudge's center. This will take about 50 minutes to an hour. Once to temperature, stir until the butter is barely incorporated.

3. Turn the mixture out onto a work surface, scatter nuts or toffee bits atop, if using, and begin folding the fudge into itself, using a bench scraper to gather and manipulate the fudge. Continue folding until the fudge loses its luster and cools to a thick, shapable consistency.

4. Roughly shape into a loaf and let cool completely to room temperature. Cut into thick slices, in the manner of biscotti. Keep covered and refrigerated.

Tip

Required equipment: candy thermometer and probe thermometer (or a probe thermometer rated to 250°F [120°C]), bench scraper, and a smooth and nonporous work surface.

KRINGLE

PASTRY • TWO PASTRIES
PREP: 1 HOUR • CHILL: 80 MINUTES • BAKE: 40 MINUTES

The Midwest does not exist without Wisconsin. It's the cheesy linchpin of these United States—a treasure kept near to the hearts of locals who weather its winters just to bask in the might of its unparalleled summers. And whether in the metropolis of Milwaukee or the sanctity of Fish Creek in Gibraltar, America's dairy land possesses one pastry to rule them all: *Kringle*.

The treat is shaped vaguely like a toilet seat, and its startlingly elongated mass became legislatively mandated as the official state pastry in 2013. First introduced by Danish immigrants to Racine County in the 19th century, this ring of flaky, buttery goodness—filled with everything from Wisconsin cream cheese to fruity preserves—has become as essential to Wisconsin as a Sunday afternoon Packers game. The recipe here is a Racine staple, featuring a creamy center, signature golden pastry, and sweet icing atop. You'll be in on a Badger State secret when you cut yourself a slice and savor the pride of Wisco.

PASTRY

2 (¼ oz/7g) packets or 4 ½ tsp active dry yeast

¼ cup (60ml) lukewarm water

1 cup (140g) bread flour

1 ½ cups (210g) all-purpose flour

¼ cup (50g) granulated sugar

1 tsp salt

½ cup (90g) vegetable shortening, or lard, cubed

½ cup (115g) butter, cold and cubed

1 egg, beaten

¼ cup (60ml) milk

1 egg, beaten together with 3 tbsp water, for egg wash

FILLING

8oz (225g) cream cheese, room temperature

¼ cup (50g) granulated sugar

Yolk of 1 egg

1 tsp vanilla extract

Zest and juice of 1 lemon

ICING

4 cups (480g) powdered sugar

1 tsp vanilla extract

8-10 tbsp water

PASTRY METHOD

1. In a small bowl, combine the yeast and the water. Set aside.

2. In a large bowl, combine the bread flour, all-purpose flour, granulated sugar, and salt. Add the shortening, and using a pastry cutter or two butter knives, cut into the dry ingredients until the crumb is uniform. Then, add the butter and repeat until the largest pieces are the size of peppercorns.

3. Add the yeast mixture, the beaten egg, and the milk. Stir to combine before kneading in the bowl to form a cohesive yet crumbly dough, adding more flour than stated if required. Form into a rough rectangle and wrap and chill for a minimum of 1 hour.

FILLING METHOD

4. Prepare the filling by combining all the filling ingredients in the bowl of a stand mixer fitted with a paddle attachment, or in a large bowl in tandem with a hand mixer. Beat the mixture until smooth and uniform, scraping the sides of the bowl as needed, about 5 minutes. Cover and set aside.

5. Once the dough has chilled, place it on a lightly floured surface and roll away from you lengthwise to form a uniform, elongated rectangle, about 6 inches (15cm) wide and 12 inches (30cm) tall. Fold the topmost short edge down to the center, and the bottommost to the top (like a letter). Repeat this rolling and folding process two times, before wrapping the rectangle again and refrigerating for a further 20 minutes.

6. Roll and fold the chilled rectangle once more, before cutting in half crosswise. Wrap and keep ½ chilled.

7. Roll the portioned dough lengthwise to measure roughly 24 inches (60cm), keeping the width uniform at 6 inches (15cm). You should be left with a long rectangular strip of dough.

8. Distribute half the filling evenly down the center of the dough in a long strip. Allow at least 2 inches (5cm) down either side of the dough's length to remain unfilled, as well as 1 inch (2.5cm) at each of the short ends.

9. Carefully fold one length of the rectangle to cover the filling, brush the remaining unfolded side with the egg wash, and fold it over the center to seal the dough. Pinch this seam together using your fingers, as well as the two short ends.

10. Spiraling the dough for easier transport, gently transfer the dough seam-side down to a parchment-lined baking sheet before shaping it into an oval. Join the two ends together as best you can using your fingers. Loosely cover the pan with plastic wrap or aluminum foil and allow it to proof for 30 minutes. Preheat the oven to 375°F (190°C).

11. Once proofed and ready to bake, brush the entire surface of the *Kringle* with the egg wash. Bake for 20 minutes, or until golden brown. Allow the pastry to cool to room temperature on the pan.

12. Once cooled, you may transfer the baked *Kringle* to a platter and repeat steps 7 to 11 to bake the second pastry. Or, keep the remaining dough and filling refrigerated, up to 2 days, until ready to bake.

ICING METHOD

13. In a large bowl, whisk together all the icing ingredients. Pour the icing over the top of the cooled pastries and allow it to set. To serve, cut crosswise into 3-inch (7.5cm) strips.

BUNDT POUND CAKE

CAKE • 10-INCH BUNDT
PREP: 25 MINUTES • BAKE: 85 MINUTES • COOL: 2 HOURS 15 MINUTES

Way up in the nation's frosty north lies Minnesota, the land of hot dishes and ten thousand lakes. While you and I fish on water, the Minnesotan fishes on ice, and whenever we adorn winter coats, the Minnesotan chooses longer shorts. They're a polite and heavy-duty bunch, who will welcome you to their potluck with open arms and show you which of the family's dishes is a definite *you betcha* or a certain *uff da*.

They also happen to be fine inventors as far as baking is concerned, as it was Minnesota native H. David Dalquist and his company Nordic Ware who were responsible for creating the most easily recognizable icon of midcentury baking: the Bundt pan. Though any one of the state's ubiquitous casseroles and "salads" would make for a worthy entry in this cookbook, there is no denying the importance of this 1950s fluted mold with its distinctive central tube. Lauded for its even baking of heavy batters for more than seventy years, this recipe was among the first to be applied to the new pan, and would set the standard for all other Bundt cakes to follow. Buttery, rich, and almost perfect when fried by the slice, this pound cake of Minnesota affirms the state's legendary contribution to American cookery.

Tip

To serve best: Heat 3 tablespoons of butter over high heat in a skillet until just bubbling. Fry pound cake slices for about 1 minute on each side until browned and crisped. Add butter as needed for further servings. Serve with fresh fruit and a drizzle of cream.

INGREDIENTS

1½ cups (340g) butter, softened, plus more for the pan

2¼ cups (450g) granulated sugar, divided

½ tsp salt

½ tsp baking soda

2¼ cups (315g) all-purpose flour, plus more for the pan

Zest and juice of 1 orange

2 tsp vanilla extract

Yolks of 9 eggs, room temperature

Whites of 9 eggs

2 tbsp white vinegar

METHOD

1. Preheat the oven to 300°F (150°C) and liberally coat a 10-inch (25cm) Bundt pan with softened butter, ensuring the entire pan and all crevices are covered. Dust with flour to coat and tap out any excess.

2. In the bowl of a stand mixer fitted with a paddle attachment, or in a large bowl in tandem with a hand mixer, beat the butter until it lightens, then beat in 1¼ cups (250g) of the sugar until pale, creamy, and uniform.

3. Beat in the salt and baking soda, followed by the flour. Add the zest and juice of the orange and the vanilla extract, followed by the egg yolks one at a time, beating until uniform. The mixture will appear lumpy.

4. In a separate clean bowl, again using a hand mixer or stand mixer fitted with a whisk attachment, beat the egg whites to soft peaks, before gradually adding the remaining cup of granulated sugar while beating. Beat to stiff peaks. Once stiff, beat in the vinegar.

5. Thoroughly mix ⅓ of the egg whites into the batter, before gently folding in the remaining ⅔.

6. Turn into the prepared Bundt pan and bake for 75 to 85 minutes, or until a toothpick inserted into the cake's center can be removed cleanly. The cake should be nearly brown in color.

7. Place the pan on a wire rack to cool for 15 minutes, before inverting onto a wire rack to cool completely to room temperature before slicing, about 2 hours.

Great Plains

Fly over these states and you might believe
that bypassing them all leaves nothing to grieve.
But those on the plains take it in stride,
the Dakotas and Cornhuskers, Missouri beside.
In Kansas, the heartland, they'll surely endear,
despite the notion there's nothing here.
These lands feed the nation from seed to cake,
so missing these, friends, is a grave mistake.

OMAHA

This is a good-hearted place. It's the kind of city that phones to check you've made it home safely and brings you a plate of warm food whenever you're sick. So friendly and hospitable are the passersby and shopkeepers that it might stand to frighten city slickers habituated by urban apathy. Here, couples stroll riverfronts with dogs in tow while children hurl frisbees over flowers in bloom. It all unfurls like a townscape once seen in 1950, yet she is assuredly fluent in modernity. Omaha rises from Nebraska's flatlands and perches herself along the Missouri River with a handsome grace that belies the state's modesty. It's the ideal place to taste the Great Plains, especially if you're partial to overalls or straws of wheat in the mouth. Omaha is the true heart of the heartland and home to the firm handshake of Americana.

Kool-Aid Pie with municipal coreopsis flowers, Heartland of America Park, Omaha.

KOOL-AID PIE

ICEBOX PIE • 9-INCH PIE
PREP: 20 MINUTES • BAKE: 12 MINUTES • CHILL: 3 HOURS

To a giant plastic pitcher, its rim etched and toughened by years of use, I watched my two older brothers, Tyler and Jason, add an obscene amount of grape Kool-Aid, deepening the liquid within to a dark purple. Disregarding the instructions, a bushel of sugar was haphazardly added—and with a hollow, gritty strain that adheres itself to memory—the syrupy potion was stirred to life, neither light nor the pleas of dentistry piercing its deep dark. Looking back, it's easy to see why I possess nearly as many fillings in my mouth as I do teeth: 23 to 28, as of writing.

Many of us share a story like this, and across the generations, memories of manning Kool-Aid stands, homemade popsicles, and the familiar, sweet bite of an ice-cold glass makes Kool-Aid synonymous with our childhoods. You might not know that it's Nebraska to whom we owe thanks for these memories, specifically the city of Hastings in Adams County, where Edwin Perkins introduced the world to Kool-Aid and helped bring about its rapid elevation to a household name in 1927.

Hastings is proud of this history and even hosts a "Kool-Aid Days" festival every summer, complete with a parade, the world's largest Kool-Aid stand, and a contest to determine which child can imbibe Kool-Aid the fastest without croaking. Nebraska even crowns a Miss Kool-Aid Days as a monarchal figurehead in service to her community. Who says Americans aren't privy to monarchies?

In honoring both Nebraska and Mr. Perkins, I present to you a testament to Kool-Aid's versatility in an equally as American icebox pie. Simple, tangy, and downright refreshing, may it hereby be a cheers-worthy companion of your summers evermore.

CRUST
1½ cups (165g) graham cracker crumbs

¼ cup (50g) granulated sugar
½ cup (115g) butter, melted

FILLING
1 (14oz/396g) can sweetened condensed milk

1 (0.13oz/3.6g) packet grape Kool-Aid drink mix (or any flavor)

⅛ tsp salt

Juice of 1 lemon

1 (8oz/225g) tub Cool Whip, thawed, or 1 cup (235ml) heavy cream, to be whipped

CRUST METHOD
1. Preheat the oven to 375°F (190°C).

2. In a medium bowl, combine all the crust ingredients and mix until the mixture is a uniform consistency, like that of wet sand.

3. Evenly press the crumb mixture into a 9-inch (23cm) pie dish, ensuring the sides are well covered.

4. Bake for 10 minutes. Remove from the oven and place on a wire rack to cool completely. Crust must be cool prior to filling.

FILLING METHOD
5. In a large bowl, whisk together the condensed milk, Kool-Aid mix, salt, and lemon juice.

6. Using a spatula, fold in the whipped topping until uniform. If using heavy cream instead of whipped topping, place the cup of cream in the bowl of a stand mixer fitted with a whisk attachment, or in a large bowl in tandem with a hand mixer, and mix until stiff peaks form. Fold in the whipped cream until uniform.

7. Pour into the cooled pie shell and refrigerate overnight, or for a minimum of 3 hours. The pie is well suited to freezing and may be served frozen. Serve with a dollop of whipped cream or topping, and garnish with a lemon wedge.

Tip

If you don't wish to make your own crust, you can use a store-bought graham cracker pie crust.

A slice of *Kool-Aid Pie* on a
hammock, Heartland of
America Park, Omaha.

Holding one of the *Butter Brickle Bricks* next to the birthplace of butter brickle: The Blackstone Hotel, South 36th Street, Omaha.

BUTTER BRICKLE BRICKS

ICE CREAM BAR • 9×13-INCH
PREP: 40 MINUTES • BAKE: 15 MINUTES • CHILL: 3 HOURS

O'er the United States' mountains and plains, whispers of a lost ice cream flavor still hang low about grocery store aisles. Once an institution from out Omaha way, trucked in and checked out by the happy numbers, the legend of butter brickle is said to still be scribbled upon shopping lists as if by ghostly reflex. It was invented in the late 1920s at the Blackstone Hotel on South 36th Street in Omaha by marrying vanilla ice cream with pieces of South Dakota's butter brickle toffee candy bar. It was a simple beginning for a flavor that soon latched itself to the appetites of the Midwest.

Mysteriously, butter brickle vanished as quickly as it arrived, with rapid acquisitions and liquidations ceasing its manufacture in the 1970s. Even the Blackstone, a landmark of the city where Nixon announced his bid for presidency in 1968, was shuttered and fallowed for office space by 1980. Today butter brickle has been reduced to a vestigial trademark, but the feisty city of Omaha refuses to let it go. Here you'll find local creameries proudly serving and attempting to reacquaint the masses with small-batch brickle, and the Blackstone Hotel, now rebranded as a Kimpton, is a proud warden of its place in the annals of ice cream history.

If you are lucky enough to know butter brickle, then this treat will be a welcome addition to your brickled obsessions. If not, then prepare yourself for a true Omaha legend, as this recipe introduces you to an easy creation of the revered ice cream, as well as a most-scrumptious vehicle for its consumption.

CRUST
2 cups (240g) all-purpose flour
½ tsp salt
¾ cup (70g) rolled oats
¾ cup (165g) packed brown sugar

2 cups (120g) chopped pecans or walnuts
1 cup (225) butter, melted
2 cups (470ml) thick caramel sauce or topping, divided

FILLING
2 quarts (1.9L) vanilla ice cream
1 (8oz/226g) bag Heath "Bits O' Brickle" toffee bits
1 tbsp molasses

CRUST METHOD

1. Preheat the oven to 400°F (200°C) and lightly grease the bottom of a 9×13-inch (22×33cm) baking pan. Place the ice cream on the counter, as it will need about 30 minutes to soften.

2. In a large bowl, combine the flour, salt, oats, brown sugar, and nuts. Pour in the melted butter and stir until uniform.

3. Evenly and firmly press half of the mixture into the bottom of the prepared pan. Spread the remaining half over a separate, ungreased cookie sheet or flat baking tray.

4. Bake both for 15 minutes, or until the crust and the crumble appear golden brown. Remove and let the crumble on the sheet pan cool. To the still-hot crust, drizzle roughly half (1 cup/235ml) of the caramel sauce over top, as evenly as you can. Set aside to cool.

FILLING METHOD

5. Place the softened ice cream into a large bowl and beat smooth with a large spoon until creamy and uniform. Beat in the toffee bits and the molasses.

6. Dollop the softened ice cream over the cooled crust and level. It should be smooth enough to spread evenly without unseating the crust.

7. Sprinkle the crumble evenly atop the packed ice cream, followed by the remaining half of the caramel sauce.

8. Cover the pan and place in the freezer overnight or for a minimum of 3 hours before serving. Cut into squares and serve from the pan.

A butter brickle brick on a bricked stoop, Arbor Street, Omaha.

THE RUNZA

Nebraska is a notoriously flat state that everyone seems to cite as the most boring through which to drive. I can attest that Interstate 80, which spans her width, is very much capable of slowing time to a glacial pace. Yet, it is a fool's folly to judge a place on the basis of how pleasant it is to bypass. It'd be equivalent to judging the quality of a swimming pool while remaining fully clothed on the deck. One has to jump in, and Nebraska's steamy Runza gives you the opportunity to go straight into the deep end.

Few can resist the juicy embrace of a warm, meat-filled pocket. After all, is that not how you and I ended up here? The Cornhusker State certainly agrees. Their meaty filling encased in fluffy bread is a direct descendent of traditions brought by Volga Germans who settled throughout the Midwest between 1870 and 1914. From their melding cuisines, we see many variations on the filled bread and bun: krautrunz, pirozhki, pirok, and bierocks, but here, the Runza is king.

Runza rose to fame as a trademark for the chain of restaurants by the same name founded by Sally Everett of Sutton, NE. With a recipe from her Volga German father's family, and out of its first location in Lincoln, Sally turned her family's recipe into the beloved sandwich it is today. Our Runza is an approved original built on the solid foundations of stewed beef, cabbage, and onion, all baked with love within a white-bread bun.

FILLING
1lb (450g) ground beef

1 medium white or yellow onion, finely chopped

1 garlic clove, minced

2-3 tsp cracked black pepper

1 tsp salt

2 cups shredded green cabbage (about ½ of a large head)

DOUGH
½ cup (120ml) milk

½ cup (120ml) water

½ cup (100g) granulated sugar

½ cup (90g) vegetable shortening, or lard

2 (¼oz/7g) packets or 4 ½ tsp active dry yeast

¼ cup (60ml) lukewarm water

4 ½ cups (630g) all-purpose flour

1 tsp salt

2 eggs, beaten

FILLING METHOD
1. Preheat the oven to 325°F (165°C).

2. In a Dutch oven or large oven-safe pot, add the beef and cook on the stovetop over medium-high heat until browned, about 8 minutes. Remove the beef from the pan and place in a nearby bowl, discarding roughly half of its fat in the process.

3. Into the remaining fat, add the onion, garlic, salt, and pepper. Place back over medium-high heat and sauté until tender and fragrant, about 5 minutes.

4. Reintroduce the beef, along with the shredded cabbage. Cook briefly on the stovetop until the cabbage just begins to wilt, about 5 minutes.

5. Cover with the lid and cook in the oven for 2 hours.

DOUGH METHOD
6. In a saucepan, combine the milk, ½ cup (120ml) water, sugar, and shortening. Over medium heat, cook and stir until the sugar is well dissolved and the shortening has melted. Remove from the heat to cool.

7. In a small bowl, combine the yeast with the ¼ cup (60ml) of lukewarm water and stir together. In the bowl of a stand mixer fitted with a dough hook, or in a large bowl in tandem with a hand mixer, combine the flour and the salt. Pour in the milk mixture (which should now be cool enough to touch), the yeast mixture, and the eggs.

Feeding *The Runza* to the sculpture *Dream* by Jun Kaneko, Gene Leahy Mall, Omaha.

8. Begin combining and kneading the dough for 5 minutes on a medium speed. The dough will remain somewhat soft and sticky.

9. Gather the dough into a ball, transfer to a clean, lightly greased bowl, and cover with plastic wrap or aluminum foil. Let rise for a minimum of 1½ hours. After this, your filling should be ready.

ASSEMBLY METHOD

10. Once your filling has cooked for 2 hours and your dough has risen for 1½ hours, turn off the oven, remove the filling, and take the lid off of your pot. Line a full-size baking sheet with parchment paper.

11. While the filling cools, dust a workspace with flour, transfer and punch down the dough, and pinch off a golf ball-size piece.

12. Using a floured rolling pin, roll out each piece to a circle roughly 7 inches (18cm) in diameter.

13. To fill, place this rolled circle in a standard cereal or soup bowl that has been rubbed with butter so as to form a basket shape. Place 3 to 4 tablespoons of filling in the center and pinch the edges together to form an oblong bun, reminiscent of a burrito. The amount of filling used should allow for easy closing of the dough without spillage.

14. Place the formed bun, seam-side down, on the prepared baking sheet. The bun's longest edge should be parallel to that of the sheet.

15. Repeat this process of pinching, rolling, and filling, keeping the counter floured and bowl buttered. Allow at least 1 inch (2.5cm) between the placed buns; 12 will fit snugly on a full-size baking sheet.

16. Once you have filled the sheet, allow the Runzas to proof for about 20 minutes. Meanwhile, preheat the oven to 375°F (190°C).

17. Once proofed, bake for about 30 minutes, or until the tops are golden brown.

18. Let cool briefly on the pan before enjoying warm. If not consumed on the same day, the room temperature runzas should be individually wrapped or stored in an airtight container and either refrigerated and consumed within 5 days, or frozen. They may be reheated in the oven or the microwave.

SMÖRBAKELSER

COOKIE · 2 DOZEN
PREP: 30 MINUTES · BAKE: 25 MINUTES

Smack dab in the middle of Kansas, you'll find a town they call Little Sweden: Lindsborg. Here you can squeeze into knee breeches as you sample lutefisk, walk the rows of carved Dalecarlian horses, celebrate Vaffeldagen, and tour the Swedish Heritage Museum to learn about why a third of this town has Scandinavian roots. If that's not your style, you can head to the Smoky Valley Roller Mills, a historic milling site built in 1898 that once churned out sacks of Kansas Winter Wheat flour by the score. Though it no longer operates, the loving people of Lindsborg cattle-prod the Victorian machinery to life every May during Millfest, where giddy pensioners and bored children stare on as the beleaguered mill begs to be put out of its misery.

In 1961, this Kansas immigrant town produced one of my favorite community cookbooks, *Measure for Pleasure*. It's a bounty of Midwestern and Scandinavian cuisine with some unholy matrimonies of the two thrown in for good measure. Thanks to the local Bethany College, you can still buy subsequent editions today, and it is to them and to Lindsborg whom I owe thanks to for introducing me to the first recipes for *Smörbakelser*, a Swedish-American take on shortbread.

Smörbakelser is made from a simple yet finely crafted ratio of ingredients that results in a most-pleasing experience, as you bite off mouthfuls of buttery crumb. My suggestion is to use a high-quality, daffodil-yellow butter to truly appreciate the flavor of this shortbread. With any luck, you'll soon be tipping your hat in Lindsborg's direction.

INGREDIENTS

1 cup (225g) good-quality, European-style or Irish butter, softened

⅓ cup (65g) granulated sugar

Yolks of 2 eggs

2 cups (280g) all-purpose flour

¼ tsp salt

Coarse-grained sugar, for coating

METHOD

1. Preheat the oven to 300°F (150°C) and line a baking sheet with parchment paper.

2. In a large bowl, beat the butter until it lightens, about 1 minute. Slowly add the sugar and cream well. Beat in the egg yolks. Add the flour and salt and mix until a stiff, pliable dough begins to form, kneading in the bowl with your hands until barely uniform. Do not overmix.

3. Gather the dough and press it into a flat disk on a lightly floured worktop with your hands. Close any seams that open on the sides.

4. Further roll the dough out to an even thickness of ½ inch (1.3cm). Cut with a fluted, round cookie cutter, roughly 1½ inches (4cm) in diameter. Gently free the cut cookies from the counter with a thin turner or offset spatula and transfer to the prepared baking sheet. Scraps may be rolled once more. The cookies do not spread and may all be baked at once.

5. Sprinkle on and very gently press coarse-grained sugar into the tops of each cookie, but do not deform them.

6. Bake for 25 to 30 minutes, or until the shortbread begins to lightly color. Let cool completely to room temperature on the baking sheet before enjoying. Store at room temperature in an airtight container.

Smörbakelser in a municipal shrub of flowers, North Kansas Avenue, Topeka.

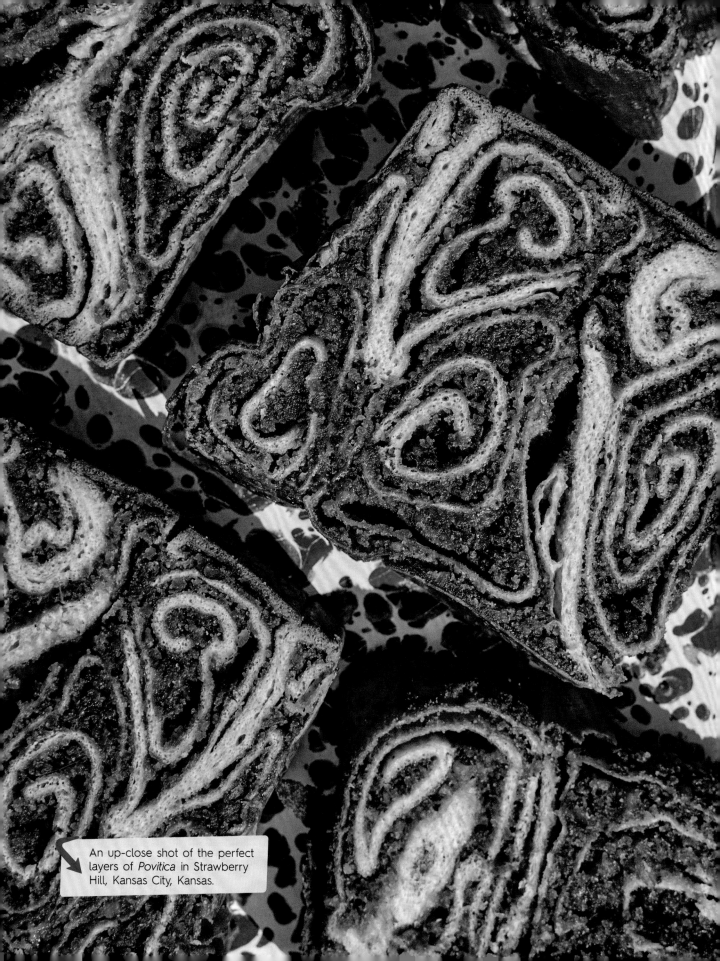

An up-close shot of the perfect layers of *Povitica* in Strawberry Hill, Kansas City, Kansas.

POVITICA

BREAD • 9×5-INCH LOAF
PREP: 3 HOURS 30 MINUTES • BAKE: 1 HOUR 10 MINUTES

Down a ways from a place called Strawberry Hill in KCK, there's a flat parcel of land where the Kaw and Missouri Rivers meet. Here, five massive meatpacking plants once ran at full steam during a lucrative industrial boom in 1890, spurring a massive emigration of Slavic nationals to settle in the area, which became known as the West Bottoms. Slavic and Croatian culture grew alongside Kansas City, until a major flood in 1903 forced relocation from the ramshackle worker accommodations upward to Strawberry Hill, a neighborhood that's now celebrated for its importance to KCK's immigrant beginnings.

In today's Kansas City, you'll find this story continues in the form of a truly special bread called *Povitica* (Pova-teet-sa). Its most-famed proprietor is the Strawberry Hill Baking Company, who bakes it in eye-watering numbers using their grandmother's recipe: a version of Potica (Po-teet-sa), brought to the US in 1903. It's a delicately layered nut bread that's become a fixture of the area ever since the business was established in 1984.

Our recipe has been proudly amalgamated from that of babas, nonas, and grandmas of Wyandotte, Leavenworth, and Johnson Counties, granting us the opportunity to knead, roll, and fill *Povitica* in a terrifying-yet-excitingly complicated process. Slicing it open to reveal the intricate, nutty filling feels as if you've won a prize, and you're sure to enjoy it, as long as you can bring yourself to eat such an artful dish.

BREAD

2 (¼oz/7g) packets or
   4½ tsp active dry yeast
¼ cup (60ml) lukewarm water
¼ cup (55g) butter
½ cup (120ml) milk

¼ cup (50g) granulated sugar
¾ tsp salt
Yolks of 2 eggs
2¼ cups (315g) all-purpose flour

FILLING

½ cup (120ml) honey
½ cup (115g) butter, melted
   and slightly cooled
Yolk of 1 egg

¼ tsp baking soda
2 cups (240g) walnut halves,
   toasted and finely ground in
   a food processor or grinder

EXTRA INGREDIENTS

3 tbsp butter, melted

1 egg, beaten together with
   3 tbsp water, for egg wash

BREAD METHOD

1. In a small bowl, mix together the yeast and the lukewarm water and set aside. In a small saucepan, combine the butter and the milk, and cook over medium heat to scald. The mixture should be steaming, but not brought to a boil.

2. Once the milk has been scalded and the butter melted, transfer to a large bowl and mix in the sugar and the salt. Once the mixture is cool enough to touch (below 110°F/43°C), mix in the yolks followed by the yeast mixture. Add the flour and mix well. A spongy ball of dough should begin to form.

3. Transfer to a clean, lightly greased bowl, cover, and allow to rise for a minimum of 2 hours. The dough should double in size. When the dough is near the end of the rise, begin preparing the filling.

FILLING METHOD

4. In a medium bowl, mix together the honey, melted butter, egg yolk, and baking soda until uniform. Mix in the walnuts. If the mixture is not thin enough to spread easily, add water 1 tablespoon at a time. Set aside.

RECIPE CONTINUES . . .

ASSEMBLY METHOD

5. Clear off a suitable and level workspace on the counter or table that is at least 3×3 feet (1×1m). Dust with flour, or alternatively use a dusted clean sheet or large pastry cloth.

6. Gather the risen dough, center it on the workspace, and with a lightly floured rolling pin, roll out to a rectangle roughly 20 inches (51cm) across and 10 inches (25cm) tall. As you are rolling, make sure to rotate and move around the disk of dough on the floured surface to keep the bottom from sticking.

7. Once you have reached the required size, brush the surface of the dough with a bit of the melted butter. This will aid in stretching. Keep the remainder of the melted butter nearby and enough flour on the counter surrounding the dough to aid while you stretch.

8. The object of this step is to stretch the dough as thin as possible to a rough rectangle that is 4 times the length of the loaf pan, and twice its length in width, around 3×2 feet (1m×0.6m). With the dough buttered, stretch with a completely open palm or the backside of a closed fist. You should do this from above, and below, by gently lifting the dough off the counter and tugging, this also helps to ensure the dough is not sticking. As you interact with the dough, you will find how best it wants to stretch. Sparingly brush melted butter where you need help, and avoid stretching areas that have become transparent. If using a sheet or pastry cloth, stretching from below becomes easier.

9. Once you have stretched the dough to roughly 3 feet (1m) across and 2 feet (0.6m) high, or as near as you can get without tearing, evenly dollop the filling in spoonfuls across the surface of the dough. Leave a 1-inch (2.5cm) border along the perimeter without filling. Then gently spread out the placed filling with your fingers.

10. Begin uniformly rolling up the sheet, starting at its longest edge. Roll into a long snake of dough. Grease your loaf pan.

11. Form a "U" shape with the snake of dough by folding in half. Place the bottom of the "U" in one end of the pan, running its arms up the other end, and then slinking the tops of the "U" over themselves, so that a cross section of the loaf will be that of 4 circles. If you were unable to stretch the dough to this length, forming an elongated "S" in the pan is just as suitable.

12. Let proof for a further 30 minutes while you preheat the oven to 350°F (180°C). Once proofed, brush the top of your dough with the egg wash.

13. Bake for 15 minutes, before reducing the temperature to 300°F (150°C) and baking for a further 45 to 55 minutes, or until the top of the bread is a dark, golden brown. The bread may be covered with aluminum foil if it is browning too early.

14. Remove from the oven and allow to cool in the pan for at least 30 minutes, before turning out onto a wire rack to cool completely. Once completely cool, slice with a sharp serrated knife from the loaf's bottom, so as to not shred the top.

Standing before a mural of Mathias Splitlog, a founding Native American contributor to the Strawberry Hill neighborhood, Central Ave, Strawberry Hill, Kansas City, Kansas.

GOOEY BUTTER CAKE

BAR • 9×13-INCH
PREP: 1 HOUR 30 MINUTES • BAKE: 40 MINUTES

Like its two differing pronunciations of Missouri and Missourah, the Show-Me State has two differing recipes for this beloved homegrown cake. The original yeasted *Gooey Butter Cake* was born in St. Louis during the Great Depression, where hearsay tells the tale of a city baker who jumbled up his coffee cake's butter ratio, and instead of abject failure, the resulting "mistake" became an unlikely hit. Missourians also know of a thinner and sweeter yellow cake variety that was popularized after the midcentury. This "ooey gooey butter cake" often calls for boxed cake mix and cream cheese.

I appreciate both, but locals from St. Louis to Kansas City are certainly dogmatic about which they prefer. This *Gooey Butter Cake* is the original, just like the type you're likely to encounter in your *great*-grandmother's recipe cards. Whereas the cakey version is the one you're sure to find at potlucks, at family gatherings, and in your *grand*mother's spiral-bound cookbooks.

CRUST

1 (¼ ounce/7g) packet or
  2¼ tsp active dry yeast
3 tbsp lukewarm water
½ cup (115g) butter
½ cup (120ml) milk

¼ cup (50g) granulated sugar
¾ tsp salt
1 egg, beaten
2 cups (280g) all-purpose flour

FILLING

1 cup (225g) butter, softened
2 cups (400g) granulated sugar
2 eggs
1 tsp vanilla extract

1 cup (140g) all-purpose flour
¼ cup (60ml) evaporated milk
½ cup (120ml) corn syrup
Powdered sugar, for dusting

CRUST METHOD

1. In a small bowl, mix together the yeast and the lukewarm water and set aside. In a small saucepan, combine the butter and the milk, and cook over medium heat to scald. Mixture should be steaming, but not brought to a boil.

2. Once the milk has been scalded and the butter melted, transfer to a large bowl and mix in the sugar and the salt. Once the mixture is cool enough to touch, mix in the beaten egg and the yeast mixture. Add the flour and mix well. A sticky, spongy dough should begin to form.

3. Grease a 9×13-inch (23×33cm) baking pan very lightly, transfer the dough to the center of the pan, and using hands wetted with water, pat and stretch the dough over the pan's bottom to form an even crust. Cover the pan with plastic wrap or aluminum foil and let rise in a warm place for a minimum of 1 hour.

FILLING METHOD

4. Once the dough has risen, preheat the oven to 350°F (180°C).

5. In a large bowl, cream together the butter and the sugar until light and fluffy. Beat in the eggs, followed by the vanilla extract.

6. Mix in the flour alternately with the evaporated milk, before mixing in the corn syrup. Beat the mixture until uniform and smooth.

7. Spread this filling evenly atop the risen dough and bake for about 40 minutes, or until the edges appear golden brown. Remove and let cool in the pan completely to room temperature before attempting to serve. Cut into bars and serve from the pan, liberally dusted with powdered sugar.

St. Louis' *Gooey Butter Cake* in arch-rival territory: Kansas City, Missouri.

Dirt Cake in the dining room of the Byers Mansion, Independence Avenue, Kansas City, Missouri.

DIRT CAKE

DESSERT • 12–15 SERVINGS
PREP: 20 MINUTES

I once received an outraged letter from a Missouri woman who informed me that I'd made a dirt cake wrong in one of my videos. Not because I'd used incorrect ingredients, made inappropriate substitutions, or otherwise loused up the dessert, but because I'd failed to serve it in a terracotta plant pot. Ridiculous? Maybe, but I couldn't dismiss the logic that a *dirt* cake should rightfully be attributed to a pot meant to hold soil. So, I thanked her kindly for her letter and informed her that I'd serve my coffee cakes in percolators and my jacket potatoes on coat hangers moving forward. Jokes aside, this letter instilled in me the realization that a dish worth getting upset over is coequal with a dish that has meaning—and the *Dirt Cake* sure means something to Missourians.

Missouri has adopted this "cake" as its own, proudly penning the bulk of the USA's recipes for the Midwestern marvel. Like the state, the dessert is a basket case of alternating puddings, Cool Whip, crushed cookies, and gummy worms half-dug into "dirt." An absurd description to any outsider, but a mouthwatering treat for those in the know.

Today's recipes typically involve fewer ingredients, but in exchange for an added 2 minutes, I think you'll prefer this 1990s method of incorporating butter and cream cheese. In the name of food safety, I recommend against the plant pot, but no matter the vessel, may you prize the *Dirt Cake* as I do for its ability to diffuse seriousness. It's sure to lighten the mood and coax just a smidge of youth from those poker-faced characters in our lives.

INGREDIENTS

2 (3oz/85g) packets vanilla instant pudding mix

3 cups (710ml) milk, cold

1 (8oz/226g) package cream cheese, softened

½ cup (115g) butter, softened

1 cup (120g) powdered sugar

1 (8oz/226g) tub Cool Whip, thawed

40 Oreo sandwich cookies (460g), finely crushed to make about 4 cups crumbs (do not remove filling)

A few Oreo sandwich cookies, roughly broken, for decoration

Gummy worms, at your discretion (optional)

METHOD

1. In a large bowl, whisk together the instant pudding and the milk until combined. Set aside.

2. In a separate large bowl, beat together the cream cheese and the butter until uniform. Add the powdered sugar and beat well. Add the pudding mixture and whisk until uniform. Fold in the Cool Whip.

FOR INDIVIDUAL SERVINGS

To sundae dishes, sherbert bowls, or other glassware, layer a portion of cookie crumbs, followed by a larger portion of pudding. Top with crumbs. Decorate with broken cookie bits and gummy worms, should you choose.

POTLUCK STYLE

To an ungreased 9×13-inch (23×33cm) casserole dish or baking tray, spread about ⅔ of the crumbs evenly across the bottom to form a crust. Evenly dollop the pudding mixture on top, using a downward force to spread flat with a spatula. Sprinkle the remainder of the crumbs on top, followed by the broken cookie bits. Decorate with gummy worms, should you choose, and portion by spoon.

BLARNEY STONES

PETIT FOUR • 20 SMALL CAKES
PREP: 1 HOUR • BAKE: 35 MINS • CHILL: 2 HOURS

You might've heard about Blarney Castle. It's a medieval stronghold in County Cork, Ireland, that's become famous for one unassuming block of limestone. People journey to kiss the stone as it's rumored to give "the gift of the gab." But have you also heard there's a slab of this Irish castle that lies 3,800 miles (6,000km) away in the middle of Emmetsburg, Iowa?

Largely settled by the Irish during the potato famine of the 1840s and '50s, Emmetsburg is proud of its Irish ties. It's been an official sister city of Dublin since 1962, and every St. Patrick's Day, Emmetsburg celebrates with a gusto incongruous with its tiny population of 4,000, even welcoming a member of the Irish Parliament to preside over the jubilee.

It was during one of these visits in 1966 when, in conjunction with local governments, Irish TWA stewardess Paddy Horan was comically asked to bring a stone from Blarney Castle in a massive suitcase aboard their charter. Nearing 100 pounds, the slab was delivered and commemorated successfully right in the yard of the Palo Alto County courthouse on Broadway Street, where it remains today.

Fascinated by the stone, the folks of Iowa decided to name a dessert of their own creation after it. These edible *Blarney Stones* are rich, feathery squares of yellow cake enrobed in vanilla buttercream and rolled in a healthy layer of roasted salted peanuts. They are petit fours I could eat in droves, and don't you think for a minute that it needs to be anywhere near St. Patrick's Day to warrant enjoying them.

CAKE
4 eggs
¾ cup (180ml) vegetable oil
1½ cups (300g) granulated sugar
2¼ cups (315g) all-purpose flour

½ tsp salt
1 tsp baking powder
½ cup (120ml) milk

BUTTERCREAM & TOPPING
1½ cups (340g) unsalted butter, softened
4 cups (1lb/480g) powdered sugar
1½ tsp vanilla extract

1-3 tbsp milk, to thin if needed
3 cups finely chopped salted peanuts

CAKE METHOD
1. Preheat the oven to 350°F (180°C). Grease a 9×13-inch (23×33cm) pan.

2. In a large bowl, whisk together the eggs, oil, and sugar until smooth.

3. In a separate large bowl, combine the flour, salt, and baking powder. Fold into the egg mixture alternately with the milk.

4. Turn into the prepared pan and bake for 30 to 35 minutes, or until a toothpick inserted into the center can be removed cleanly. Allow to cool in the pan for 15 minutes, before inverting onto a wire rack to cool completely.

5. Once completely cool, cut the cake into squares: 5 slices across the pan's length and 4 by its width will yield 20 squares. Clean the knife after each cut to prevent tearing.

6. Freeze the cakes for a minimum of 2 hours before frosting.

BUTTERCREAM & TOPPING METHOD
7. In the bowl of a stand mixer fitted with a paddle attachment, or in a large bowl in tandem with a hand mixer, beat the butter on high speed until smooth, about 3 minutes.

8. Gradually beat in the powdered sugar ¼ cup (30g) at a time. Once all the sugar has been incorporated, add the vanilla extract and beat for 5 minutes longer, until completely uniform. If the frosting is too thick, milk may be added to thin. Keep the frosting in this bowl.

9. Set out a large parchment paper-lined workspace to hold the finished petit fours. Place the chopped peanuts in a small bowl.

10. Using a thick kebab skewer or butter knife, pierce a frozen cake square so as to easily apply frosting to all sides with a spatula. Hold the skewered piece in one hand while applying frosting with the other. The cakes may also be held with the fingers if you do not mind the mess.

11. Sprinkle handfuls of peanuts over the frosted squares, working over the bowl of nuts and covering all sides.

12. Remove from the skewer and place the least attractive side face-down on the parchment. Repeat. Like any buttercream-frosted treat, these petit fours may be kept covered at room temperature if cool enough. Otherwise, they should be kept refrigerated.

Happy is a fine descriptor for South Dakota and its people. They're so chipper that their level of positivity would be downright foreboding in any horror-movie setting. The first South Dakotan I ever met was Alie Martin, who studied with me at the University of Wyoming. She introduced me to the delightful *Kuchen* and corrected my pronunciation to the proper South Dakota way (koog-en or koo-kin). From the small town of Eureka in McPherson County to the sprawling metro of Rapid City, I learned that *Kuchen* was cherished the state over for its warm-hug-on-a-plate reputation.

The dish was created by early German settlers brought to the Dakotas by the Homestead Act of 1862 and is now among the most visible of the Dakota states' well-ingrained German heritage. This is why North Dakotans also stake their claim on the tart, but it was South Dakota that officially made *Kuchen* their state dessert in 2000.

While kuchen can define almost any cake in its native country of Germany, South Dakota's *Kuchen* refers to a singular yeasted pastry with a custard topping, either with or without fruit and streusel. Relatively flat and unassumingly beige, *Kuchen*'s looks certainly belie its lovable taste. This recipe will raise an eyebrow to the merits of South Dakota and give insight as to why the people who live here are so darn happy all the time.

KUCHEN

TART · TWO 9-INCH PASTRIES
PREP: 3 HOURS · BAKE: 45 MINUTES

PASTRY

⅓ cup (80ml) milk

1 (¼oz/7g) packet or 2¼ tsp active dry yeast

3 tbsp lukewarm water

¼ cup (50g) granulated sugar

½ tsp salt

1 egg, beaten

2 cups (280g) all-purpose flour

FILLING

4 cups sliced fruit: apples, peaches, plums, apricots, etc.

3 eggs

1 cup (235ml) milk

½ cup (100g) granulated sugar

STREUSEL

⅔ cup (135g) granulated sugar

⅔ cup (90g) all-purpose flour

1 tbsp ground cinnamon

½ tsp ground nutmeg

½ cup (115g) butter, cold and cut into pieces

PASTRY METHOD

1. In a small saucepan, scald the milk over medium heat. Meanwhile, mix together the yeast and the lukewarm water in a small bowl.

2. Once the milk has been scalded, transfer to a large bowl and mix in the sugar and the salt. Once the mixture is cool enough to touch, mix in the egg and the yeast mixture. Add the flour and mix well. A moderately sticky but cohesive dough should begin to form.

3. Transfer the dough to a lightly greased bowl, cover with plastic wrap or aluminum foil, and let rise in a warm place for a minimum of 2 hours. For a heartier crust, you may also choose to let it rise in the fridge overnight, taking it out of the fridge at least 30 minutes before the following step.

4. Have ready two 9-inch (23cm) pie pans. Punch down and divide the dough in half, dust the countertop or workspace, and roll each ball to a flat circle that extends generously beyond the outer rim of your pie pans, about 10½ inches (26cm).

5. Being mindful of the center, transfer each circle to a pie pan and gently press the pastry into the sides and up to the edge, finally crimping to the rim to form the crust.

6. Preheat the oven to 350°F (180°C).

FILLING METHOD

7. Divide your fruit of choice between the 2 pie pans and place within.

8. In a large bowl or pourable vessel, combine the eggs, milk, and sugar, and whisk thoroughly. Pour ½ in each pie pan to cover the fruit.

STREUSEL METHOD

9. In a separate large bowl, combine all of the streusel ingredients and rub together with your fingers to form a uniform consistency, like that of wet sand. Divide and evenly sprinkle atop each pie.

10. Bake for 40 to 45 minutes or until golden brown. If the crust begins to brown too early during baking, it may benefit from being shielded with aluminum foil. Allow to cool completely to room temperature before slicing. Keep refrigerated.

BUTTER BRICKLE CAKE

LAYER CAKE • TWO 9-INCH LAYERS
PREP: 1 HOUR • BAKE: 45 MINUTES

CAKE

1 cup (225g) butter, softened

½ cup (100g) granulated sugar

½ cup (110g) packed brown sugar

1 (3.4oz/96g) box butterscotch instant pudding mix

4 eggs

3 cups (420g) all-purpose flour

½ tsp salt

2 tsp baking powder

1 cup (235ml) milk

1 (8oz/226g) bag Heath "Bits O' Brickle" toffee bits (1 heaping cup)

FILLING & FROSTING

1½ cups (355ml) heavy cream

¼ cup (55g) brown sugar, sifted to remove lumps

½ tsp cream of tartar

½ tsp vanilla extract

1 (8oz/226g) bag Heath "Bits O' Brickle" toffee bits (1 heaping cup), divided

CAKE METHOD

1. Preheat the oven to 350°F (180°C). Grease two 9-inch (23cm) cake pans.

2. In a large bowl, cream together the butter and the sugars until light and fluffy. Beat in the pudding mix, followed by the eggs.

3. In a separate large bowl, combine the flour, salt, and baking powder, and add to the creamed mixture alternately with the milk. Lastly, fold in the toffee bits.

4. Turn into the prepared pans and bake for 35 to 45 minutes, or until a toothpick inserted into the centers can be removed cleanly. Cool in the pans for 10 minutes, before transferring to a wire rack to cool completely.

FILLING & FROSTING METHOD

5. In the bowl of a stand mixer fitted with a whisk attachment, or in a large bowl in tandem with a hand mixer, whisk the heavy cream, brown sugar, cream of tartar, and vanilla extract to smooth, stiff peaks.

6. Prepare a suitable place to assemble the cake, keeping in mind how it will be served. Ideally, use a cake stand with a cake board. You may use a long serrated knife to remove any doming if you wish.

7. Spread a suitable amount of frosting atop the first cake, about ¼ of the total. Then sprinkle about ½ of the toffee bits on top of this to form the filling.

8. To form the second layer, place the second cake atop the first and spread the remaining frosting across the wall and top of the assembled cake. Alternatively, the frosting may be added to a piping bag and frosted in this fashion.

9. Finally, press handfuls of the remaining toffee bits into the wall of the cake, reapplying any which do not stick. Serve at once. Keep leftovers by the slice refrigerated in airtight containers.

Mention Butter Brickle to any older South Dakotan, and you'll watch their brow elevate as they endure flashbacks to the legend it once was. From the heart of 1920s Sioux Falls, confectionery brothers James and Henry Fenn churned out their chocolate-coated butter brickle toffee bar to test the waters, and what followed was pure pandemonium. Everyone from bankers to infants to infant bankers would babble for Butter Brickle in the golden wrapper. The fad would later burst Sioux Falls' metaphorical levees when two hours south in Omaha, NE, the Blackstone Hotel had the bright idea to crush pieces of the bar and mix it into their ice cream, starting what would become a national Butter Brickle Ice Cream craze.

Other candymakers may have held similar patents, like the Woodward Candy company in Council Bluffs, IA, but Butter Brickle was firmly cornered by the Fenn brothers. Unfortunately, in 1971 their company folded, and the Butter Brickle formula was sold to the highest bidder. Sioux Falls had suddenly lost an icon.

Like a phoenix from the ashes, Betty Crocker, in all her formless and disembodied wisdom, revived Butter Brickle in the 1990s with a line of Butter Brickle cake mix. This cake became a favorite of your grandmother's bridge parties. Despite this second wind, brickle's history repeated itself when the mix was eventually discontinued. In salute to both the Fenn Brothers and South Dakota, I'd like to reinvigorate brickle fever with this recipe, which recreates a cake lost to the decades. Chock-full of caramel flavors and toffee crunches with a slightly worrisome 1970s shade of orange, this cake is ready to transport you back to yesteryear's Sioux Falls.

HONEY ROUGH RIDERS

ICEBOX COOKIES • 2 DOZEN
PREP: 20 MINUTES • CHILL: 2 HOURS • BAKE: 20 MINUTES

If you know one thing about North Dakota, you're doing better than most. Two? Then you must be a Rough Rider State intellectual. But it seems that only the most learned scholars know that North Dakota leads the nation in the production of honey! Even some Dakotans remain unaware that their state churned out more than 31 million *pounds* of honey in 2022 alone. That's more than a large 8-ounce supermarket jar of honey getting filled every second, every day of the year. Why this fact isn't as celebrated as, say, the California raisin, I don't know. But allow me the liberty to help remedy this and highlight a comparatively obscure recipe in celebration of these North Dakotan apiculturists.

To be clear, knoephla soup is *the* North Dakota dish, but a savory soup is of little use to both this book and to beekeepers like Mackrill Honey Farms in bustling Wells County. They sell honey by the 55-gallon bucket and probably run their cars on the stuff. In truth, honey has always been a part of the kitchen, but too often it's only a teaspoon there and a tablespoon here. Beekeepers statewide have a vested interest in the proliferation of recipes that really take honey by the hand and give it a good farmer's shake. Something that these peculiar, shortbread-like *Honey Rough Riders* achieve swimmingly.

INGREDIENTS

1 cup (225g) good-quality, European-style or Irish butter, softened

1 cup (340g) honey

1 cup (135g) cornstarch

¼ tsp salt

2½ cups (350g) whole wheat flour

1 egg white, beaten together with 1 tbsp water for egg-white wash

½ cup (60g) walnuts, finely pulsed in a food processor

METHOD

1. In a large bowl, beat together the butter and the honey until creamy and well combined. Beat in the cornstarch and the salt, then mix in the whole wheat flour.

2. Transfer the dough to a tray lined with parchment paper and form a rough log. Refrigerate for at least 1 hour.

3. Dust the counter or workspace with cornstarch, and with lightly starched hands, roll the chilled dough into a long log about 15 inches (38cm) in length, cut in half, cover, and freeze for at least 1 hour.

4. When ready, preheat the oven to 300°F (150°C) and line a baking sheet with parchment paper. Have the bowl of egg-white wash nearby. Scatter the processed walnuts over a cutting board.

5. Remove one log from the freezer and brush its circumference with egg-white wash. Roll this log in the processed walnuts, manually covering any spots missed.

6. Cut the log into 12 equal rounds, transfer to the prepared baking sheet, and bake for 20 to 22 minutes, or until the tops of the cookies no longer appear wet. Allow to cool completely on the baking sheet before rolling, slicing, and baking the remaining chilled dough. Store in an airtight container at room temperature.

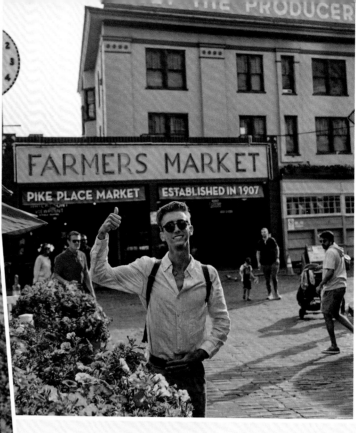

West

MOUNTAIN WEST · SOUTHWEST
PACIFIC NORTHWEST

MONTANA

YELLOWSTONE

YELLOWSTONE
NATIONAL
PARK

WYOMING

UTAH

COLORADO

NEW MEXICO

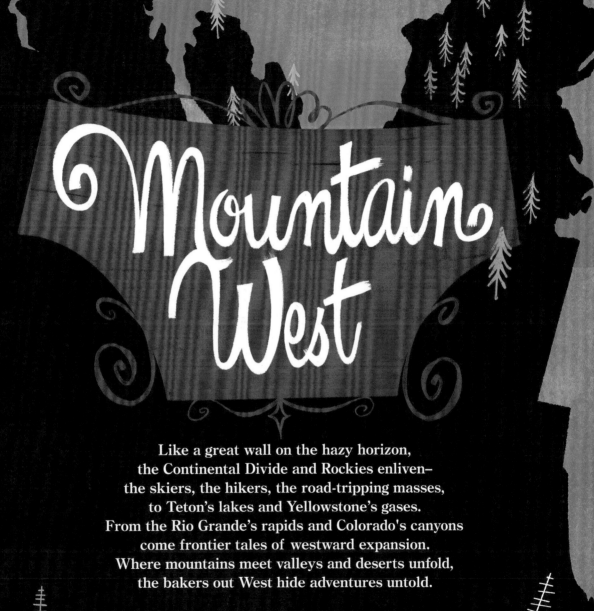

Mountain West

Like a great wall on the hazy horizon,
the Continental Divide and Rockies enliven–
the skiers, the hikers, the road-tripping masses,
to Teton's lakes and Yellowstone's gases.
From the Rio Grande's rapids and Colorado's canyons
come frontier tales of westward expansion.
Where mountains meet valleys and deserts unfold,
the bakers out West hide adventures untold.

YELLOWSTONE

It is summer in America. The meddlesome children have been thoroughly stuffed into the RV, crammed with picnic supplies, sunscreen, and ball caps, and with a coughing refrain, the engine rumbles up to the toll gate of the greatest national park in the West. The name Yellowstone carries a renown unmatched by any other road-trip destination, and pulling up to its many timber-frame lodges and stone-sided outposts is a pilgrimage that fulfills the longtime values of American recreation. While sitting in the lobby of the towering Old Faithful Inn, it's easy to envision past generations sitting there beside you, enthralled by the very same escape to these great outdoors their parents had once shown them. Here, lodgepole pine throngs the air alongside sulphured gusts, as the low rumble of geysers signal nature's ever-present grandeur. Overlooking the iridescent tableau of geothermal pools, you might spot grazing bison in the distance, or herds of elk, which make up only a small part of this park's incredible fauna. Speak tales around campfires or speak no words at all, the scope of Yellowstone can breathe life and steal breath all at once.

Huckleberry Scones on deadfall, Biscuit Basin, Yellowstone National Park.

HUCKLEBERRY SCONES

BISCUIT • 1 DOZEN
PREP: 20 MINUTES • BAKE: 12 MINUTES

From Lamar Valley to Old Faithful, the hikers and anglers of Yellowstone are powerless against the prevalence of the huckleberry. I spoke to a gentleman named Grant from Detroit one evening in the lodge and discovered he'd been unaware that the huckleberry is an actual, tangible fruit. For some reason, he'd assumed since his youth that it was a fictitious literary device or pseudonym for any carefree boy whose surname may or may not be Finn. It wasn't until he saw the pervasiveness of huckleberry jams and syrups in Yellowstone's gift stores, or the huckleberry margaritas and milkshakes elsewhere in the park, that he made the startling discovery that this fruit is in fact quite real.

Grant from Detroit needed help. There are far too many ways to consume the huckleberry here, and despite the fact that Yellowstone occupies but a small portion of Wyoming, its ubiquity in the park has attached it to the state as a whole. Late July witnesses not only Yellowstone being overloaded with huckleberry goods, but nearby Grand Teton, Jackson, and Bridger-Teton National Forests, too. My vote is that you might as well indulge in that which is ripe for the picking. Descend into the bush and get yourself some of the star ingredient in these buttery, crumbly, and lemony slices of teatime delight.

INGREDIENTS

2 cups (280g) all-purpose flour

1 tsp baking soda

½ tsp salt

½ cup (100g) granulated sugar

Zest of 1 lemon

½ cup (115g) butter, cold and cubed small

½ cup (120ml) buttermilk

1 cup (150g) huckleberries

METHOD

1. Preheat the oven to 400°F (200°C) and line a baking sheet with parchment paper.

2. In a large bowl, combine the flour, baking soda, salt, sugar, and lemon zest. Add the butter and rub the dry mixture into the butter with your fingers until the mixture is uniformly crumbly and there are no overly large pieces of butter remaining.

3. Add the buttermilk and the huckleberries and mix until the dough is barely combined. If the dough feels too dry, add an additional tablespoon of buttermilk at a time until the dough becomes cohesive.

4. Divide the formed dough in half (this is best done with a scale) and form each into a ball. Do not overhandle the dough.

5. On the prepared baking sheet, flatten each ball to make a rough disk 1½ inches (4cm) in height and cut each disk into 6 wedges (done easily by cutting the disks in half, followed by an "X"). Keep the wedges in a disk formation, but separate them slightly before baking.

6. Bake for about 12 minutes, until their edges are lightly golden and well-defined.

Tip

In lieu of huckleberries, raspberries, blackberries, and blueberries can be used.

Scones and a disgruntled raven at Biscuit Basin, Yellowstone National Park.

 Enjoying *Outdoorsman Bars* next to the Opal Pool, Yellowstone National Park.

OUTDOORSMAN BARS

BAR • 9×13-INCH PAN
PREP: 20 MINUTES • BAKE: 25 MINUTES • COOL: 40 MINUTES

INGREDIENTS

½ cup (135g) creamy peanut butter

½ cup (115g) butter, melted

½ cup (100g) granulated sugar

½ cup (170g) honey

2 tsp vanilla extract

½ cup (80g) flaxseeds or chia seeds

¼ cup (70g) all-purpose flour

1 tsp ground cinnamon

4 cups (400g) quick-cooking oats

½ cup mini chocolate chips (optional)

1 egg, beaten together with ¼ cup
    (60ml) water, for egg wash

OPTIONAL FROSTING

1 cup (120g) powdered sugar

2–3 tbsp water

Grand Prismatic Spring

METHOD

1. Preheat the oven to 350°F (180°C) and line a 9×13-inch (23×33cm) baking pan or casserole dish with a parchment sling. The two short edges of the pan should be left exposed so there is no bunching of the parchment. Lightly grease the exposed sides.

2. In a large bowl, add the peanut butter, melted butter, and sugar, and mix well. The mixture will be runny. Beat in the honey and the vanilla extract, then mix in the flaxseeds.

3. Add the flour, cinnamon, oats, and chocolate chips, if using. Mix very well, ensuring everything is evenly moistened. This is best done with a butter knife, crisscrossing and mixing thoroughly.

4. Turn the granola mixture into the prepared pan. Wet your hands and fingers in the egg wash and pack the mixture down firmly and evenly. The mixture should be smoothly packed, its entire surface evenly wetted with egg wash, with no straggler bits around the edges. Note that you will not need all the egg wash.

5. Bake for about 22 minutes, or until the very edges begin to noticeably brown. Place the pan on a wire rack to cool for at least 40 minutes before lifting the edges of the parchment sling and placing it flat on a cutting board. Test to see if the sheet granola will fold before lifting, and if so, cool for longer before reattempting. With a sharp knife, cut the sheet of granola lengthwise, before slicing crosswise into rectangular bars. Clean the knife after each cut. Carefully transfer the bars to a wire rack to cool completely. Store in an airtight container.

OPTIONAL FROSTING METHOD

6. If drizzling with frosting, place a sheet of parchment paper or aluminum foil below the wire rack. Combine the powdered sugar with the water in a small bowl and mix until thick but liquid. If the mixture is too thick, more water may be added in very small amounts. Add more powdered sugar, if the opposite occurs.

7. Transfer the frosting to a piping bag with a very narrow tip, arrange the bars side by side, and drizzle across their surface in a zigzag pattern. Let the frosting set before storing the bars in an airtight container.

Outdoorsman Bars and the Grand Prismatic Spring, Yellowstone National Park.

To fully grasp Wyoming means to meet her out of doors—something that's rather easy to do considering there aren't many doors here to begin with. I've had the great pleasure of spending many summer days hiking Wyoming. Favorites of mine include the desertlike landscapes of Curt Gowdy and Vedauwoo, or ascending the 12,000-foot Medicine Bow Peak in the state's southeast. Most recently, I've done as the tourists do and experienced the reverence of Jenny Lake in the Tetons and the wonders of old Yellowstone—quintessential stops on the American summer road trip.

During these outings, especially the several-day treks or extended campouts, a hearty snack becomes a pretty important object of affection. Campers here tend to have lists of fun and inventive recipes that aid in abating that post-hike hunger, most of which involve the campfire, but a few recipes, like this one, are drummed up before the adventure begins. These *Outdoorsman Bars* allow you to bake a Wyoming camping trip's worth of chewy snacks that take up little space. Chockablock full of oats and seeds, these honey-bound bars are thankfully just as tasty as they are useful to provide sustenance on the go.

Muffins before the Teton Range, Mormon Row Historic District, Jackson Hole.

Naturally, as the least populous state, Wyoming has some impressive swaths of nothingness. The early Mormon settlers found their trek through Wyoming so incomprehensibly barren that it made a desolate and arid lake of *salt* seem preferable in comparison. But Wyomingites thrive on vastness. It's home to cowpokes, homesteaders, and ranchers—real-life cowgirls and cattlemen who raise, breed, and sell livestock for their daily bread upon lands with acreages in excess of my home country. Not just with cows, either, as on the outskirts of dear Laramie, there's a bison ranch where good friends of mine work hard to keep bison tagged, trailers loaded, and the devil's rope (electric fence) operational. I've even personally bottle-fed a baby bison named Jolene. So yes, Wyoming is known for the sunscreen-caked tourists who come to its lands to frolic obtusely close to wildlife for Instagram, but it is simply a daily routine for the local rancher.

Immediately familiar to locals and friends of Wyoming is the lowly chokecherry. Named for its astringent bite, it's one of few fruits that's reliably encountered in the wild throughout the state. For a week or two every August, the small, deep-red berries inundate the kitchens of homesteaders and stain the teeth of snacking foragers across the plains. Yet, with their awful pit-to-flesh ratio, they are well suited only to make jam and jelly. In this manner, chokecherry preserves have become a fixture of Wyoming's pantries and have necessitated a slew of inventive recipes that seek to exhaust the endless supply. Wheat bran, with its thirsty and moisture-loving properties, is the perfect ingredient to allow a muffin to be sweetened almost entirely with these preserves. So if you're seeking a not-too-sweet, earthy, hardy, and hearty bran muffin for your breakfast and buttering pleasure, Wyoming's *Chokecherry Homestead Muffins* are pleased to serve.

CHOKECHERRY HOMESTEAD MUFFINS

MUFFIN • 1 DOZEN
PREP: 30 MINUTES • BAKE: 15 MINUTES

INGREDIENTS

2 cups (140g) wheat bran

1 cup (320g) chokecherry jam, preserves, or jelly

1½ cups (355ml) milk

½ cup (120g) vegetable oil

¼ cup (55g) brown sugar

2 eggs

1½ cups (210g) whole wheat flour

1½ tsp baking powder

½ tsp salt

½ tsp baking soda

¼ tsp ground allspice

¼ cup (25g) rolled or quick-cooking oats, for topping, if desired

METHOD

1. Preheat the oven to 425°F (220°C), and thoroughly grease both the wells and the top of a standard muffin pan. Use a trusted baking spray or apply a thin layer of solid shortening. Do not use liners for this recipe.

2. To a large bowl, add the wheat bran.

3. In a medium saucepan, whisk the chokecherry jam until smooth over medium heat while slowly pouring in the milk. Bring to a low simmer until steaming and bubbling around the pan's edge, stirring occasionally. Pour over the wheat bran and whisk together.

4. Whisk in the oil, sugar, and eggs.

5. In a separate bowl, mix together the flour, baking powder, salt, baking soda, and allspice. Add to the wet wheat-bran mixture and fold until just combined.

6. Using a trigger-release ice cream scoop or large cookie scoop, fill the muffin wells to their rims, creating a mound in the center that exceeds the well. Sprinkle oats on top for decoration, if desired.

7. Place in the oven, immediately reduce the temperature to 400°F (200°C), and bake for about 15 minutes, until the muffin-top edges have browned or until a toothpick can be removed from a muffin's center with only a few crumbs.

8. Cool in the pan for 10 minutes, before placing the muffins on a wire rack to cool completely. You should be able to twist and pick the muffins up. There shouldn't be any sticking of the muffin tops, but if so, attempt to free their undersides with a knife.

9. If you have batter left over, repeat the process, but be sure to wipe off excess grease and debris from unoccupied muffin wells to prevent burning and acrid smells.

Tip

In lieu of chokecherry jam, you may substitute with any fruit jam of your choosing.

Chokecherry Homestead Muffins and the iconic T.A. Moulton Barn, just outside of Grand Teton National Park.

Laramies and my 1963 Cadillac Series 62, "Ernest," photographed in Laramie.

Wyoming
LARAMIES

COWBOY COOKIE • 2½ DOZEN
PREP: 30 MINUTES • BAKE: 14 MINUTES

Of all the questions I get asked during these fortunate minutes in the limelight, the question of how I came to be in Laramie, Wyoming, from my home island of Bermuda is by far the most prevalent. It was the first thing the wonderful Dave Jorgenson asked me in Washington, DC when I was on stage celebrating the release of *Baking Yesteryear* in 2023. I of course told him, "By plane," but his question was really: Why would someone with such a sunbaked birthright go to a place an American might consider a wrong turn off the interstate? Well, in choosing a US university at which to study, I knew I wanted a "real" experience, not a major metro filled with the worldly and the urbane. All I did was stare down a map of the US, pointed to the area with the least amount of text, and applied to whatever school was nearest. In many ways, it was a joke, but at every step I felt compelled to keep following through.

By complete luck and foolishness, I found the University of Wyoming and the town of Laramie—the hidden gem of the Mountain West. It's a place where lifted diesels roll coal down Grand Avenue, McDonald's orders are retrieved on horseback, and red beams of the western sunset set brick facades aglow in a downtown built by lawmen and outlaws. Come summertime, the place blooms like a prairie rose: days are spent out among the pines, and nights are enjoyed perched upon a warm curb, watching fools on the footbridge attempt to throw a beer to the passing Union Pacific's engineer.

Laramie is so much more a character in my life than it is a setting. It continuously makes me smile, just as it continuously stays the same over the changing years. Because of this, I've always wanted to name something after it as a way to say thanks. So, I hereby present my recipe for a cookie I've been making for friends and family in this very town for almost a decade: my own take on the state's favorite cowboy cookie, born right here in Laramie. If you're ever left wanting for a different cookie, then my chunky *Laramies* — which are a blend of toasted coconut and graham cracker nuttiness, complete with pockets of gooey chocolate—might just give you a taste of that which I hold so dear.

INGREDIENTS

1½ cups (180g) pecan halves

2 cups (170g) unsweetened shredded coconut

1 cup (225g) butter

1 cup (220g) brown sugar

1 cup (200g) granulated sugar

2 eggs

2 tsp vanilla extract

1 tsp almond extract

2 cups (280g) all-purpose flour

2½ cups (275g) graham cracker crumbs

½ tsp baking soda

½ tsp salt

12oz (340g) semisweet chocolate bar (1½ Baker's bars)

METHOD

1. Preheat the oven to 350°F (180°C) and line a baking sheet with parchment paper. Spread the pecans and coconut flat on the sheet, and toast in the oven for 8 minutes. Let cool on the baking sheet as you continue. Set aside.

2. In a large bowl, cream together the butter, brown sugar, and granulated sugar until light and fluffy. Beat in the eggs, followed by the extracts.

3. In a separate large bowl, combine the flour, graham cracker crumbs, baking soda, and salt. Add to the creamed mixture and mix until thoroughly combined. The dough should be dry and stiff.

4. With a sharp knife, chop the chocolate into small chunks, leaving some pieces fairly large. Add to the dough. Chop the toasted pecan halves and add them to the dough, along with the coconut. Mix the dough well, using your hands to knead in the ingredients if needed.

5. Using an ice cream scoop or large cookie scoop (#40), drop the dough in large 3-tablespoon portions onto the baking sheet, allowing at least 2 inches (5cm) between each. Bake for 12 to 14 minutes, until the edges appear well-defined. Allow to cool on the baking sheet for 10 minutes, before transferring to a wire rack to cool completely. Repeat with the remaining dough.

Laramies in my 1963 Cadillac, photographed in Laramie.

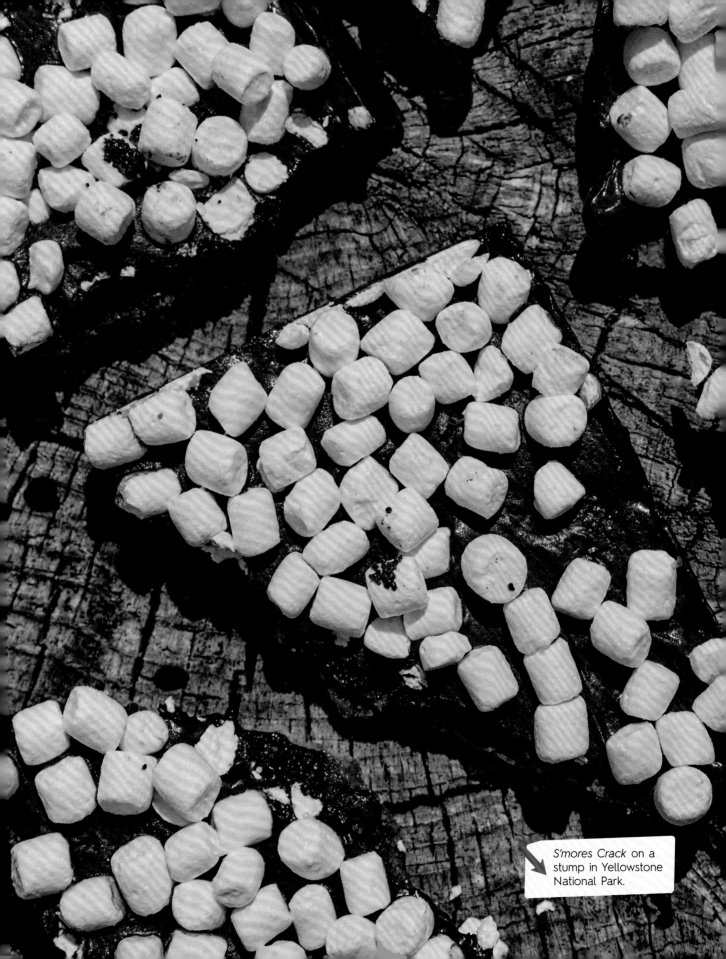

S'mores Crack on a stump in Yellowstone National Park.

S'MORES CRACK

CONFECTION • 2LB
PREP: 20 MINUTES • BAKE: 10 MINUTES • COOL: 30 MINUTES

With two cows for every Montanan, open space is ordinary, and dating is difficult—most of the options have four legs. Perhaps this is why Montanans are known for their penchant for spending time in nature, nursing broken hearts and peculiar infections. Like in Wyoming and Colorado, the Rocky Mountains reach toward the sky here, offering pristine vistas in Glacier National Park and Flathead National Forest. And there's nothing better at the end of a day exploring the great outdoors than to indulge in the signature outdoor American treat: the s'more.

Practically mandated to be consumed whenever near a campfire, s'mores are a confection of milk chocolate and partially melted marshmallows sandwiched between two graham cracker squares. Even though it's not the official state dessert, s'mores perfectly pair with Montana's bounty of outdoor treasures and have become an adored icon worthy of its breathless beauty.

There is little sense writing a recipe for s'mores, as their formula is just as ingrained in our minds as their delectability is inseparable from their campfire preparation. So, here is a Montana creation that seeks to capture a taste of the outdoors in your own kitchen. Ideally suited to be served at functions where fires may be impractical and/or excitingly illegal, *S'mores Crack* takes America's famous Christmas crack recipe and gives it a summer spin.

INGREDIENTS

12 graham cracker sheets (comprising 8 individual crackers)

1 cup (225g) butter

1 cup (200g) granulated sugar

2 cups (340g) semisweet or milk chocolate chips

2 cups (100g) mini marshmallows

METHOD

1. Preheat the oven to 350°F (180°C).

2. Line a full-size baking sheet with heavy-duty aluminum foil. Arrange a grid of graham cracker sheets in 2 rows of 6. The longest edges of the cracker sheets correspond to the shortest edges of the pan. The crackers should all be touching.

3. Vertically crease the sides of the aluminum foil to create a dam that borders the crackers.

4. In a medium saucepan over high heat, combine the butter and the sugar, stirring occasionally until it reaches a boil. Once it reaches a full boil, boil for 5 minutes without stirring. Carefully pour the mixture evenly over the graham crackers. The foil dam will prevent the syrup from spilling.

5. Immediately bake for 7 minutes.

6. Remove from the oven and quickly disperse the chocolate chips evenly over the hot crackers. Let sit for about 2 minutes until they appear melted, before carefully spreading the melted chips over the crackers in a thin, even layer.

7. While the chocolate is still hot, sprinkle the mini marshmallows over the top.

8. Let cool completely until the chocolate sets, refrigerating if necessary. Remove the foil and cut into irregular, bite-size pieces.

HUCKLEBERRY ICE CREAM

ICE CREAM • 1 QUART
PREP: 30 MINUTES • CHILL: 6 HOURS

Every summer, along the lands where Montana hugs her southerly neighbor, Wyoming, the ice cream to beat is colored pink and bespeckled with the Mountain West's most adored fruit: the huckleberry. From Missoula to Billings, Montanans eschew the two-tone vanilla and chocolate preferences of the masses in favor of fruity scoops in waffle cones from favorite ice cream shops like Wilcoxson's and Big Dipper. Having a cone of *Huckleberry Ice Cream* in your hand is the Montana equivalent of having Old Glory pinned to your lapel. You won't find a better place to acquaint yourself with it than the national park–gateway towns of Bozeman and West Yellowstone.

The state fruit tastes more or less like the blueberry, but keep this comparison to yourself, lest you face the throes of frontier justice. This red berry is noticeably tarter, and the deeper the hue, the sweeter the huckle. I imagine that the local love of the berry stems from its ephemeral nature. Despite valiant attempts, it remains an impossibility to cultivate at scale, and thus stands as the perfect thing to sample in situ. So, whenever you find yourself in Montana, be sure to make it two scoops.

Tip

In lieu of huckleberries, raspberries, blackberries, and blueberries may be used.

INGREDIENTS

Ice

½ cup (150g) ice cream salt, for churning (regular salt will work the same), more if needed

2 cups (470ml) heavy cream

1 cup (235ml) evaporated milk, chilled

½ cup (100g) granulated sugar

¼ tsp salt

½ tsp vanilla extract

1½ cups (½lb/227g) huckleberries, fresh or frozen and thawed, plus more for serving

Juice of ½ lemon

METHOD

1. Have ready 2 large bowls, the larger to be filled with ice water and salt, and the smaller, preferably metal, to be nestled within for churning of the cream. Start by filling the large bowl with a suitable amount of ice, pour about ½ cup (150g) of the ice cream salt on top, and add enough cold water to submerge the sides of the smaller bowl without overflowing.

2. To the smaller churning bowl, add the heavy cream, evaporated milk, sugar, salt, and vanilla extract. Using a hand mixer, beat the mixture for 12 minutes, making sure to incorporate any mixture that freezes to the side of the bowl. The mixture should be thick and inflated. Place the entire assembly in the freezer for 1 hour. If the large bowl does not fit, freeze only the churning bowl and add more ice and salt before step 4.

3. Meanwhile, combine the huckleberries and lemon juice in a separate bowl. Mash to a pulp using a fork or potato masher. Strain the mixture through a sieve to remove excess liquid. Reserve the huckleberry pulp.

4. Once the ice cream has chilled for an hour, scrape down the sides of the churning bowl and beat again using a hand mixer within the ice bath for 3 minutes. The mixture should deflate and become noticeably stiff. Mix in the huckleberry pulp until uniformly distributed, and transfer to a covered dish to freeze overnight or for a minimum of 5 hours before scooping to serve. Garnish with berries.

On the 24th of July, 1847, while overlooking Salt Lake Valley, the bearded and stern-faced Brigham Young thrust his cane into the earth and, with his band of merry Mormons, declared, "This is the right place," after an arduous trek west. Back east, Uncle Sam declined Young's proposed "State of Deseret" for the territory, opting for "Utah" instead. And so began the story of one of the most beatific and wondrous lands in the union. Venerated for its stunning landscapes, Utah is a state where you're never bored by the scenery. I'd be curious to now exhume Brother Young and ask him what he'd make of the fact that his exalted land has since become known for its heady infatuation with Jell-O.

Inexplicably, Utah consumes more of this fruit-flavored gelatin than anywhere else in the country. It's even been ordained in 2001's SR.5: *Resolution Urging Jell-O Recognition* bill, with the prophetic words "NOW, THEREFORE, BE IT RESOLVED that the Senate of the state of Utah recognize Jell-O as a favorite snack food of Utah."

Like the planting of Brigham's cane in 1847, the gavel of legislative justice thunders as it urges you to celebrate Utah in all its renown with the bejeweled, jiggling majesty of this recipe. A symphony of fruity flavors are set in slices of creamy lime in the fashion of stained glass. Upheld by the crunch of vanilla wafers and surrounded by caryatids of ladyfingers, this dessert of Deseret is the very last word in haute gelatin cuisine.

THE PRIDE OF DESERET

GELATIN MOLD • 10-INCH SPRINGFORM
PREP: 2 HOURS • BAKE: 10 MINUTES • CHILL: 12 HOURS

INGREDIENTS

1 (3oz/85g) packet lemon flavored gelatin

1 (3oz/85g) packet cherry flavored gelatin

1 (3oz/85g) packet orange flavored gelatin

3 cups (235ml) boiling water, divided

1½ cups (120ml) cold water, divided

1⅓ cups (150g) vanilla-wafer crumbs, finely crushed

¼ cup (50g) granulated sugar

⅓ cup (75g) butter, melted

About 30 ladyfingers, or similar elongated cookie (Biscoff wafer, Vienna cookie)

ASSEMBLY

1 cup (235ml) boiling water

2 (3oz/85g) packets lime flavored gelatin

½ cup (120ml) cold water

2¼ cups (530ml) heavy cream

METHOD

1. The night before, or at least 6 hours before the dish needs to be prepared, prepare the lemon, cherry, and orange gelatins separately by mixing their powders with 1 cup boiling water, followed by ½ cup cold water for each. Pour each mixture into their own 8-to-9-inch (20 to 23cm) square pan and refrigerate until firmly set, at least 3 hours.

2. Preheat the oven to 350°F (180°C). Line the wall of a 9-inch (23cm) springform pan with a long rectangle of parchment paper that covers its entire height.

3. In a large bowl, combine the vanilla-wafer crumbs, sugar, and melted butter, and mix until uniform. The consistency should be like that of wet sand. Press the crumbs firmly into the bottom of the springform pan and bake for 10 minutes. Place the pan on a wire rack to cool.

ASSEMBLY METHOD

4. In a large bowl, pour the boiling water over the lime gelatin. Mix in the cold water and chill the mixture in the refrigerator until thick and syrupy, but not set completely, about 30 minutes.

5. Once the lime gelatin is at this stage, whip the heavy cream until stiff in the bowl of a stand mixer fitted with a whisk attachment, or in a large bowl with a hand mixer. Reserve and set aside a small portion (about ¼ cup) to help stick the ladyfingers together in step 7. Fold the remaining whipped cream into the thickened lime gelatin until uniform.

6. Remove each of the lemon, cherry, and orange gelatins from the fridge. Using a sharp knife dipped in a nearby glass of hot water after each cut, cut the gelatin in the pans vertically and then horizontally to create a grid of small ½-inch (1.3cm) cubes. Free the sides of the pan in the same manner, and using a spatula, turn out each tray of the cut cubes into your bowl of whipped-cream lime gelatin. Gently fold to distribute and keep cool.

7. Cutting each end with a sharp knife so they stand straight, and using the reserved whipped cream to help, arrange the lady fingers vertically along the wall of the springform pan, atop the baked and cooled crust.

8. Pour the assembled gelatin mixture carefully into the prepared shell. Shake gently to level and refrigerate for a minimum of 6 hours. Unmold, remove the parchment, and slice between the ladyfingers to serve as if it were a cake. Keep refrigerated.

SUNSHINE GRANOLA

CEREAL • 2½LB
PREP: 10 MINUTES • BAKE: 40 MINUTES

Utah is the United States' playground when it comes to natural beauty: Zion, Capitol Reef, Canyonlands, Bryce Canyon, and Arches National Parks are all ripe for exploration under your wayfaring boots. Pick any direction and you'll be among sandstone scenes of oranges and reds. In Utah more than anywhere else, summer seems to strike with such a vibrancy that it's nearly unrecognizable to the state it was but six months ago.

Sharing in the palette of summer is the funny snack of granola—crumbs with a purpose. It fuels hikers, makes yogurt edible, and differentiates the crisps from the cobblers. With an almost endless variety of flavors, granola is among the most versatile and useful of baked goods to come out of simple ingredients. Why then don't we see more recipes for granola in baking books? I think it's because many don't know how easy it is to prepare at home. Personally, I started making granola after I fell to my knees in the cereal aisle the day Post discontinued Honey Bunches of Oats: Just Bunches. They say the good die young, all while those horrific grape nuts live on.

The homemade granola recipes of Utah trump them all: where golden raisins and coconut are crunched together with honeyed oats and almonds. It begs to be eaten by the fistful. Many of the modern recipes you'll find online fail to include the all-important crunchy clusters of oat or almond meal, but don't worry, Utah and I have your back with this sunshine-filled snacking masterpiece. Tailor this recipe to your liking, and you'll see that your granola soars leagues above any store-bought offering.

INGREDIENTS

½ cup (100g) solid coconut oil (substitute with vegetable shortening)

½ cup (170g) honey

½ cup (110g) brown sugar

¾ tsp salt

3 cups (240g) rolled oats

¾ cup (90g) almond or oat flour, or any fine-ground nut meal

1 cup (120g) raw almonds, chopped or slivered (or any nut of your choosing)

1 cup (85g) unsweetened shredded coconut

1 cup (200g) golden raisins (or any dried fruit of your choosing, chopped, as needed)

1 cup optional add-ins: chocolate chips, candies, sesame sticks, etc.

METHOD

1. Preheat the oven to 300°F (150°C) and line a baking sheet with parchment paper.

2. In a small saucepan, combine the coconut oil, honey, brown sugar, and salt. Cook over low heat and stir until the brown sugar is fully dissolved.

3. In a large bowl, combine the oats, almond flour, almonds, and coconut. Pour the oil-and-honey mixture over top and mix until thoroughly combined.

4. Turn the mixture onto the baking sheet and spread into an even layer. Using wet hands, press and form the mixture into a level sheet with defined borders.

5. Bake for 25 minutes. Let the granola cool on the pan for 3 minutes, before crushing, jostling, and disturbing the mixture with a wooden spoon, creating clumps and clusters to a size of your liking. Return the mixture to the oven for 10 to 15 minutes longer, until golden brown.

6. Let the granola cool completely to room temperature on the baking sheet before adding the raisins and any optional add-ins, which can be mixed in by hand on the sheet. Store in an airtight container, and consume within 3 weeks.

The people of Colorado are among the highest in the world. Denver, its capital, lies at 5,200 feet above sea level, yet many travel here to get even higher. The beloved occult airport in Denver is the most-common starting point for skiing tourists once they land in the mile-high city. These are the exciting types who flock to Colorado by the numbers just to get chapped lips and exclaim varying platitudes about *mountain air* whilst applying lotion. They travel west to the ski towns of the Rocky Mountains: locales that have become known across the nation for their powdery, picturesque resort life, and plurality of traffic circles.

While Aspen's millionaires have begun to invade Vail with their small dogs and strange sunglasses, the small and distant mountain town of Palisade remains unfettered by the après-ski claptrap. Probably because they're too busy growing peaches. Yes, you heard me, peaches in Colorado!

Palisade's unusually temperate climate, paired with the state's long summer days and cool nights, makes the peaches grown here an alluringly delicious variety. Every summer, the Rocky Mountains go wild for these peaches, giving Georgia a run for its money, and giving pie shells a most sumptuous reason to be filled. Set within an elegant custard, this bright peach pie sings a tune so sweet you're liable to be rapt face-first. It offers all things peachy and creamy with Palisade's best.

PALISADE PEACHES N' CREAM PIE

PIE • DEEP 9-INCH PIE
PREP: 40 MINUTES • BAKE: 1 HOUR • COOL: 90 MINUTES

PIE

1 single-crust Pie Crust (page 17)

4 large Palisade peaches, or other fresh peaches, peeled, cored, and cut into small pieces, or 2 (15oz/425g) cans sliced peaches in juice (not syrup), drained

1 egg

Yolks of 3 eggs

¾ cup (180ml) heavy cream

¼ cup (60ml) milk

¾ cup (150g) granulated sugar

2 tbsp cornstarch

Zest of 1 lemon

TOPPING

1 cup (180ml) heavy cream, for topping

¼ cup (30g) powdered sugar, for topping

PIE METHOD

1. Preheat the oven to 350°F (180°C).

2. Fit your prepared pie crust in a deep 9-inch (23cm) pan, crimp the edges, line with parchment paper, and fill with pie weights or dry beans. Bake for 15 minutes. Place the pan on a wire rack to cool, then remove the pie weights and paper.

3. In a small saucepan, add the cut peaches and cook over medium heat until they begin to release their juices and simmer. Cook for 15 minutes while stirring occasionally, until they are soft and can be easily mashed with a fork. Reduce the heat to very low, mash them together, and keep warm.

4. In a small bowl, beat together the egg and egg yolks. Set aside.

5. In a separate larger saucepan, add the cream, milk, sugar, and cornstarch. Bring to a boil over medium-high heat while whisking constantly. After 3 minutes, the mixture should thicken substantially. Reduce heat to very low, and using a ladle, slowly pour about ½ cup (120 ml) into the beaten eggs while whisking constantly to temper them. Whisk the tempered eggs back into the cream mixture.

6. Add the mashed peaches, their juices, and the lemon zest to the tempered cream mixture. Return the heat to medium and cook for a further 5 minutes, stirring often.

7. Transfer the filling to the pie crust and bake for 40 minutes. Allow the pie to cool completely to room temperature in the pan set atop a wire rack before preparing the topping.

TOPPING METHOD

8. In the bowl of a stand mixer fitted with a whisk attachment, or in a large bowl in tandem with a hand mixer, beat the heavy cream and powdered sugar to smooth, stiff peaks.

9. Decoratively spread the whipped cream in peaks on top of the cooled pie and to the pie crust's edge. Alternatively, you may use a piping bag and decorate the pie in this manner. Serve at once. Store refrigerated.

BIZCOCHITOS

ROLLED COOKIE • 6 DOZEN SMALL COOKIES
PREP: 35 MINUTES • CHILL: 20 MINUTES • BAKE: 11 MINUTES

I learned about this cookie one evening at a dinner party in my grandfather's home in Santa Fe, New Mexico. The heads of the table insisted that *Bizcochitos* required orange juice in the dough, while others lobbied that brandy was essential and could not be superseded. The outlier who argued for neither but instead suggested orange zest was summarily bound and gagged. I was eleven at the time and couldn't care less, as the distracted adults offered no resistance against my inhalation of these small cookies, which—being coated in cinnamon sugar—could likely contain all three and be just as good.

The bizcochito, the official state cookie of New Mexico, was born in 19th-century Santa Fe de Nuevo México after the turbulent last days of the Viceroyalty of New Spain. A wonderfully spiced rolled cookie resembling the Spanish mantecado shortbread or the Mexican pan de polvo, the bizcochito is imbued with the licorice-like sweetness of aniseed with a moreish, melt-in-your-mouth texture.

Celebrated for more than a century, the folks in New Mexico consider *Bizcochitos* an essential part of any festivity, particularly around Christmastime. Despite many variations throughout the years, be it orange juice here or brandy there (brandy is superior, by the way), New Mexicans are unwavering in their declaration that there is no bizcochito without lard, but I've had much success with vegetable shortening whenever neutral-tasting lard is hard to come by. Above all else, be sure to roll your *Bizcochitos* thin, unless you want to be ground up and plastered into the adobe.

INGREDIENTS

1 cup (180g) vegetable shortening, or lard

⅔ cup (130g) granulated sugar

1 egg

3 tbsp brandy

3 cups (420g) all-purpose flour

2½ tsp ground aniseed

1½ tsp baking powder

½ tsp salt

1 tbsp ground cinnamon mixed with ¾ cup (150g) granulated sugar, for dredging

METHOD

1. Preheat the oven to 350°F (180°C) and line a baking sheet with parchment paper.

2. In a large bowl, beat the shortening until smooth and uniform. Slowly add the sugar in small additions and cream together very well. Beat in the egg, followed by the brandy.

3. In a separate large bowl, combine the flour, aniseed, baking powder, and salt. Add to the creamed mixture and mix until no streaks of flour remain. Gather the dough into a cohesive ball.

4. Cover the bowl, or wrap the dough in plastic wrap, and chill in the fridge for 20 minutes and no longer.

5. Dust a clean counter or workspace with flour, turn out the chilled dough, and first press the dough to a rough, flat disk using your palms, closing any seams that open on the side. Then, with a lightly floured rolling pin, roll out the dough to a thin sheet of about ¼-inch (0.6cm) thick. The shape is unimportant.

6. Using a fluted cookie cutter, cut out small circular cookies no more than 1½ inches (3.8cm) in diameter. You may also use the rim of a small glass, like a shot glass or spice container. Transfer the cut cookies to the prepared baking sheet. As they do not appreciably spread, a full-size sheet should accommodate 2 dozen.

7. Bake for 11 minutes, or until lightly golden. Allow the cookies to cool on the pan for 2 minutes before dredging each through the prepared mixture of cinnamon and sugar. Set dredged cookies on a wire rack to cool completely. Repeat with the remaining dough and store baked cookies in an airtight container.

While Route 66 gets all the love and attention, its southerly neighbor Route 60 is a comparatively forgotten thoroughfare. If Bobby Troup hadn't written "Get Your Kicks on Route 66!" singing about Flagstaff, Arizona, and Gallup, New Mexico, we could've just as easily been singing about Route 60's Show Low, Arizona, and Pie Town, New Mexico.

Sixty miles south of Gallup, US Route 60 started as a cattle path connecting New Mexico to Arizona. In 1922, WWI veteran Clive Norman set up shop along the road, offering provisions and his homemade dried apple pies. This "Pie Town" became the weary traveler's respite. But after agricultural failings in the late '40s and the adoption of the Interstate Highway Act in 1956, all attention shifted north, and by the 1990s, Pie Town was pie-less—a criminal loss.

Then in 1995, a family on a road trip across sunny Route 60 became so dismayed that Pie Town had no pies, they resolved to purchase a trading post and put pie back on the menu. Soon enough, Kathy Knapp and her mother were baking up nothing but pies at the Pie-O-Neer, and by the 2010s, top sellers like cherry and coconut cream were served by the dozens. But it was a New Mexico apple-and-green-chile pie that garnered the most attention from motorists.

With my love of all things wild, wacky, and wonderful, I, too, am enthralled by this New Mexican riff on America's beloved apple pie. Featuring the gentle heat of Hatch chiles, a cheddar crust, and a sweet, brown sugar crumble, this pie ticks all the boxes. I think you'll find its tantalizing flavor combination an unlikely hit, and as Kathy Knapp argued in 2021, this now-pervasive New Mexican thrill should be considered as the official state pie by the powers that be.

HATCH CHILE & CHEDDAR APPLE PIE

PIE • 9-INCH PIE
PREP: 45 MINUTES • CHILL: 40 MINUTES • BAKE: 55 MINUTES • COOL: 30 MINUTES

CRUST

1⅓ cups (185g) all-purpose flour

¼ tsp salt

⅓ cup (75g) butter or vegetable shortening (62g), cold and cubed

1 cup (120g) grated sharp cheddar cheese, packed

4–6 tbsp cold water

FILLING

3 large green apples, peeled, cored, and sliced

1 large green Hatch chile, roasted, seeded, and chopped, or ½ cup (80g) drained and chopped canned green chiles

Juice of 1 lemon

¾ cup (150g) granulated sugar

½ tsp salt

½ tsp ground cinnamon

¼ tsp ground nutmeg

¼ cup (35g) cornstarch

CRUMBLE

½ cup (70g) all-purpose flour

½ cup (110g) brown sugar

¼ cup (55g) butter, cold and cubed

½ cup (75g) chopped walnuts

CRUST METHOD

1. Combine the flour and salt in a large bowl. Using a pastry cutter or a fork, cut ½ the butter into the flour until the mixture is uniform. Add the remaining butter and repeat until the largest pieces are the size of peppercorns. Add the cheddar and water, and mix until the dough forms a ball. If the mixture does not hold its shape when squeezed in the hand, additional water may be added. Form a disk of dough resembling a hockey puck, wrap in plastic wrap, and chill for at least 40 minutes.

2. Turn the disk onto a lightly floured board, and with a floured rolling pin, roll out from the center of the dough to form a circle that extends at least 2 inches (5cm) beyond the rim of a 9-inch (23cm) pie pan. While rolling the disk of dough, turn occasionally and lightly flour beneath to prevent sticking. Once the size is adequate, fold the dough gently in half over the rolling pin and center into the pie pan before patting into place to form the crust. Trim the edges evenly, leaving roughly a 1-inch (2.5cm) overhang beyond the rim. Flute or crimp to the rim and trim any excess. Refrigerate until ready to fill.

FILLING & CRUMBLE METHOD

3. Arrange the oven rack to the position below that of the middle, but above the bottommost. If your oven does not allow this, leave the rack in the middle position. Preheat the oven to 425°F (220°C).

4. To a large saucepan over medium-high heat, add the apples and the chiles and cook until the apples begin to release their juices. Then, stir in the remaining filling ingredients and mix until combined. Once the mixture is simmering and bubbling throughout, reduce to low heat and continue cooking, stirring occasionally, for 8 minutes. It should begin to thicken substantially. Meanwhile, prepare the crumble.

5. In a medium bowl, combine the flour and the brown sugar, then add the butter. Rub the dry mixture into the butter with your fingers or a pastry cutter until the mixture is a uniform consistency like that of wet sand. Mix in the walnuts.

6. Spoon the apple filling into the prepared and chilled crust, leaving any excess liquid behind in the saucepan, and evenly distribute the crumble on top.

7. Bake the pie for 10 minutes, then lower the heat to 375°F (190°C) and bake for 30 to 40 minutes, or until the filling is bubbling at the crust's edge and the crumble has browned nicely.

8. Place the pie on a wire rack to cool for at least 30 minutes before slicing. Serve warm.

NEVADA

CALIFORNIA

PALM
SPRINGS

HAWAII

ARIZONA

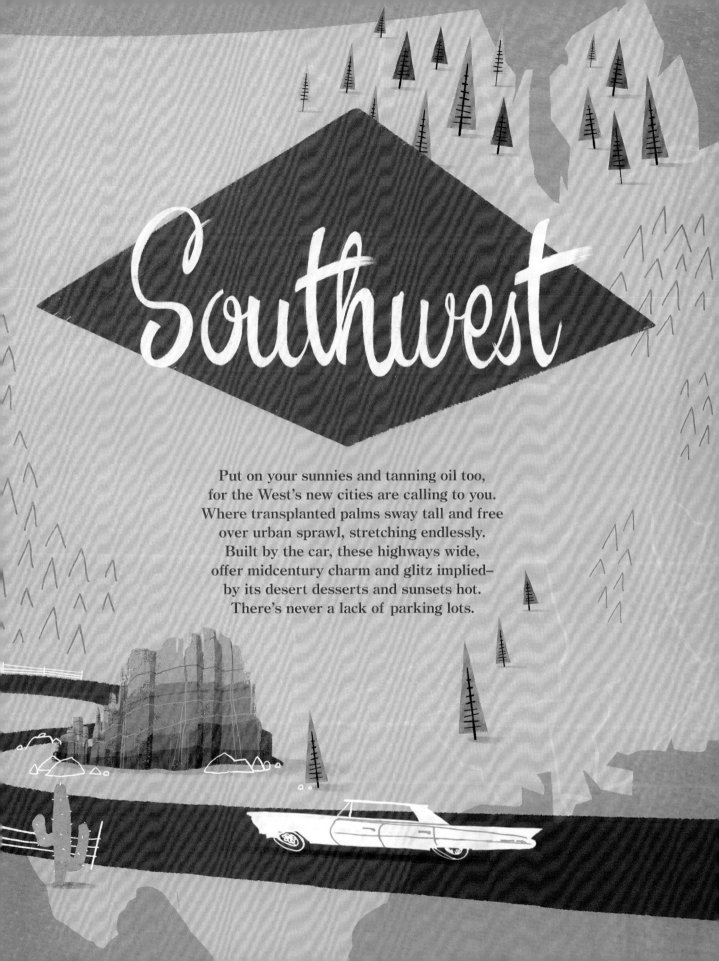

Southwest

Put on your sunnies and tanning oil too,
for the West's new cities are calling to you.
Where transplanted palms sway tall and free
over urban sprawl, stretching endlessly.
Built by the car, these highways wide,
offer midcentury charm and glitz implied–
by its desert desserts and sunsets hot.
There's never a lack of parking lots.

PALM SPRINGS

Gay is the day you're hit with Palm Springs heat beneath the California rays. Sun-drunk by the pool or scoring birdies on the green, the sunglassed wink of the Coachella Valley always encourages you to take a load off. This desert enclave and its resort city sisters are more a lifestyle than a destination. Semi-reclined and with zinced noses, everyone here keeps tabs on what's new, and whether Patricia's husband has yet to kick the bucket. Here, the shirts are linen and their collars camp—like Palm Canyon Drive and its breezeway blocks that trace the clean lines of midcentury gloss. This is unadulterated, silver-screened California-living in retrospective—it's leisure done the glamorous way. The air of Palm Springs is easygoing and aimed squarely at life's pleasures, for it's too damned hot to be concerned with much else.

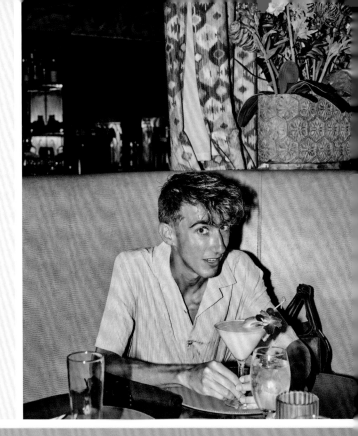

A slice of chiffon, Racquet Club Estates, Palm Springs.

CHIFFON OF GRAPEFRUIT

CHIFFON CAKE • 10-INCH TUBE
PREP: 30 MINUTES • BAKE: 1 HOUR • COOL: 2 HOURS

L auded as "the first really new cake in a hundred years," the chiffon was unveiled to the nation's housewives by dry-goods overlord General Mills in 1948. Though it debuted with orange, it was Hollywood's popular "Grapefruit Diet" of the '40s which led grapefruit to become the archetypal California chiffon from the start. Twenty-one years prior, California insurance salesman Mr. Harry Baker—no doubt stirred to change his career by his befitting surname—experimented tirelessly in his kitchen within the Windsor Square neighborhood of Los Angeles. The City of Angels has a way of convincing people they're destined for more than papers and policies, and so Baker sought to improve upon the fitting angel food cake: a dish known for its texture, not its richness. He wanted both, and succeeded to this end. In 1927, Baker discovered that vegetable oil combined with beaten egg whites created a rich cake sporting a moist, airy texture.

You might chuckle at such a simple revelation, yet someone somewhere had to be the one to do it first. The chiffon's merits were evident when the famous Brown Derby restaurant in Hollywood began to pay Baker to provide them with his cakes, and it was further affirmed when General Mills got wind and paid Baker a hefty sum to hand over the secret recipe. And so it was, undulating outward from the San Andreas fault in waves of cookbooks, pamphlets, and brochures. This Angeleno wonder—the first recipe of its kind—pushed the 1950s into a tizzy. Your guests are sure to step back into the midcentury when you serve this proud California creation.

INGREDIENTS

2 cups (260g) cake flour

1 cup (200g) granulated sugar

1½ tsp baking powder (use ¾ tsp if baking at or above 5,000 feet)

Zest and juice of 1 grapefruit

1 tsp vanilla extract

¼ cup (60ml) vegetable oil

Yolks of 7 eggs

Whites of 9 eggs

½ tsp salt

1 tsp cream of tartar

½ cup (60g) powdered sugar

Cream or whipped cream, for serving

METHOD

1. Place the oven rack to one position below center and preheat the oven to 325°F (165°C). Have ready a clean 10-inch or 9½-inch (25 or 24cm), 2-piece angel food pan, but do not grease it.

2. In a large bowl, combine the flour, sugar, baking powder, grapefruit zest and juice, vanilla extract, oil, and egg yolks. Beat until smooth and uniform. Set the batter aside.

3. In the bowl of a stand mixer fitted with a whisk attachment, or in a large bowl in tandem with a hand mixer, add the egg whites, salt, and cream of tartar, and beat to soft peaks. Then begin adding the powdered sugar 2 tablespoons at a time, beating until stiff.

4. Thoroughly mix ⅓ of the beaten egg whites into the batter before gently folding in the remaining ⅔. Turn into the pan, place on the positioned rack, and bake for 45 to 55 minutes, or until the top of the cake springs back when poked gently with a finger.

5. Remove from the oven, invert, and let cool upside down using the pan's feet, or centered on its elongated tube. If your pan has neither, it may be suspended via a narrow-necked bottle through the tube. Let cool for a minimum of 2 hours.

6. Right the cake, and using a thin, narrow knife, like a boning or fillet knife, free the adhered cake from the wall of the pan by running the knife along its circumference, keeping it flush and parallel to the wall. Pull the cake out by the tube, free the top with the knife, and serve with whipped cream or drizzled with cream.

Chiffon, cactus, and breezeway facades, Racquet Club Estates, Palm Springs.

Polvorones Rosas and Seward Johnson's *Forever Marilyn* outside the Palm Springs Art Museum, Palm Springs.

POLVORONES ROSAS

COOKIE • 2 DOZEN
PREP: 30 MINUTES • CHILL: 1 HOUR • BAKE: 15 MINUTES

Mention "Coachella" in conversation and most will assume you're referring to a music festival where thousands rabble yearly to post pictures from the desert and desperately affirm to themselves and others they're not losing their fleeting youth. In truth, Coachella is the valley where desert-dwelling Californians differentiate themselves from the pouting, mirror-loving socialites of Los Angeles. Shielded by the San Jacinto Mountains from the cacophony of LA, this low desert tract encompasses not only Palm Springs, but Rancho Mirage, La Quinta, and Cathedral City, towns that form part of the Desert Empire: a place where Hollywood stars once built their desert retreats to sip and sun their woes away. Here, like most of the Southwest, there are the bakeries, and then there are the *panaderias*.

Hispanic influence defines most of that which makes this desert grand. You see it in the mission architecture, the names of the region, and in the baked goods. Step out of the touristy bakeries of downtown Palm Springs, and one can indulge in the panaderias that fulfill the many sweet-toothed needs of the locals, like Las Tres Conchitas in Coachella, where the Mexican delights of conchas abound.

I've studied hard so I can present to you one of the more lighthearted and joyfully quizzical creations of panaderias across these sands. Colored pink and befitting of both the kitschy sensations of Palm Springs and the levity of the Coachella Valley, *Polvorones Rosas* are Mexican pink sugar cookies that delight the eyes and the simple snacking pleasures of those here both young and old. When in this Googie desert, why settle for a cookie that is anything *but* pink?

INGREDIENTS

½ cup (115g) butter, softened

½ cup (90g) vegetable shortening, or lard

¾ cup (150g) granulated sugar, plus ½ cup (100g), for topping

½ tsp salt

1 tbsp imitation vanilla flavoring, preferably clear

Red food coloring or pink gel food coloring

2 cups (280g) all-purpose flour

1 tsp baking soda

1 tsp baking powder

METHOD

1. In a large bowl, cream together the butter, shortening, granulated sugar, and salt until light and fluffy. Beat in the vanilla flavoring.

2. Add several drops of red food coloring and mix until the creamed mixture is a lipstick red. If using a pink gel coloring, conservatively drip it in until the mixture is pink.

3. In a separate large bowl, combine the flour, baking soda, and baking powder. Add to the creamed mixture in two additions and mix until no streaks of flour remain. As the dough becomes drier, switch to kneading in the bowl with your hands.

4. Divide the dough in half, and on a very lightly floured surface, roll each half into a log about 6 inches (15cm) long. Wrap the logs with plastic wrap and refrigerate for 1 hour.

5. Preheat the oven to 350°F (180°C) and line a baking sheet with parchment paper. Add the remaining ½ cup (100g) granulated sugar to a wide bowl for topping.

6. Remove one log from the fridge and roll further to a perfect cylinder, if needed. Using a sharp knife, cut the log into 12 equal rounds. Dip the tops of each round into the bowl of sugar to thoroughly coat and place them sugar side up on the baking sheet, allowing at least 2 inches (5cm) between each. Sprinkle a little extra sugar on top.

7. Bake for 13 to 15 minutes until their edges are well-defined and the cookies' surfaces have cracked. If you've refrigerated the logs for over an hour, they may require slightly more time. Allow them to cool on the baking sheet for 5 minutes, before transferring them to a wire rack to cool completely. Repeat from step 6 to bake the remaining dozen.

Polvorones Rosas,
Palm Springs.

Alexander serving polvorones poolside, Racquet Club Estates, Palm Springs.

Scooping up *Date Cream* while beating the heat in Palm Springs.

DATE CREAM

FROZEN CUSTARD · 1 QUART
PREP: 30 MINUTES · CHILL: 4 HOURS

Beneath the scalding rays, California's Colorado Desert is home to those who like to live life on the recreational side. Here the sun is king, golf is the people's choice, and sweltering heat is the norm. Daily temperatures easily hit 110°F from May through September, which render northerners mute and inanimate as they adhere themselves to air conditioners and wail for the nonexistent water. Should you leave your car unshielded during midday, seating yourself inside will give you a taste of what many turkeys face every Thanksgiving. But, rising above this heavy mirage, the calm and stately date palm reaches to the cloudless blue and rains down pure desert gold in the form of the date: the crown jewel of desert fruits.

In years past, the folks in the Coachella Valley bowed in reverence to the date palm. It built their towns, paved their roads, and concurrently held their gazes and dotted their peripheries. However, time has been unkind to the date, and it is now branded as fogey and old-fashioned, or relegated purely to the health foodies. It's been downgraded to the status of a happy fixture: present and defining of the valley, but overlooked in favor of whatever frilly, du jour nonsense currently transfixes the youth. I cannot idly stand for this. So here, I happily present the fan-favorite 1955 *Date Cream*, which I first made on TikTok in the summer of 2021. With much of its weight being that of dates, paired with a unique mix of cream and evaporated milk, *Date Cream* is an unbelievably creamy custard that will soothe away the sweat from your brow and envelop you in a cool California reprieve.

INGREDIENTS

2 cups (470ml) heavy cream

1 cup (200g) granulated sugar

¼ cup (35g) cornstarch

¼ tsp salt

1 cup (235ml) evaporated milk

Yolks of 4 eggs

1½ cups (225g) pitted dates, ground to a paste in a food processor

1 tbsp vanilla extract

3 tbsp butter, cut into pats

METHOD

1. Place a long and shallow dish, such as a casserole dish, into the freezer to chill.

2. In the top of a double boiler filled with simmering water, add the heavy cream to begin heating.

3. To a separate large saucepan, add the sugar, cornstarch, and salt. Whisk in the evaporated milk and heat over medium heat, stirring often, until the mixture boils. Boil for 3 minutes. Once boiled, carefully mix it into the heavy cream atop the double boiler and cook for 15 minutes, stirring occasionally.

4. In a small heatproof bowl, vigorously beat the egg yolks with a whisk. Using a ladle or a suitably large spoon, take about ¼ cup of the hot cream mixture and add it to the beaten eggs while whisking to temper them. Slowly whisk the tempered egg mixture back into the cream mixture in the double boiler. Continue to cook for 10 minutes longer.

5. Remove the bowl from the double boiler and whisk in the ground dates. Add the vanilla extract and the butter and stir until the butter has fully melted and incorporated.

6. Pour the mixture into the long and shallow dish from the freezer. Return it to the freezer, and agitate the mixture every hour by stirring and pulling the freezing edges of the mixture inward. Repeat four times. Serve as you would ice cream.

MOJAVE NUGGETS

CONFECTION • 1½LB
PREP: 30 MINUTES

Plastered across health blogs, vegan Pinterest boards, and YouTube tutorials, the date-based protein ball is all the rage. With gaped mouths and astonished looks at its all-natural fruit-and-nut ingredients, it's as if the current food scene has stumbled across a most innovative creation. But nothing's new under the sun, especially under the sun that shines on the Mojave and Colorado Deserts. Here this same combination of ingredients has been known for almost a century as the date roll, and even longer in the Middle East as various date candies and confections by other names.

When dates are macerated into a paste, often in tandem with nuts and coconut, the result is an effortlessly moldable base that can be rolled, decorated, and presented in quaint boxes as gifts. This is precisely what California institutions like China Ranch Date Farm in Tecopa and Shield's Date Garden in Indio—two of my most favorite places in the world—have been making for years. If your Christmas gift has ever been an array of coconut-sheathed date confections with a single almond atop, you're likely dealing with someone who's spent time on these warm sands.

With the majority of this confection's weight being sugar, the aforementioned health nuts would rather not see the date as candy, but that's precisely what you'll be signing up for when you make these *Mojave Nuggets*. Sweet, protein-filled, and delectably Californian, call them whatever you'd like so long as you remember the revered date and the desert that made them oh-so-very popular.

INGREDIENTS

1 cup (150g) toasted almonds

1½ cups (225g) chopped, pitted dates

¼ tsp salt

3 cups (255g) desiccated coconut, divided

¼ cup (85g) mesquite honey (any type may be used), or agave nectar

¼–⅓ cup (30-60g) fine almond flour

Blanched or slivered almonds, for decoration

METHOD

1. In a food processor, pulse and grind the almonds fine. Add the dates, salt, and 2 cups (170g) coconut. Pulse until a uniform paste is formed. Transfer to a large bowl and thoroughly mix in the honey. (Without a food processor, one may mince the almonds and dates to a fine paste using a food chopper or blender, before mixing in the 2 cups coconut and honey in the same manner.)

2. Starting with ¼ cup (30g), add the almond flour and knead it in by hand until the mixture is only slightly sticky.

3. Divide the mixture in half, and on a clean surface, roll each half to a long cylinder roughly 1 inch (2.5cm) in diameter. Cut into 2-inch (3cm) portions, rolling each in the remaining 1 cup (85g) coconut. Top each log with a blanched or slivered almond and keep in an airtight container.

Mojave Nuggets at the Moorten Botanical Garden, Palm Springs.

Arizona
PIÑON TART

TART • 10-INCH TART
PREP: 20 MINUTES • BAKE: 1 HOUR • COOL: 3 HOURS

Each region in the US has its own preference for nuts. Georgia has pecans, Hawaii likes macadamias, and Washington, DC prefers politicians. The sunny state of Arizona has proven unique for its love of the pine nut, commonly referred to in these parts as piñon, the seed of the pinyon pine tree. Though popular in savory Southwestern entries inspired by Native American cuisine, the tiny pine nut is seldom used in the typical American baked good. For one, its flavor is as subtle as it is complex, and toasting it is practically required to make its buttery notes apparent. Pine nuts are also impressively expensive, owing to their labor-intensive extraction from pine cones, something the trees often take 20 years or more to produce. In fact, pine nuts can be considered the most expensive nut globally, surpassing pistachios, cashews, and even macadamias in cost.

It is thus safe to say that this Arizona *Piñon Tart*, with its primary constituent of pine nuts, is a rare treat to be relished. It is all the things one wants out of a deeply rich dessert. Its sweetness is full-bodied like pecan pie, yet the buttery depth to piñon's nuttiness offers several more layers for your taste buds to explore. It is perhaps the bougiest of desert desserts, and though my wallet wails whenever I desire it, there's a good reason I come back to the *Piñon Tart* time and time again.

INGREDIENTS

1 single-crust Pie Crust (page 17)

1 egg, beaten together with 3 tbsp water, for egg wash

2 eggs

½ cup (110g) brown sugar

1 tbsp cornstarch

½ tsp ground cinnamon

½ tsp salt

1 tsp vanilla extract

½ cup (175g) unsweetened applesauce, room temperature

3 tbsp butter, melted

Zest and juice of 1 lemon

1½ cups (215g) pine nuts, toasted

METHOD

1. Preheat the oven to 350°F (180°C). Fit the prepared pie crust into a 9½- or 10-inch (28 or 33cm) tart or quiche pan with a removable bottom. Using a fork, press a few holes into the bottom of the pie crust, then line with parchment paper, fill with dried beans or pie weights, and bake for 12 minutes. Allow to cool slightly before carefully removing the weights and parchment. Brush the bottom and the sides with egg wash and return to the oven for a further 4 minutes. Set on a wire rack to cool.

2. In a large bowl, thoroughly whisk together the remaining ingredients, save for the pine nuts, in the order given until well combined. Evenly distribute the pine nuts into the pie crust, before pouring the filling in over top.

3. Bake for 45 to 55 minutes, or until only the center of the pie wobbles slightly when jostled. Place the pan on a cooling rack and allow to cool for a minimum of 3 hours before uncoupling and slicing. The tart will neither set nor be sliceable while warm.

PRICKLY PEAR CHEESECAKE

CHEESECAKE • 9-INCH SPRINGFORM
PREP: 30 MINUTES • BAKE: 12 MINUTES • CHILL: 6 HOURS

Among the many icons of the Southwestern deserts, the cactus is without question the most recognizable. Look at a map of cacti distribution and you may be surprised to learn they are (for the most part) only native to the Americas. It's no wonder that Arizona visitors make a big point about getting a photo with them, even if it risks a few pricks.

I'm a big fan of the cactus. And having ascended to Wasson Peak in Saguaro National Park many times over, I hereby declare Arizona as the seat of the cactus crown. Here, the mighty saguaro (sah-warro) cactus is the de facto silhouette of the entire species. With an average height of 40 feet (12m), saguaro are looming deities of the arid and the parched. This height makes access to their fruit rather difficult, which is why we concern ourselves hereto with the more down-to-earth, and equally as abundant, prickly pear cactus.

A joy to look at, and a horror to fall into, the waist-high prickly pear is an edible pain in the Arizonan ass. Its paddles, called nopals, can be prepared in a variety of savory dishes, while its fruit has become celebrated for its rich purple hue and sweet taste. Should you meet the unfortunate fate of winding up in any Arizona tourist trap, you'll surely be assaulted by all things prickly pear, and many tourists have left Sonoran storefronts with jars of prickly pear jellies and preserves in hand. While the commercialization of the prickly pear in this unromantic manner is somewhat upsetting, I suppose it's preferable to the fate of those who unwittingly reach for the fresh fruit, only to be greeted by the painful handshake of needles that lodge themselves firmly into the skin.

CRUST
1½ cups (165g) graham cracker crumbs
¼ cup (50g) granulated sugar
½ cup (115g) butter, melted

CHEESECAKE
3 (8oz/226g) packages cream cheese, room temperature
¾ cup (185g) sour cream
¼ tsp salt
1 cup (235ml) heavy cream
1 cup (120g) powdered sugar
1 cup (320g) prickly pear jelly, divided

CRUST METHOD
1. Preheat the oven to 375°F (190°C).

2. In a medium bowl, combine the crust ingredients and mix until uniform. Press the mixture into the bottom and partway up the sides of a 9-inch (23cm) springform pan. Bake for 12 minutes. Remove the pan from the oven and let cool completely on a wire rack.

CHEESECAKE METHOD
3. In the bowl of a stand mixer fitted with a paddle attachment, or in a large bowl in tandem with a hand mixer, beat together the cream cheese, sour cream, and salt until creamy and uniform. Set aside.

4. In a separate bowl, again using a mixer, switch to a whisk attachment and whip the heavy cream and powdered sugar to smooth, stiff peaks.

5. Fold the whipped cream into the cream-cheese mixture until uniform.

6. Spread ⅔ cup (210g) prickly pear jelly evenly over the cooled crust, before turning the cheesecake mixture over top. Smooth the surface, before dolloping the remaining ⅓ cup (110g) jelly in small mounds over the top. Using a butter knife or skewer, swirl these dollops into the top of the cheesecake to create a decorative effect.

7. Refrigerate overnight or for a minimum of 6 hours. Gently run a sharp knife along the edges of the springform pan before uncoupling and serving cold.

No place seems more perfectly suited to motoring than the United States. Whether carbureted, fuel-injected, or—God forbid—electrified, this country's vast ribbons of asphalt deliver the best road-trip experience on earth. Contrarians can cite the potholes, traffic, or endless construction with good merit, but recall any memorable story from your past travels and you'll find the imperfections are what define the indelible, not the lack thereof. The same is true of Arizona's Dateland. It isn't a town so much as it's a pit stop: one that's hot, dusty, and eerily lonesome. But, where other travel centers offer burned coffee and stale chocolate bars, Dateland bakes up and shakes down their groves of date palms into desserts, candies, and milkshakes to soothe your desert rambles.

Dateland's trees were planted in the 1930s and grew alongside the community when the military operated the Dateland Air Force Auxiliary Field during WWII. It's from the wives of these servicemen that our recipe originates. Chewy oatmeal cookies with a hint of cinnamon, sweetened and softened by the bountiful date and iced with a homestyle kiss, these are as top-tier as the top guns of the airfield. The base may be shuttered, but Dateland continues to wink at travelers along the empty expanse of Arizona's I-8. You won't find any thrills here, but the respite of this desert snack in hand can make a barren road feel like home.

DATELAND ICED OATIES

COOKIE • 2½ DOZEN
PREP: 1 HOUR • CHILL: 30 MINUTES • BAKE: 14 MINUTES

COOKIES

1½ cups (225g) chopped dates, divided

2 eggs

2 cups (180g) rolled oats, divided

1 cup (225g) butter, softened

1 cup (220g) brown sugar

⅓ cup (65g) granulated sugar

2 tsp vanilla extract

2 cups (280g) all-purpose flour

½ tsp salt

1 tsp baking powder

1 tsp baking soda

½ tsp ground cinnamon

ICING

1½ cups (180g) powdered sugar

3 tbsp water

COOKIES METHOD

1. In a food processor, combine 1 cup (150g) dates, the eggs, and 1 cup (90g) rolled oats. Pulse until a smooth and uniform paste is formed.

2. In a large bowl, cream together the butter, brown sugar, and granulated sugar until light and fluffy. Beat in the vanilla extract, followed by the date-and-oat paste.

3. In a separate large bowl, combine the flour, salt, baking powder, baking soda, and cinnamon. Add to the creamed mixture, mixing until no streaks of flour remain, before mixing in the remaining dates and oats. Cover and chill the dough for a minimum of 30 minutes.

4. Preheat the oven to 350°F (180°C) and line a baking sheet with parchment paper.

5. Portion the chilled dough by tablespoon or cookie scoop (#40) and roll between the hands to form a uniform ball. Place on the prepared sheet and bake for 12 to 14 minutes, or until the edges of the cookies begin to darken and crispen. Allow the cookies to cool on the pan for 5 minutes, before transferring to a wire rack to cool completely. Repeat with the remaining dough.

ICING METHOD

6. Prepare the icing by mixing together the powdered sugar and the water in a small bowl until smooth and uniform. It should be the consistency of heavy cream. More sugar or water may be added to reach the desired consistency. Place a sheet of aluminum foil or parchment paper beneath a separate wire rack to catch any drippage.

7. Grabbing each cooled cookie, dip only the tops of each into the icing. After allowing any excess to drip back into the bowl, place the cookies dipped side up on the wire rack to set. Repeat, and store in an airtight container once the icing has set.

SILVER MINER'S PIE

PIE • 9-INCH PIE
PREP: 30 MINUTES • BAKE: 1 HOUR • COOL: 3 HOURS

Thousands of fortune-seekers once trekked long and far with pickaxe in hand to stake their claims of silver and gold from the hills of Nevada. It is only now, through the billions dumped yearly into the slots and tables of Las Vegas, that they've begun to pay her back. Nevada hosts hundreds of decaying gold and silver towns, all fittingly and imaginatively named after minerals. Famous ones like Rhyolite and Ruby Hill have become destinations for ghost-town hunters and mine spelunkers, while some retain populations yet, like charming Goldfield and Tonopah. The town of Goodsprings, south of Vegas, has even achieved a cult status thanks to its depiction in *Fallout: New Vegas*, the best video game of all time. I've personally enjoyed a sarsaparilla on the porch of the town's Pioneer Saloon. But how did the miners of old enjoy Nevada?

By all accounts, their primary interaction with baked goods was plain bread, as evidenced by the "Trade Tokens" of these lost company towns: coins that could only be exchanged for food and services, with stamps like *good for one loaf of bread*. Evidently, Nevada has always had a penchant for tokens and chips that aren't legal tender.

Whenever the miner *was* afforded a special treat, it was apple pie. But not the apple pie as we know it. It was a pie made from dried apples, drained of moisture and life. The result is a shockingly different taste and texture that will turn back the clock 150 years. The recipe below is perfect should you want to experience the silver years of Nevada. As a lover of the wild, wacky, and wonderful, I'm rather chuffed with the *Silver Miner's Pie*.

INGREDIENTS

1 double-crust Pie Crust (page 17)
2 cups (180g) dried apples, thinly sliced or diced
1 cup (160g) raisins
1 cup (235ml) water
3 tbsp apple cider vinegar
½ tsp salt

½ cup (100g) granulated sugar
1 tbsp molasses
1 tsp ground cinnamon
½ tsp ground allspice
1 egg, beaten together with 3 tbsp water, for egg wash

METHOD

1. In a large saucepan, combine the ingredients, save for the pie crust and egg wash. Cook over medium-high heat and bring to a boil. Boil for 5 minutes, stirring often, until the filling has thickened and reduced. Remove from the heat to cool and thicken.

2. Preheat the oven to 350°F (180°C) and fit the prepared bottom pie crust in a deep 9-inch (23cm) pan. Pour the thickened filling into the crust.

3. Fit the top crust over the filling, trim and crimp the edges, brush with the egg wash, and cut four slits around the pie's center to vent.

4. Bake for 60 minutes, or until the pie's top is a deep golden brown. Place on a cooling rack and allow to cool for a minimum of 3 hours before slicing. The pie will neither set nor be sliceable while warm.

When listing our beloved precious metals, gold and silver are always at the top. In the United States during the 1850s, the city of San Francisco welcomed thousands of Basque immigrants during the wild and opportunistic Gold Rush. But as the hills of California dried up, Nevada's legend of plentiful, untouched silver beckoned an eastward settling of towns like Elko and Winnemucca. Mining, railroading, and sheepherding were the occupations of these Basque people of Northern Spain and Southern France, and whether by choice or by Nevada's comparative isolation, the Basque communities remained and flourished well after the din of the silver mines hushed to an eerie, cobwebbed silence.

Today, the town of Elko continues to celebrate its Basque communities with festivals, cuisines, and traditions, like *Pastel Vasco* (aka Gâteau Basque): a lovely, buttery pastry that bakes cakelike as it envelops a sweet and substantial vanilla-custard filling. There are few equivalents to compare it to, though one might try to describe it as a custard pie in cake form, or a cheesecake with a pastry top. In appearance, it resembles a rustic wheel of cheese, but slice it open and you'll reveal the strata of sumptuous pastry cream. Pastel Vasco stands proud as the baked good of Nevada beyond compare, and should you deliver it onto your table, your spurs may just jingle, jangle, jingle.

PASTEL VASCO

PASTRY • 9-INCH SPRINGFORM
PREP: 2 HOURS • CHILL: 1 HOUR • BAKE: 45 MINUTES

FILLING

3 cups (700ml) whole milk

⅔ cup (130g) granulated sugar

¾ tsp salt

¾ cup (100g) cornstarch

Yolks of 9 eggs

1 tbsp vanilla extract

⅓ cup (80ml) triple sec or any citrus liqueur

½ cup (115g) butter, softened, cut into pats

1 egg, beaten together with 3 tbsp water,
    for egg wash

DOUGH

¾ cup (170g) butter, room temperature

¾ cup (150g) granulated sugar

4 eggs

3½ cups (490g) all-purpose flour

1 tsp baking powder

¼ tsp salt

FILLING METHOD

1. In a large saucepan, whisk together the milk, sugar, salt, and cornstarch. Cook over medium heat just until it begins to simmer. Meanwhile, beat the egg yolks in a small bowl.

2. Using a ladle or suitable spoon, pour about ½ cup of the simmered milk mixture into the beaten yolks while whisking constantly to temper them. Whisk the tempered yolks back into the saucepan. Continue to cook, whisking constantly, until the mixture is boiling and significantly thickened. Remove from the heat and whisk in the vanilla extract, liqueur, and butter. Cool slightly before transferring the filling to a bowl and covering with plastic wrap, pressing the plastic directly to the surface of the filling. Refrigerate for a minimum of 1 hour.

DOUGH METHOD

3. To make the dough, cream together the butter and the sugar until light and fluffy. Beat in the eggs.

4. In a separate large bowl, combine the flour, baking powder, and salt. Add to the creamed mixture and mix well until uniform. As it stiffens, use your hands to knead in the bowl.

5. Divide the dough in half and form each half into a rough disk. Wrap and refrigerate them for a minimum of 30 minutes. After which, you may preheat the oven to 350°F (180°C) and butter a 9-inch (22cm) springform pan. Dust with flour to coat and tap out any excess.

6. On a lightly floured work surface, roll out one of the dough disks to a circle that is roughly 4 inches (10cm) wider than the circumference of the pan. Carefully center and place the dough in the pan, allowing an even overhang, like that of a pie crust. Fill with the chilled filling.

7. Roll out the second disk of dough to the same size as the pan and place directly atop the filling. Dab the overhanging dough with a bit of water, before bringing the bottom dough up over the top to overlap and seal together.

8. Brush the egg wash over the entire top. Use the wash to smooth the seam. Ensure all exposed dough is brushed with egg wash.

9. Bake for 45 minutes, or until the surface is a deep golden brown. Cool completely to room temperature by placing the pan on a wire rack, about 2 hours. Uncouple and cut into slices.

CHOCOLATE HAUPIA PIE

TART • 10-INCH PIE
PREP: 1 HOUR • BAKE: 20 MINUTES • CHILL: 4 HOURS

SHORTCRUST

1½ cups (210g) all-purpose flour

¼ tsp salt

1 cup (225g) butter, cold and cubed

3 tbsp cold water

FILLING

½ cup (67g) cornstarch

½ tsp salt

1 cup (200g) granulated sugar (omit if using cream of coconut, below)

2 (13.5-14oz/400ml) cans coconut cream or cream of coconut

1 tsp vanilla extract

1 cup (170g) semisweet chocolate chips

TOPPING

1½ cups (355ml) heavy cream

3 tbsp granulated sugar

1 tsp vanilla extract

Shaved chocolate or cocoa powder, for garnish

SHORTCRUST METHOD

1. Combine the flour, salt, and butter in a large bowl. Working quickly, press and pinch the butter into the flour using your fingers. Once the largest pieces of butter are the size of peppercorns, add the cold water, briefly knead in the bowl to gather, form a rough disk, wrap, and refrigerate for a minimum of 30 minutes. Meanwhile, preheat the oven to 400°F (200°C). For this recipe, you will need a deep 10-inch (25cm) tart pan with a removable bottom.

2. On a lightly floured surface, roll out the chilled pastry to a diameter about 3 inches (7.5cm) larger than that of your tart pan. Center and fit the pastry, line with parchment paper, and fill with pie weights or dry beans. Bake for 15 minutes, carefully remove the weights and the parchment paper, and bake for a further 5 minutes, or until the pastry has colored. Allow the crust to cool completely to room temperature in the pan set on a wire rack.

FILLING & TOPPING METHOD

3. To a large saucepan, add the cornstarch, salt, and sugar. Whisk in the coconut cream. Cook over medium heat until the mixture begins to lightly boil. Reduce heat and lightly simmer for above 5 minutes, whisking often, or until the mixture thickens substantially. Remove from the heat and stir in the vanilla extract.

4. Pour roughly half of this mixture into a heatproof bowl and set the coconut mixture aside. Return the remaining half in the saucepan to the stove, adding in the chocolate chips. Cook over very low heat, whisking often, until the chocolate melts and the mixture is uniform.

5. First pour the chocolate mixture into your prepared crust and level, before evenly pouring the coconut mixture overtop. Refrigerate for a minimum of 4 hours.

6. When ready to serve, add the heavy cream, granulated sugar, and vanilla extract to the bowl of a stand mixer fitted with a whisk attachment, or to a large bowl in tandem with a hand mixer. Beat until stiff. Carefully remove the pie from the pan by way of its bottom, before topping the entire pie with the whipped cream. Garnish with shaved chocolate or dust with cocoa powder.

Hawaii is a living, breathing, and powerful home to those who have inhabited this Polynesian archipelago for generations. I've tried hard to fathom how a people can form such a tight bond with their physical islands, connecting them not only to their ancestors, but to the very source of life itself. My Western upbringing may limit any comprehensive understanding of Hawaii's ways. I know I'd just as quickly don a lei and utter aloha as would the next tourist, but I don't think it limits my ability to recognize a damn good dessert when I see one. And Hawaii has just that with their coconut haupia.

Far lighter than the topic of cultural commodification, haupia is a subtle, refreshing pudding that sets firm when chilled—à la blancmange. Made of coconut milk, sugar, and a thickening agent, haupia is served here just as Jell-O is served at American potlucks. As foreign influence in Hawai'i grew over time, so did haupia's adoption of American desserts, spawning creations like this *Chocolate Haupia Pie*. Here the light coconut pudding is set atop a layer of chocolate, topped with whipped cream, and held together by a buttery shortcrust pastry. This *Chocolate Haupia Pie* may be *hapa haole*, but it's 100 percent good.

ALASKA

Pacific Northwest

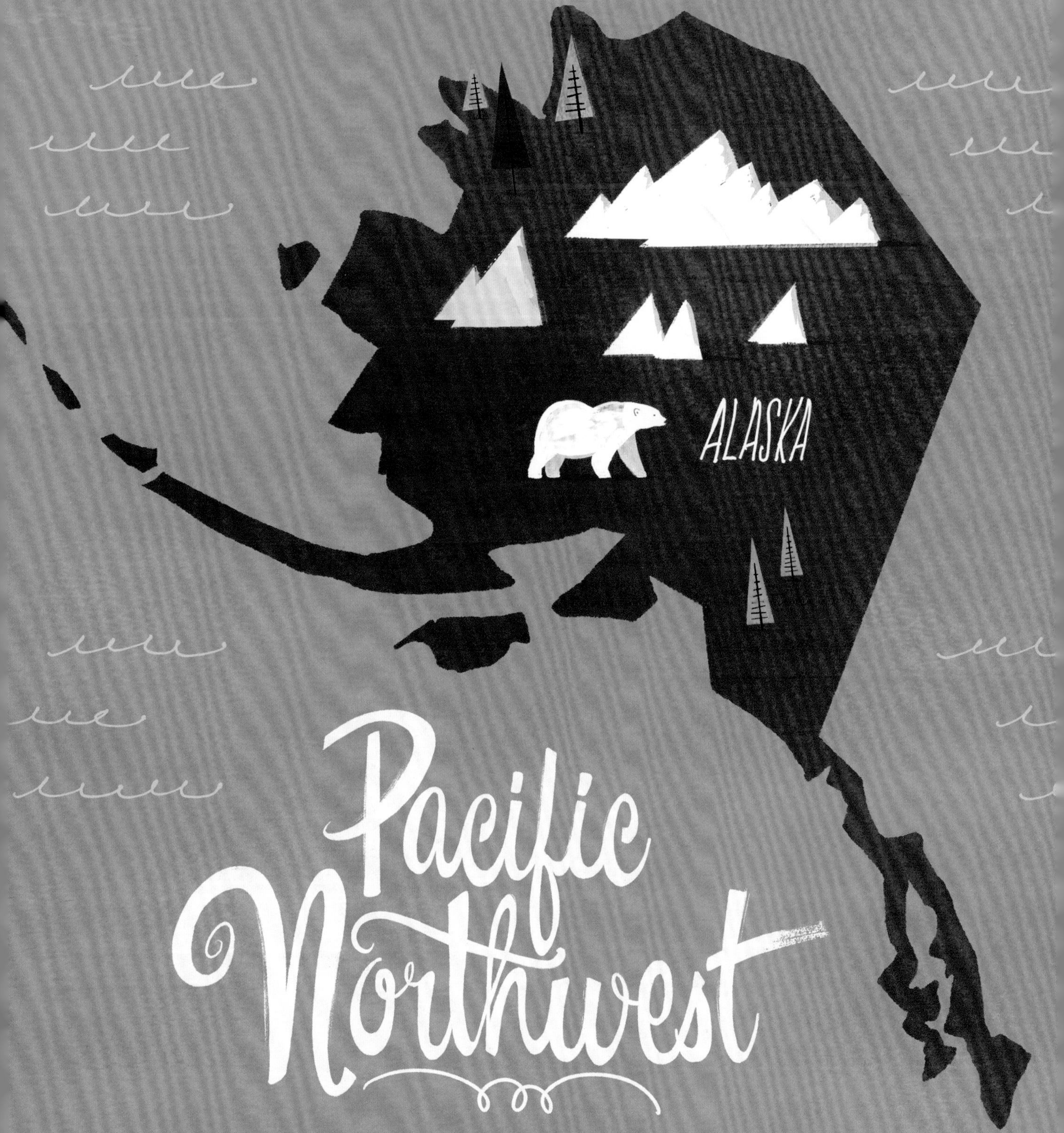

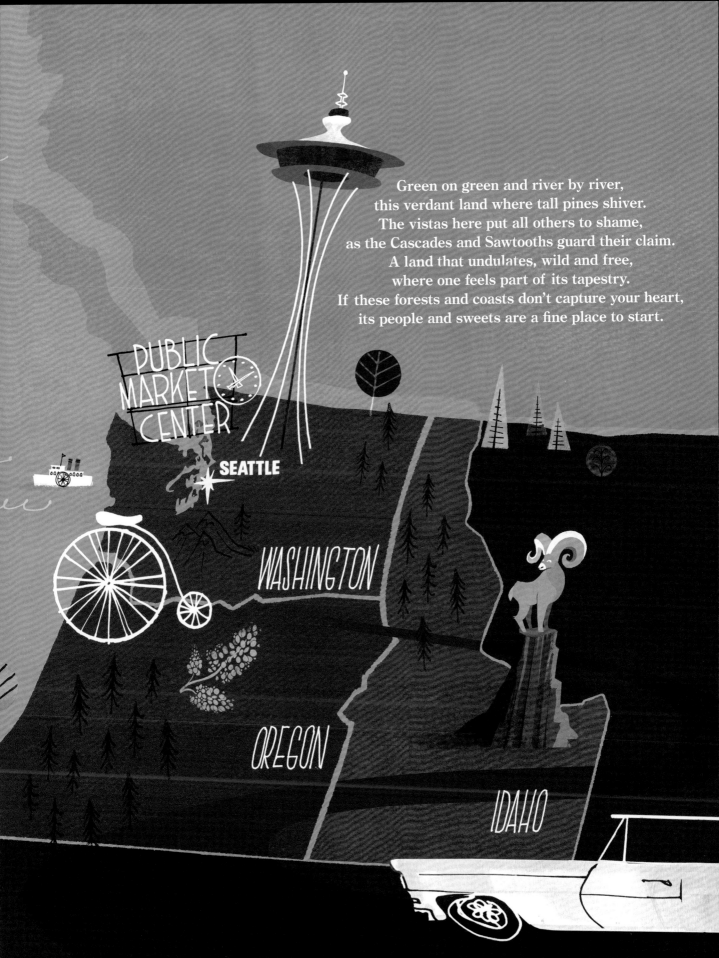

Green on green and river by river,
this verdant land where tall pines shiver.
The vistas here put all others to shame,
as the Cascades and Sawtooths guard their claim.
A land that undulates, wild and free,
where one feels part of its tapestry.
If these forests and coasts don't capture your heart,
its people and sweets are a fine place to start.

PUBLIC
MARKET
CENTER

SEATTLE

WASHINGTON

OREGON

IDAHO

Culture Capital ———————————

SEATTLE

Here is a trim and svelte city that occupies a clearing among the forests of the Pacific Northwest with the individuality of someone who's studied abroad and is proud of it. This isn't a dig; rather, it's an observation that Seattle seems to be a solid step ahead of fashion, urbanity, and cosmopolitanism. Take a coffee in its deified java joints or thrift through its artsy markets, and you'll be participating in what makes this place the nation's indie trendsetter. In lieu of celestial navigation, the Seattleite triangulates by means of their mountains, which punctuate this city's impressive horizon, guiding them to the fracas of Pike Place Market or the stunning lake vistas alongside Gas Works Park. It is an Emerald City rapt by the majesty of its surroundings—a dilettante finger on the pulse and a reverence for idyllic beauty.

Mapleine Dreams and hydrangeas, Wallingford, Seattle.

MAPLEINE DREAMS

MACAROONS • 2 DOZEN
PREP: 20 MINUTES • COOL: 4 HOURS

Mapleine is a name faded by time. A pivotal creation unveiled at the Washington State Fair in 1908, this versatile extract introduced the entire nation to the tastes of maple without ever having to interact with tree or tap. If you've ever poured table syrup over flapjacks—that is, used any "fake" maple syrup like Mrs. Butterworth's—you've felt the impact that Washington's Crescent Foods had on this nation's tastes. With just a half teaspoon of Mapleine plus sugar and water, a family could make enough table syrup for a week's worth of breakfasts. This frugality boosted morale during the Great Depression and surged Mapleine's popularity well over state lines.

Today, with pure Vermont maple syrup readily available, it's easy to overlook Mapleine as one of the earliest and most successful products of its time. But there's good reason you'll still find it on grocers' shelves, humbly standing as overseer to the new crowd of imitation flavors.

Mapleine is featured in this 1960s Puyallup original for a smooth, buttery, and maple-y macaroon which impressively contains neither butter nor maple. These dreams are filled with macadamia nuts and sweetened by butterscotch chips, an exciting new import from Hawaii and a fresh invention from Nestlé, respectively. The whimsical flavor combination they impart is as decidedly midcentury as it is moreish, packaged up for us by the Evergreen State in a unique and lovely treat.

INGREDIENTS

Whites of 3 eggs

¼ tsp cream of tartar

½ tsp salt

1 cup (120g) powdered sugar

2 tsp Mapleine, or maple extract

1 cup (130g) macadamia nuts, toasted and finely chopped (may substitute with unsalted peanuts)

1 cup (170g) butterscotch chips

METHOD

1. Preheat the oven to 375°F (190°C) and line a baking sheet with parchment paper.

2. In the bowl of a stand mixer fitted with a whisk attachment, or in a large bowl in tandem with a hand mixer, beat the egg whites, cream of tartar, and salt until frothy, before slowly beating in the sugar. Add the Mapleine and beat until stiff. Fold in the macadamia nuts, followed by the butterscotch chips. Ensure the nuts are cool, lest they loosen the egg whites.

3. Drop by level tablespoon or cookie scoop (#60) onto the prepared baking sheet, allowing about 2 inches (5cm) between each. Place in the oven. Once placed, immediately turn off the oven, leaving them to remain until the oven is completely cold (at least 4 hours). Store in an airtight container in a cool place.

Mapleine Dreams, kayakers, and geese, Gas Works Park, Fremont, Seattle.

NANAIMO BARS

BAR • 8×8- OR 9×9-INCH PAN
PREP: 30 MINUTES • CHILL: 1 HOUR

Make no mistake, the pleasant *Nanaimo Bar* is a shining star of British Columbian bakery. It is without question a Canadian invention. But touring the bakeries of Seattle, you'd never know it. Of course, one is ever-cognizant here of the shared waters with our northern friends, and just as BC license plates dot the roads, what is cuisine without a little neighborly influence?

This tale of shared sweet tooths emanates from the city of Nanaimo on Vancouver Island about 130 miles northwest of Seattle. It tells of a bake-less, three-tiered bar of crunchy, sweet, coconutty delight that members of the Women's Auxiliary to the Nanaimo General Hospital contributed to a fundraising cookbook in 1952. The first recipes were simply called "Chocolate Squares" in this cookbook, but these bars from Nanaimo transcended the Salish Sea and captured the attention of Seattleites just the same as their BC brethren, earning their name in the process. Though the old Nanaimo Hospital on 388 Machleary Street met the wrecking ball in 2017, the Auxiliary and its famed bars live on.

LAYER 1
½ cup (115g) butter
¼ cup (50g) granulated sugar
¼ cup (30g) cocoa powder
¼ tsp salt
1 egg, beaten

1 ¾ cups (190g) fine graham cracker crumbs
½ cup (55g) sweetened shredded coconut
½ cup (60g) walnuts, toasted and finely chopped

LAYER 2
½ cup (115g) butter, softened
2 cups (240g) powdered sugar
¼ cup (60ml) cold milk

¼ cup (45g) powdered vanilla instant pudding mix, or custard powder (like Bird's)
2 tbsp cornstarch

LAYER 3
1 cup (170g) semisweet chocolate chips

¼ cup (60ml) heavy cream

LAYER 1 METHOD
1. Line an 8-inch (22cm) or 9-inch (23cm) square pan with a parchment sling.

2. In the top of a double boiler filled with simmering water, melt the butter. Mix in the sugar, cocoa powder, and salt. Add the egg while mixing. Mix until uniform.

3. Remove the bowl from the double boiler and add the graham cracker crumbs, coconut, and walnuts. Mix until stiff and uniform.

4. Transfer the mixture to the prepared pan and pat firmly and evenly to make the first layer.

LAYER 2 METHOD
5. In a large bowl, beat the butter and the powdered sugar until fluffy. Whisk in the milk. Whisk in the pudding mix and cornstarch, whisking thoroughly until the mixture becomes pale and fluffy and no longer contains lumps. Evenly spread across the first layer. Place the pan in the freezer as you prepare the third layer.

LAYER 3 METHOD
6. Combine the chocolate chips and heavy cream in the top of a double boiler filled with simmering water. Once melted, stir until uniform. Pour atop the chilled second layer, tilt the pan until level, and refrigerate for a minimum of 1 hour, or until the chocolate appears set.

7. Once the chocolate has set, allow the pan to sit at room temperature for about 10 minutes, before freeing the exposed sides with a sharp knife, lifting the sheet out by the parchment sling, and cutting into bars. Cutting while too cold can result in the chocolate cracking.

Nanaimo Bars and the city skyline along Elliott Bay, Seattle.

Nanaimo Bars aboard the Seattle-Bainbridge Island Ferry, traveling across Puget Sound.

Sharing *Seattle Coffee Crèmes* sitting alongside Elliott Way, Seattle.

Seattle Coffee Crèmes at Pike Place Market, Seattle.

There's no city quite like the Emerald City. With one foot in the door of all things modern and pioneering, and the other in the evergreen wonders of Cascadia, waking up here on the Puget Sound reminds one that the world is very much something to be explored. The looming mountains offer the promise of adventure, and the waves of the sound whisper the nearness of faraway lands. It's all very literary until one steps into the cacophony of Pike Place Market and gets an albacore tuna thrown in the face. That's one way to wake up from the dream of Seattle.

The other more practical way to be snapped awake is with Washington's love for coffee. Everyone knows of Starbucks as Seattle's homegrown giant, but the city and state's love for arabica goes far beyond a single name. Coffee here is much more a decided ritual than the drive-through relay race at your local java joint, which may be why coffee as a calculated flavor in bakery is the Washingtonian's specialty. Here, this love is on full display with rich, chewy, and perfectly spiced coffee cookies hugging a sweet vanilla-bean filling. *Seattle Coffee Crèmes* are the sandwich cookies for the sophisticated urbanite, and with an appreciable dose of caffeine in each, they might just be for anyone who wants a pick-me-up and a delicious treat in one.

SEATTLE COFFEE CRÈMES

SANDWICH COOKIE • 2 DOZEN
PREP: 1 HOUR • BAKE: 12 MINUTES

COOKIES

1 cup (225g) butter, softened

1 cup (200g) granulated sugar

½ cup (110g) brown sugar

Yolks of 3 eggs

1 tsp vanilla extract

1 shot (2oz/60ml) espresso, cooled,
   or 3 tbsp coffee liqueur

3 tbsp instant coffee granules

2½ cups (350g) all-purpose flour

½ tsp salt

2 tsp ground cinnamon

1½ tsp ground cardamom

½ tsp baking powder

½ tsp baking soda

FILLING

½ cup (115g) unsalted butter, softened

2¼ cups (270g) powdered sugar

1 tsp vanilla bean paste

COOKIES METHOD

1. Preheat the oven to 350°F (180°C) and line a baking sheet with parchment paper.

2. In a large bowl, cream together the butter and the sugars until light and fluffy. Beat in the egg yolks, followed by the vanilla extract, cooled espresso, and instant coffee granules.

3. In a separate large bowl, combine the flour, salt, cinnamon, cardamom, baking powder, and baking soda. Add to the creamed mixture and mix until a stiff dough forms.

4. Drop by rounded tablespoon or cookie scoop (#40) onto the prepared baking sheet, allowing about 2½ inches (6cm) between each, and bake for 10 to 12 minutes, or until the cookies have puffed and their edges appear defined. Allow them to cool on the baking sheet for 5 minutes before carefully transferring to a wire rack to cool completely. They will be soft until cooled.

FILLING METHOD

5. In the bowl of a stand mixer fitted with a whisk attachment, beat the butter until it lightens, about 2 minutes. Then, slowly beat in the powdered sugar ¼ cup (30g) at a time. Add the vanilla bean paste and beat until smooth and stiff.

6. Transfer the filling to a piping bag (the tip is unimportant) and apply a heaping tablespoon of filling to the center of a cookie's flat bottom. With the tip of the bag barely touching the cookie surface, pipe without moving the bag until a uniform dollop is formed. Sandwich together with another cookie to make each crème. Repeat. Keep airtight in a cool place, and refrigerate if storing for more than 2 days.

ICE CREAM POTATO

DESSERT • 4 SERVINGS
PREP: 1 HOUR 15 MINUTES

The drive-in diner was once a neon-lit staple of 1950s America. Here, one could park their chromed land yachts, crank down the window, and order fries and malts to be delivered via roller skates and enjoyed on a special tray called a car hop. Once humans grasped the challenging concept of vehicle cup holders, the drive-in became the drive-thru, spelling the end of drive-ins, and ubiquitously spelling "through" incorrectly. In Boise, Idaho, however, the drive-in endures, where the Westside Drive-In on State Street serves up milkshakes and burgers alongside their most famous creation: the *Ice Cream Potato*.

Idahoans seemingly receive visions of potatoes in their dreams, so it's only fitting that here in Boise, they feel it necessary to mold ice cream into the shape of a potato, cover it in cocoa powder, and serve it sliced open in the style of a baked potato: loaded with sour cream (whipped cream) and chives (green sprinkles). It is the creation of chef Lou Allen, who's been operating the Westside Drive-In since 1994. It has quickly sprouted into an Idaho icon. You might argue that it's nothing but a way to deliver ice cream, but ask anyone if they prefer a cone or a cup, and you'll find that it's often the method of serving that defines ice cream's adoration. And here, with the *Ice Cream Potato*, stands the potato state's offering to America's ice cream ingenuity.

INGREDIENTS

1 (1.5qt/1.42L) tub French vanilla ice cream, ideally a circular tub

1 cup (120g) cocoa powder

Canned whipped cream, for topping

Chocolate syrup, for topping

Green sprinkles, or any desired topping, such as crushed cookies, nuts, etc.

METHOD

1. Place 4 soup bowls lined with plastic wrap in the freezer to chill for 30 minutes. Line a sizable section of the counter with parchment or wax paper.

2. On a clean surface, like a plastic cutting board, cut away the ice cream tub to free the ice cream. Quarter the ice cream and quickly form each quarter into the shape of a potato using clean hands.

3. Either by placing the cocoa powder on the parchment, or applying with your hands, liberally coat each ice cream "potato" in cocoa powder. Place the coated potatoes in the chilled bowls. Let chill for 30 minutes while you ready the whipped cream, chocolate syrup, and sprinkles for topping. Have a knife at the ready.

4. When ready to serve, take each coated potato out of their bowls and coat again in cocoa powder. Using the knife, cut a wedge into the top of each potato to resemble a split baked potato. Atop the wedge, pile whipped cream, and garnish with chocolate syrup and green sprinkles. Serve at once.

POTATO MACAROONS

MACAROONS • BAKER'S DOZEN
PREP: 20 MINUTES • BAKE: 20 MINUTES

Idaho is a state in reverence to the tuber. Here, the potato is bowed before and prayed to. By all accounts, it seems to run the entire operation with a starchy fist. While New York has the Metropolitan Museum of Art, Idaho has the Potato Museum, which you can visit after you watch a game at the Potato Bowl and stay at the Potato Hotel. Seemingly in place of a state government, the Idaho Potato Commission makes sure Idahoans and outsiders alike never forget about Americans' favorite vegetable à la Orwell's 1984, as it fervently lobbies for potato domination and literally controls the trademark for "Idaho" whenever it's used in tandem with a potato product. This is apt, considering that 13 billion pounds of potatoes are produced in the state yearly.

This Idaho recipe is equally insane and is likely the most bizarre in this book, as it is a macaroon of rice and potatoes, which sounds more like a dinner than it does any sweet treat. As it bakes, you'll smell the allure of potato chips, yet biting into them reveals a chewy, sweet, and tantalizing combination of spud and chocolate. *Potato Macaroons* are a playful take on the beloved Boise-produced Idaho Spud candy bar, except this macaroon's creator must've wanted to remedy the fact that the Idaho Spud contains no actual potato. So, I implore you to take a chance on this truly far-out cookie and pay your tithe to Idaho's patriotic church of the tuber.

MACAROONS

Whites of 3 large eggs

¼ tsp cream of tartar

½ tsp salt

¼ tsp baking powder

¾ cup (150g) granulated sugar

1 tsp vanilla extract

⅔ cup (40g) potato flakes (also called instant potato flakes)

1 cup (29g) puffed rice cereal, like Rice Krispies

1 cup (85g) unsweetened shredded coconut

COATING

1½ cups (255g) dark chocolate chips

1 tsp vegetable shortening, or coconut oil

1 cup (85g) unsweetened shredded coconut

MACAROONS METHOD

1. Preheat the oven to 350°F (180°C) and line a baking sheet with parchment paper.

2. In the bowl of a stand mixer fitted with a whisk attachment, or in a large bowl in tandem with a hand mixer, beat the egg whites, cream of tartar, salt, and baking powder until frothy, before slowly beating in the sugar. Add the vanilla extract and beat until stiff peaks form. Fold in the potato flakes, rice cereal, and 1 cup (85g) unsweetened shredded coconut.

3. Drop by rounded tablespoon or cookie scoop (#60) onto the prepared baking sheet, allowing about 2 inches (5cm) between each, and bake for 20 minutes, or until the macaroons are lightly colored.

4. Cool completely to room temperature on the baking sheet.

COATING METHOD

5. In the top of a double boiler filled with simmering water, add the chocolate chips and the shortening, stirring once melted until uniform. Then, set the burner to its lowest setting.

6. Take a cooled macaroon and coat each half laterally by dipping it in the melted chocolate. Sprinkle each coated half with the shredded coconut and place on a wire rack to set. Store airtight in a cool place.

Oregon
BING BARS

BAR • 9×9-INCH PAN
PREP: 45 MINUTES • BAKE: 35 MINUTES

Nobody appreciates the state of Oregon more than the young Oregonian. Their enthusiasm for the Beaver State way of life borders on mania. You'll find these granola hipsters by the droves as they weave through farmer's markets and eco-chic craft breweries with their foreign talk of upcycling and conscious consumerism.

The good people of Oregon have every right to be proud, as the scenes of Pacific beauty here are speckled gold and green as the sun dances through her forests and mountainscapes. It's to be expected that such a picturesque state also claims ownership of America's most beatific cherry: the bing.

Perfected in Milwaukie (*not* Milwaukee) in Clackamas County during the 1870s, this cultivar bred by orchardman Seth Lewelling and his Manchurian foreman Ah Bing has since become a symbol of the state, and the early summer months in Oregon are practically painted in shades of deep red, as the cherry dominates produce bins. This recipe in celebration of the Bing was given to me during a most hospitable welcome to the state when I visited Beaverton on the book tour for *Baking Yesteryear* in 2023. They're cheery cherry bars that allow you to bake, slice, and savor the flavors of summer in Oregon, and they're one of the many reasons I'm thankful for the Pacific Northwest.

FILLING
3 cups (450g) pitted and chopped Bing cherries

¾ cup (150g) granulated sugar
Zest and juice of 1 lemon

CRUST
1½ cups (210g) all-purpose flour
½ tsp salt
1 cup (220g) brown sugar
1 cup (90g) rolled oats

¾ cup (170g) butter, cold and cubed

1 egg, beaten together with 3 tbsp water, for egg wash

FILLING METHOD
1. To a medium saucepan, add all the filling ingredients and cook over medium heat, stirring until the cherries release their liquid. Increase heat to medium-high and boil until significantly reduced and jam-like, stirring often, about 20 minutes. Remove from the heat and allow to cool to lukewarm as you continue.

CRUST & TOPPING METHOD
2. Preheat the oven to 350°F (180°C) and line an 8-inch (20cm) or 9-inch (23cm) square pan with a parchment sling. Ensure there is no bunching of the parchment.

3. In a large bowl, combine the flour, salt, brown sugar, oats, and butter. Using a pinching motion, rub the dry mixture into the butter until the mixture is a uniform consistency, like that of wet sand, and no large lumps of butter remain. Divide the mixture in half.

4. Firmly press half of the crumb mixture into the bottom of the pan. Pour and spread the cherry filling overtop.

5. Spread the remaining crumbs evenly atop. Pack gently. Evenly drizzle then brush on the egg wash as best you can. (Some crumbing is okay.)

6. Bake for 30 to 35 minutes, until the top is golden brown and the edges begin to darken significantly. Cool completely to room temperature in the pan before freeing the two exposed sides with a sharp knife, lifting the parchment sling out and onto a cutting board, and cutting into squares or rectangular bars.

BAKED ALASKA

DESSERT • 6 SERVINGS
PREP: 30 MINUTES • BAKE: 5 MINUTES

If there's one word to describe Alaska, it would be impenetrable. From its thick-walled forests and jagged coastlines, to its deathly seas and unforgiving climes, Alaska has rightly earned its title of the Last Frontier. Those who live here are hardy, and their way of life is far from what is assumed by the cruising and hiking tourists who see the state from a purely recreational lens. This does not diminish Alaska's beauty, but rather underlines that waking up to this Western might on the daily takes real resolve.

The quizzical *Baked Alaska* is much like the tourist's assumption of these lands. It is not the real Alaska, yet it has become the accepted notion of the state. Inspired no doubt by the cold and mighty peaks of the Alaska Range, it features a meringue piled high atop ice cream and pound cake. The real head-scratcher is that this chilly dessert is baked in an oven! Such brazen contradiction is what makes the *Baked Alaska* special, and since its inception in the 19th century, it has been high on the list of kitschy and characterful desserts. Our recipe is a midcentury "cheat" for the dish, making use of frozen pound cake, which aids in easy preparation. With browned peaks, a buttery base, and a cool reprieve, this classic dessert is all you need to cheers to the eminence of the 49th state.

INGREDIENTS

1 (16oz/453g) frozen pound cake loaf

1 pint (470ml) Neapolitan ice cream, or any desired flavor

Whites of 4 eggs

¼ tsp salt

½ tsp cream of tartar

½ cup (100g) granulated sugar

METHOD

1. Remove the frozen pound cake from its packaging and slice it horizontally, creating one top and one bottom half. Place the bottom half on a wooden cutting board, and evenly distribute the ice cream atop, either by scoops, or by removing the ice cream from its container and cutting it to size. Place the top half of the pound cake on top and return to the freezer.

2. Preheat the oven to 500°F (260°C) or to its highest temperature.

3. In the bowl of a stand mixer fitted with a whisk attachment, or in a large bowl in tandem with a hand mixer, beat the egg whites, salt, and cream of tartar to soft peaks. Slowly beat in the sugar 2 tablespoons at a time until stiff, glossy peaks are achieved. Transfer the meringue to a piping bag with a tip of your choosing.

4. Remove the loaf from the freezer and cover the sides with thick, vertical stripes of meringue. Top the loaf by piping large peaks atop. No part may be left exposed.

5. Bake until the meringue's peaks are browned, no more than 3 to 4 minutes. For a more dramatic presentation, the meringue may be torched after baking to brown further. Serve and slice immediately.

Tip

It is customary to bake the *Baked Alaska* on a wooden cutting board to insulate the dessert and to offer a nicer presentation when serving. This will not harm your cutting board, but you may choose to bake it on a baking sheet if you prefer.

CONCLUSION

Admirable America, you bake like nobody's watching. You add sugar to sugar, marshmallows to salads, and peanut butter to everything else. No other country could get away with naming pies after mud or cupcakes after disgraced presidents, yet you do it with a poise that both awes and bemuses. Your oft-irreverent approach to nutrition reflects a deeper reverence to life's core pleasures, and while some may mistake this for wanton disregard, I see it as your wise acknowledgement that there's plenty of time to be responsibly boring once dead.

Baking Across America has proven to me that the wild, wacky, and wonderful bakes that I encounter in old cookbooks certainly originate from your wild, wacky, and especially wonderful places. These locales from coast to coast inspire the collective awe of this nation and the vibrant people who make it so. Americans write recipes like love letters, and by making and enjoying them, one can connect directly to the essence of what makes every place in the United States feel like home.

Yes, this is a cookbook, but it's also a book about sunburned summer evenings, elbow-deep in *Gooey Butter Cake* and dodging Missouri cicadas. It's about toasting a sazerac to New Orleans, and trying to find positive things about Ohio. It's equal praise to the honk of the eighteen-wheeler as it is to the toll of the Liberty Bell, because there is no single way to feel a sense of belonging across these great lands—only a recognition and a nurturing of whatever form that might take. And for me, as for many Americans, it starts with dessert.

 Clockwise from top left: Boston, New Orleans, Hot Springs National Park, Seattle, Palm Springs, and Washington, DC.

ACKNOWLEDGMENTS

To every individual who has ever watched my half-witted material—whether willingly or unwillingly—across TikTok, Facebook, Instagram, and YouTube: thank you most kindly. This is no broad stroke; rather, this book couldn't have been dreamed of, let alone realized, without you. I'm forever grateful for you, my audience—young and old—as you've afforded me my lifelong dream of entertaining and the opportunities that come with it. Because of you, my time in the online sphere continues to be nothing short of an immense pleasure.

To Alexander Rigby: the best editor in the business and the caring mastermind behind the concept of *Baking Across America*. A book as grand and adventurous as this requires untold amounts of patience, professionalism, and vision—all of which you embody. Under no other editor could *Baking Across America* be brought to full life, and I owe you my utmost gratitude.

To Mackenzie Smith: our photographer. You not only brought the vibrance of this country and its bakes to vivid color, but you did so with spontaneity and goodheartedness. You've changed how I view both food and the world—through light, shadow, and emotion.

To Kailey Stalder: my friend and baking confidant. Without you, this book would've simply been called *Across America*. We could not have pulled off this feat if it weren't for your grace, care, and kitchen knowledge. Some of the best moments spent working on this book were had in those many kitchens with you.

To my granny, Peggy Hollis. I've never known a love so kind as yours, and should I ever grow to be but a fraction of the person you are, I'll have lived a good life.

To my father, Bruce Wayne Hollis. The older I get, the more I realize this "luck" I've been afforded isn't luck at all, but rather the traits you instilled in me from the very start. I love you, Dad.

To my mother, Shawn Lea. I have grown into the person I am only because you have afforded me love, the world, and more. I love you so very much, Mom.

To Jane Ryan. You have a heart of gold, and your warmth and support have been a quiet strength through the writing of this book.

To Mike Sanders, whose kindliness, support, and championing of my writing prospects make such a career warm and enjoyable.

To William Thomas, whose thoughtful design makes this book among the most handsome of its kind.

Thanks to The Original Oyster House in Spanish Fort, AL; Cafe Du Monde and Brennan's Restaurant in New Orleans, LA; Strawberry Hill Baking Company in Merriam, KS; and Runza at 50th & Center in Omaha, NE, for their wonderful cooperation and business.

To the staff of Mrs. Betty's Fried Chicken in Butler, GA; Jay Abdulwahed of the Palmer House in Chicago, IL; Darnell Joyce Western in Palm Springs, CA; Cowboy Moving & Storage and Laramie Lawnery in Laramie, WY, and the many others whose kindness during our adventures made such a feat enjoyable.

Thank you to Brandon Campbell for lending his expertise in illustrating the beautiful maps in our book.

To Jennifer Harbster, Clay Smith, Zach Klitzman, and Susan Reyburn. Thank you for your warm hospitality during my visit to the Library of Congress. Your boundless expertise in cookery past gives credence to the field as a whole. While I am but a hobbyist, you are the professionals and keepers of this important literature.

To Bob Binkerd and Bill Bridges. Over the years you two turned my 1963 Cadillac 'Ernest' from an antique into a daily driver, and only through you both was my car able to be captured within, and on the cover of this book. Thank you.

Thank you to Dr. Ben Markley, whose tutelage taught me the nuances of hard work, manners, and poise in applied entertainment.

To my best friend and cousin, Chad Nelmes. I will never laugh as hard as I laugh whenever I'm with you.

The *Baking Across America* team, from left to right: Mackenzie, Kailey, Dylan, and Alexander.

Thank you to my friends Nate, Parker, Tony, Alie, Aidan, Jordan, Jake, Aida, Kirsten, Brendan, Jalyn, Will, Maria, Kingslea, and Hannah.

And to the old friends who deserve more than the sporadic contact of a reclusive writer: Peter, Kelton, Adrien, Shantell, Trystan, Mark, Maia, and Ben.

Thank you to all of my family and friends at home in Bermuda, to Sue and Stephen in Arizona, and to John and Amy in Missouri.

To the town of Laramie, Wyoming. You are what makes my heart for small town America beat.

To my barber Shelby, who has bestowed unto me the haircut featured in every picture within this book.

Thank you to Bobby Naugle, Brandon Fox, Christine Parker, and Bob Cowan for your help and good spirits during our various travel shoots.

To Ben Mitsack, who kindly traveled to little Laramie to help make the cover of this book.

To the staff at DK, thank you for making my tours, travel, and all things behind-the-scenes such a lovely endeavor.

To the pharmaceuticals finasteride and dutasteride. You arrested my hair loss at 19 and have kept it upon my head for a decade. The shape of my head is such that I would not have gained notoriety bald.

To tinnitus. Though I cursed your arrival in 2022, your constant company and the fear of silence you instilled in me has spurred heretofore unknown productivity.

Thank you again to DK and Penguin Random House, for giving me the opportunity to be an author. I am grateful as can be.

CREDITS

The cookbooks listed below were used to reference methodologies, ingredients, and recipe names, with their recipes workshopped and combined to create the entries in *Baking Across America*.

The Compendium Of Cookery and Reliable Recipes - 1890 | E. C. Blakeslee, Emma Leslie and Dr. S. H. Hughes

Picayune's Creole Cookbook - 1900 | *The Times-Picayune of New Orleans*, Louisiana

Grand Union Cook Book: Reliable Recipes For Hundreds Of Tempting Dishes - 1902 | Margaret Compton

Presidential Cook Book: Adapted From The White House Cook Book - 1908 | The Werner Company of Akron, Ohio

A New Book Of Cookery - 1912 | Fannie Merritt Farmer

The Boston Cooking-School Cook Book (Revised Edition) - 1919 | Fannie Merritt Farmer

Woman's Institute Library Of Cookery - 1921 | Woman's Institute of Domestic Arts and Sciences Inc. Scranton, PA

Modern Priscilla Cook Book: One Thousand Home Tested Recipes - 1924 | Various contributors

Rumford Complete Cookbook - 1925 | Lily Haxworth Wallace

Recipes and Instructions For Hotpoint Electric Ranges - 1926 | Bernice Lowen

Good Housekeeping's Book Of Meals Tested, Tasted, and Approved - 1930 | Good Housekeeping Institute

The Art of Cooking and Serving - 1937 | Proctor and Gamble Co.

Ruth Wakefield's Toll House Tried and True Recipes - 1938 | Ruth Wakefield

The New England Yankee Cookbook - 1939 | Imogene Wolcott

All About Home Baking (3rd Edition) - 1939 | Consumer Service Department of the General Foods Corporation

The Household Searchlight Recipe Book (18th Edition) - 1945 | *The Household Magazine of Topeka*, Kansas

The Stamford Cook Book (2nd Edition, Revised) - 1947 | The Stamford Hospital Aid Society of Stamford, Connecticut

The United States Regional Cookbook - 1947 | Edited by Ruth Berolzheimer

Blue Ribbon Cook Book: For Everyday Use In Canadian Homes - ca. 1947 | Blue Ribbon Manufacturing Company

Our Favorite Recipes By the Ladies Of St. John's Ev. Lutheran Church (53095) - 1949 | Various contributors

The Household Searchlight Recipe Book (22nd Edition) - 1949 | *The Household Magazine of Topeka*, Kansas

Charleston Receipts (28th Printing) - 1950 | The Junior League of Charleston

A Treatise on Baking - 1950 | Julius E. Wihlfahrt and Robert W. Brooks

The Women's Auxiliary to the Nanaimo Hospital Cookbook - 1952 | Women's Auxiliary to the Nanaimo Hospital, BC

Epicurean Sparklers - 1956 | Ways and Means Committee of the San Diego Chapter - Executives' Secretaries Inc.

Stove Pilot Volume II: Favorite Recipes From Maxwell - 1958 | Officers Wives Club, Maxwell A.F.B. Montgomery, AL

Recipes from Old Virginia (17th Printing) - 1958 | Virginia Association for Family and Community Education

Favorite Recipes: Dodge County Extension Clubs - 1962 | Mrs. G. H. Rawlings and various contributors

What's Cooking in Middletown, OH - 1963 | The Fenwick Roosters

The Memphis Cook Book - 1963 | The Junior League of Memphis, Inc. Memphis, Tennessee

A Campbell Cookbook: Cooking With Soup - 1963 | Campbell Soup Company, Inc.

Cooking the Holiday Inn Way (3rd Edition) - 1964 | Ruth M. Malone

Ladies' Home Journal Dessert Cookbook - 1964 | Edited by Carol Traux

American Legion Auxiliary: 1965 Recipe Calendar - 1965 | Various contributors

Culinary Arts Institute Encyclopedic Cookbook (New Revised Edition) - 1965 | Edited by Ruth Berolzheimer

Farm Journal's Complete Pie Cookbook - 1965 | Edited by Nell B. Nichols

Love and Knishes: An Irresponsible Guide to Jewish Cooking (Fawcett Crest Edition) - 1967 | Sara Kasdan

Reynolds Wrap Creative Cooking With Aluminum Foil (2nd Printing) - 1967 | Eleanor Lynch

Lamesa's Recipe Roundup (5th Printing) - 1968 | Mary Martha Circle of the First Presbyterian Church of Lamesa, TX

Favorite Recipes of Episcopal Churchwomen: Desserts - 1968 | Various contributors

Imperial Sugar Company 125th Anniversary Cookbook - 1968 | The Imperial Sugar Company, Sugar Land, Texas

German-American Cookery: A Bilingual Guide (3rd Printing) - 1969 | Brigitte Schermer Simms

Mrs. Rasmussen's Book Of One-Arm Cookery with Second Helpings (3rd Printing) - 1970 | Mary Laswell

The Complete American-Jewish Cookbook (Revised Edition) - 1971 | Anne London and Bertha Kahn Bishov

The Cape Cod Cookbook (Dover Edition) - 1971 | Suzanne Cray Gruver

Typically Texas: A Collection Of Recipes Used By Rural Electric Co-Op Members - 1971 | Edited by Mary Graham

The Thrifty Cook: Tasty Budget Recipes By The Food Editors Of Farm Journal - 1974 | Edited by Nell B. Nichols

A Texas Hill Country Cookbook (8th Printing) - 1976 | Cookbook Committee of the Blue Haven Foundation

Pots, Pans, Pot Herbs - ca. 1976 | Agnes Scott

Women's Circle Home Cooking Periodical - 1976–1981 | Various issues, various contributors

Kinkaid Cooks Y Cocineras - 1977 | Parents and Friends of the Kinkaid School, Houston, TX

Toll House Tried and True Recipes - 1977 | Ruth Wakefield

Come Cook with Nanook - 1978 | University Women's Association of the University of Alaska (UAF)

Christ Church Cook Book: Savannah, Georgia - 1978 | Arthur Gordon, Mrs. Lawrence Lee, various contributors

Treasured Slovenian and International Recipes - ca. 1978 | The Progressive Slovene Women of America

In the Forks Of Hanover (23047) - 1979 | Friends and parishioners of Fork Church

Easy Homemade Desserts with Jell-O Pudding - 1979 | General Foods Corporation

The Philadelphia Orchestra Cookbook - 1980 | Various contributors

The Amish Way Cookbook - 1981 | Adrienne F. Lund

Secret Recipes of Telephone Pioneers - 1982 | South Carolina Chapter No. 61 - Telephone Pioneers of America

Rainbow of Recipes - ca. 1984 | Various contributors

Trinity Lutheran Church: Laramie, Wyoming 1884-1984 - 1984 | Various contributors

Holidays A La Carte: Recipes For Holidays Year Round - 1987 | ESA Women International

Heavenly Delights: Christian Unity Church (44044) - ca. 1987 | Ladies Christian Unity of Grafton, OH

Historic Hot Springs Collections - 1987 | Judy Giddings and June Simmons

Recipes Old and New: The East Eddington Community Church (04428) - ca. 1990 | Various contributors

Cooking In the Rockies II: Bethlehem Lutheran Church (80501) - 1991 | Various contributors

Measure for Pleasure, Featuring Hyllningsfest Smorgasbord, Lindsborg, KS. - 1991 | The Bethany College Auxiliary

Sharing Our Best: A Collection of Recipes from E Gordon St. Baptist Church (30436) - 1996 | Various contributors

Family Favorites: W. M.'S Of Grace Assembly Florissant, Missouri (63033) - ca. 2002 | Various contributors

A Taste of Heaven: Bethel Lutheran Church 35th Anniversary Cookbook (68106) - 2000 | Various contributors

Sidewinder's Snake "Bites": Twenty-Nine Palms Elementary School Cookbook - 2007 | 29 Palms Elementary PTO

Granger United Methodist Church: (44256) Granger Delights - 2008 | Various contributors

Ladies Of the Covered Dish: Yucca Valley United Methodist Church (92284) - 2008 | Various contributors

* *Strawberry Pretzel Salad* credited to the editor's mother and grandmother, Christine Parker and Teddie Cowan

* *Piñón* courtesy of Dr. Hernán Padilla and Atlas Van Lines International

* *The Brownie* courtesy of the Palmer House hotel in Chicago, Illinois

* *Sorghum & Honey Pecan Pie* adapted from an index-card recipe from an unknown writer

INDEX

A

Adduci, John, 170
Alabama, 136
    Mobile Bay Peanut Butter &
        Chocolate Chip Pie, 137
    The Prized Lane Cake, 139–140
Alaska
    Baked Alaska, 305
Albertson, Julie, 128
Allen, Lou, 298
Almond Joy Bars, 44
Anezin, Augustine, 25
Arbuckle Mountains (Oklahoma),
    155
Arches National Park, 248
Arizona
    Dateland Iced Oaties, 277
    Piñon Tart, 273
    Prickly Pear Cheesecake, 274
Arkansas
    Possum Pie, 147–148
    Searcy County Chocolate Rolls,
        151
    The Vanilla Wafers of North
        Little Rock, 152
armamentarium, 14–15
    egg whites (beating of), 15
    heavy cream (beating of), 15
    milk (scalding of), 15
    nuts (toasting of), 15
    oven temperature, 14
    toothpick test, 14
Atomic Cake, 171–172
Augusta Chronicle, 93
Aunt Sallie's Frozen Cream, 71

B

Bainbridge Island ferry, 334
Baked Alaska, 305
baked desserts
    Peach Cobbler, 90
Baker, Harry, 261
Baker Chocolate Company, 130
Baking Yesteryear, 240, 302, 322, 326
Bananas Foster, 119
Barrens (Maine), 35
bars
    Bing Bars, 302
    The Brownie, 175
    Charleston Chewies, 109
    Gooey Butter Cake, 212
    Lowbush Blueberry Buckle, 35
    Mississippi Mud, 132
    Nanaimo Bars, 292
    Outdoorsman Bars, 234
    Strawberry Pretzel Salad, 53
Battle of Bunker Hill, 25
Beaver State. *See* Oregon
Beignets, 13, 114
Benne Wafers, 106
Berger, Henry, 72
Berger Cookies, 72
Berkeley Springs (West Virginia), 13
Betty Crocker, 221
Bienville, Jean-Baptiste Le Moyne
    de, 121
Big Dipper, 244
Bing, Ah, 302
Bing Bars, 302
Biscuit Basin (Yellowstone), 230
biscuits
    Huckleberry Scones, 231
Bizcochitos, 252
Black Heritage Trail, 33

Black Magic Tomato Cake, 68
Blackstone Hotel (Omaha), 201, 202
Black Walnut Bread, 163
Black Walnut Festival (West
    Virginia), 163
Black & White Cookies, 67
Blange, Paulus Lodivicus, 119
Blarney Stones, 216–217
Boston, 22–23
Boston Cream Pie, 25–26
Bourbon Bread Pudding, 159
breads. *See also* quick breads;
    stuffed breads
    Povitica, 209–210
Brennan, Owen, 119
Brennan's (New Orleans), 120
Brown, Joseph and Lucretia, 32
Brown Derby restaurant, 261
The Brownie, 13, 175
Bryce Canyon National Park, 248
Buckeyes, 182
Bumpy Cake, 185
Bundt Pound Cake, 193
Bunker Hill, 25
Bush, Laura, 128
Butter Brickle Bricks, 202, 330
Butter Brickle Cake, 220
Buttermilk Pie, 128
Byers Mansion, 214

C

cakes. *See also* ice cream cakes; layer
    cakes
    Black Magic Tomato Cake, 68
    Boston Cream Pie, 13, 22, 25–26
    Bumpy Cake, 185
    Bundt Pound Cake, 193
    Chiffon of Grapefruit, 261

Jam Cake, 160
    Pastel Vasco, 281
    Texas Sheet Cake, 127
Calas, 121, 122
Calas Café, 121
California
    Chiffon of Grapefruit, 261
    Date Cream, 269
    Mojave Nuggets, 270
    Polvorones Rosas, 264
Canyonlands National Park, 248
Capitol Reef National Park, 248
Carnegie, Andrew, 50
casseroles
    Piñón, 96, 97
Cathedral of Learning, 55
cereal
    Sunshine Granola, 248
Charleston Chewies, 109
cheesecakes
    Coffee Milk Cheesecake, 47
    A New York Cheesecake, 60
    Prickly Pear Cheesecake, 274
Cherry Winks, 186
Chess Pie, 101
Chicago, 168–169
Chicago Athletic Association Hotel, 330
Chicago Theatre, 173
Chickasaw National Recreation Area (Oklahoma), 155
Chiffon of Grapefruit, 261
China Ranch Date Farm, 270
Chocolate Haupia Pie, 282
Chokecherry Homestead Muffins, 237
Churchill Downs, 161
Cider Doughnuts, 39
City of Brotherly Love. See Philadelphia
Coachella Valley, 264
Coffee Milk Cheesecake, 47
Colonel Sanders, 161
Colorado, 250
    Palisade Peaches n' Cream Pie, 251
Colorado Desert, 269, 270
confections

Almond Joy Bars, 44
Buckeyes, 182
Irish Potato Candy, 56
Mackinac Island Fudge, 189
Mojave Nuggets, 270
Nashville Goo Clusters, 156
Pralines, 125
S'mores Crack, 243
Connecticut
    Almond Joy Bars, 44
    Snickerdoodles, 43
cookies. See also cowboy cookies; icebox cookies; rolled cookies; sandwich cookies
    Berger Cookies, 72
    Black & White Cookies, 67
    Cherry Winks, 186
    Dateland Iced Oaties, 277
    Joe Froggers, 32
    Polvorones Rosas, 264
    Smörbakelser, 206
    Snickerdoodles, 43
    The Toll House Inn Chocolate Chip Cookies, 28
    The Vanilla Wafers of North Little Rock, 152
Cool Whip, 16
Cornhusker State. See Nebraska
corn syrup, 16
cowboy cookies
    Laramies, 240
Cranberry Loaf, 30, 31
Crescent Foods, 289
Culture Capitals
    Boston, 22–23
    Chicago, 168–169
    Hot Springs, 144–145
    New Orleans, 112–113
    Omaha, 196–197
    Palm Springs, 258–259
    Pittsburgh, 50–51
    Savannah, 84–85
    Seattle, 286–287
    Washington, DC, 74–75
    Yellowstone, 228–229
cupcakes
    Watergate Cupcakes, 77–78
Curt Gowdy, 235

D

Dallas Morning News, 130
Dalquist, H. David, 193
Date Cream, 269
Dateland (Arizona), 276
Dateland Iced Oaties, 277
DeBaufre Bakeries, 72
Delaware
    Aunt Sallie's Frozen Cream, 71
desserts
    Baked Alaska, 305
    Dirt Cake, 13, 215
    Ice Cream Potato, 298
Dirt Cake, 13, 215
Dixie, 138
doughnuts
    Cider Doughnuts, 39
Dream, 205

E

egg whites (beating of), 15
Elliott Way (Seattle), 295
Emerald City. See Seattle
Everett, Sally, 204
Everglades, 94

F

Fenn, James and Henry, 221
Flathead National Forest, 243
flavored gelatin mixes, 16
Florida
    Key Lime Pie, 94
Ford, Gerald, 77
Ford, Henry, 189
Forever Marilyn, 263
Forsyth Fountain, 91
Forsyth Park (Savannah, Georgia), 13
Foster, Richard, 119
Freedom Trail (Boston), 13, 22, 27
French Quarter (New Orleans), 115
Fried Pies, 155

fritters
  Beignets, 114
  Calas, 122
  Hush Puppies, 93
frozen custards
  Date Cream, 269

G

Garden District (New Orleans), 124
Gas Works Park (Seattle), 291, 334
gelatin, flavored (mix), 16
gelatin molds
  The Pride of Deseret, 247
  Waldorf En Stase, 63
Gene Leahy Mall, 205
General Foods, 16
General Mills, 261
Georgia
  Hush Puppies, 93
  Peach Cobbler, 90
  Sorghum & Honey Pecan Pie, 87
Georgia Queen, 92
German, Samuel, 130
German's Chocolate Cake, 131
ghost-town hunters, 278
Glacier National Park, 243
Gold Rush, 280
Gooey Butter Cake, 212
Govan, Romy, 93
Graham, Sylvester, 16
graham crackers, 16
Grand Ole Opry, 157
Grand Prismatic Spring
  (Yellowstone), 235
Grand Teton National Park, 231, 238
Granite State. *See* New Hampshire
Great Lakes, 166–193
  Illinois
    Atomic Cake, 171–172
    The Brownie, 175
    Lemon Fluff, 177–178
  Indiana
    Hoosier Pie, 181
  Michigan
    Bumpy Cake, 185
    Cherry Winks, 186
    Mackinac Island Fudge, 189

Minnesota
  Bundt Pound Cake, 193
Ohio
  Buckeyes, 182
Wisconsin
  Kringle, 190–191
Great Plains, 194–223
  Iowa
    Blarney Stones, 216–217
  Kansas
    Povitica, 209–210
    Smörbakelser, 206
  Missouri
    Dirt Cake, 215
    Gooey Butter Cake, 212
  Nebraska
    Butter Brickle Bricks, 202
    Kool-Aid Pie, 199
    The Runza, 204–205
  North Dakota
    Honey Rough Riders, 223
  South Dakota
    Butter Brickle Cake, 220
    Kuchen, 219
Green Mountain State. *See* Vermont
Gullah Geechee Home Cooking, 106

H

Harbster, J.J, 126
Hatch Chile & Cheddar Apple Pie,
  255
Hawaii
  Chocolate Haupia Pie, 282
Heartland of America Park, 198,
  200
heavy cream (beating of), 15
Hershey's, 44
Homestead Act of 1862, 218
Honey Rough Riders, 223
Hoosier Pie, 181
Horan, Paddy, 216
Hot Springs, 144–145
Hot Springs Mountain Tower, 326
Hot Springs National Park, 146, 149,
  150
Huckleberry Ice Cream, 244, 334

Huckleberry Scones, 231
Hummingbird Cake, 105
Hush Puppies, 93

I

icebox cookies. *See also* cookies
  Honey Rough Riders, 223
icebox pies. *See also* pies
  Kool-Aid Pie, 199
  Maple Creemee Pie, 40
  Mobile Bay Peanut Butter &
    Chocolate Chip Pie, 137
  Possum Pie, 147–148
ice cream
  Aunt Sallie's Frozen Cream, 71
  Huckleberry Ice Cream, 244
  Ice Cream Potato, 298
ice cream cakes
  Butter Brickle Bricks, 202
Idaho
  Ice Cream Potato, 298
  Potato Macaroons, 301
Illinois
  Atomic Cake, 171–172
  The Brownie, 175
  Lemon Fluff, 177–178
Indiana
  Hoosier Pie, 181
ingredients of America, 16
  Cool Whip, 16
  corn syrup, 16
  flavored gelatin mixes, 16
  graham crackers, 16
  instant pudding mixes, 16
  Jell-O, 16
  molasses, 16
  whipped topping, 16
instant pudding mixes, 16
Iowa
  Blarney Stones, 216–217
Irish Potato Candy, 56

J

Jackson Cookie company, 152
Jam Cake, 160

Jamey Aebersold Jazz Camp, 158
Jell-O, 16, 246
Joe Froggers, 32
Johnson, Seward, 263
Jolson, Al, 138
Jorgenson, Dave, 240

K

Kaneko, Jun, 205
Kansas
    Povitica, 209–210
    Smörbakelser, 206
Kellogg, John Harvey, 186
Kellogg, W.K., 186
Kentucky
    Bourbon Bread Pudding, 159
    Jam Cake, 160
Kern's Kitchen, 161
Key Lime Pie, 94
Klum, Stephen, 182
Knapp, Kathy, 254
knoephla soup, 223
Kool-Aid Pie, 199
Kringle, 190–191
Krispy Kreme, 102
Kuchen, 219

L

Labadie's Bakery (Maine), 37
Lane, Emma Rylander, 138
Laramies, 240
Last Frontier. *See* Alaska
layer cakes. *See also* cakes
    Atomic Cake, 171–172
    Butter Brickle Cake, 220
    German's Chocolate Cake, 131
    Hummingbird Cake, 105
    The Prized Lane Cake, 139–140
    Red Velvet Cake, 64
layer chiffons
    Lemon Fluff, 177–178
Lemuria Books, 326
L'Enfant, Charles, 74
Lewelling, Seth, 302
Lincoln, Abraham, 75

Lindsborg (Kansas), 206
Loop Da Loop, 170
Louis XIV (king), 114
Louisiana
    Bananas Foster, 119
    Beignets, 114
    Calas, 122
    Pralines, 125
Lowbush Blueberry Buckle, 35

M

macaroons
    Mapleine Dreams, 289
    Potato Macaroons, 301
Mackinac Island Fudge, 189
Mackrill Honey Farms, 223
Madison, Dolley, 71
Maine
    Lowbush Blueberry Buckle, 35
    Whoopie Pies, 36, 37
Maple Creemee Pie, 40
Mapleine Dreams, 289
Martha's Vineyard, 31
Martin, Alie, 218
Maryland
    Berger Cookies, 72
Massachusetts
    Boston Cream Pie, 25–26
    Cranberry Loaf, 30, 31
    Joe Froggers, 32
    The Toll House Inn Chocolate
        Chip Cookies, 28
Medicine Bow Peak, 235
Meggett, Emily, 106
Michigan
    Bumpy Cake, 185
    Cherry Winks, 186
    Mackinac Island Fudge, 189
Mid-Atlantic, 48–79
    Delaware
        Aunt Sallie's Frozen Cream, 71
    Maryland
        Berger Cookies, 72
    New Jersey
        Black Magic Tomato Cake, 68
        Black & White Cookies, 67

    A New York Cheesecake, 60
    Red Velvet Cake, 64
    Waldorf En Stase, 63
    Pennsylvania
        Irish Potato Candy, 56
        Shoofly Pie, 59
        Strawberry Pretzel Salad, 53
    Washington, DC
        Watergate Cupcakes, 77–78
Midwest, 164–223
    Great Lakes, 166–193
        Atomic Cake, 171–172
        The Brownie, 175
        Buckeyes, 182
        Bumpy Cake, 185
        Bundt Pound Cake, 193
        Cherry Winks, 186
        Hoosier Pie, 181
        Kringle, 190–191
        Lemon Fluff, 177–178
        Mackinac Island Fudge, 189
    Great Plains, 194–223
        Blarney Stones, 216–217
        Butter Brickle Bricks, 202
        Butter Brickle Cake, 220
        Dirt Cake, 215
        Gooey Butter Cake, 212
        Honey Rough Riders, 223
        Kool-Aid Pie, 199
        Kuchen, 219
        Povitica, 209–210
        The Runza, 204–205
        Smörbakelser, 206
milk (scalding of), 15
Minnesota
    Bundt Pound Cake, 193
Mississippi
    Mississippi Mud, 132
Mississippi River, 133
Missouri
    Dirt Cake, 215
    Gooey Butter Cake, 212
Mobile Bay Peanut Butter &
    Chocolate Chip Pie, 137
Mojave Desert, 270
Mojave Nuggets, 270
molasses, 16
Montana

Huckleberry Ice Cream, 244
S'mores Crack, 243
MooMobile, 71
Moorten Botanical Garden, 271
Moravian Spice Cookies, 102
Mormon Row Historic District
(Jackson Hole), 236
Mountain West, 226–255
Colorado
Palisade Peaches n' Cream
Pie, 251
Montana
Huckleberry Ice Cream, 244
S'mores Crack, 243
New Mexico
Bizcochitos, 252
Hatch Chile & Cheddar Apple
Pie, 255
Utah
The Pride of Deseret, 247
Sunshine Granola, 248
Wyoming
Chokecherry Homestead
Muffins, 237
Huckleberry Scones, 231
Laramies, 240
Outdoorsman Bars, 234
Mrs. Butterworth's, 289
muffins
Chokecherry Homestead Muffins,
237

N

Nanaimo Bars, 292
Nashville, 157
Nashville Goo Clusters, 156
Nebraska
Butter Brickle Bricks, 202
Kool-Aid Pie, 199
The Runza, 204–205
Nestlé, 289
Nevada
Pastel Vasco, 281
Silver Miner's Pie, 278
New England, 20–47
Connecticut
Almond Joy Bars, 44

Snickerdoodles, 43
Maine
Lowbush Blueberry Buckle,
35
Whoopie Pies, 36, 37
Massachusetts
Boston Cream Pie, 25–26
Cranberry Loaf, 30, 31
Joe Froggers, 32
The Toll House Inn Chocolate
Chip Cookies, 28
New Hampshire
Cider Doughnuts, 39
Rhode Island
Coffee Milk Cheesecake, 47
Vermont
Maple Creemee Pie, 40
New Hampshire
Cider Doughnuts, 39
New Jersey
Black Magic Tomato Cake, 68
New Mexico
Bizcochitos, 252
Hatch Chile & Cheddar Apple
Pie, 255
New Orleans, 112–113
New York
Black & White Cookies, 67
A New York Cheesecake, 60
Red Velvet Cake, 64
Waldorf En Stase, 63
A New York Cheesecake, 60
Nixon, Richard, 74, 77
Nordic Ware, 193
Norman, Clive, 254
North Carolina
Hummingbird Cake, 105
Moravian Spice Cookies, 102
North Dakota
Honey Rough Riders, 223
Northeast, 18–79
Mid-Atlantic, 48–79
Aunt Sallie's Frozen Cream, 71
Berger Cookies, 72
Black Magic Tomato Cake, 68
Black & White Cookies, 67
Irish Potato Candy, 56
A New York Cheesecake, 60

Red Velvet Cake, 64
Shoofly Pie, 59
Strawberry Pretzel Salad, 53
Waldorf En Stase, 63
Watergate Cupcakes, 77–78
New England, 20–47
Almond Joy Bars, 44
Boston Cream Pie, 25–26
Cider Doughnuts, 39
Coffee Milk Cheesecake, 47
Connecticut, Snickerdoodles,
43
Cranberry Loaf, 30, 31
Joe Froggers, 32
Lowbush Blueberry Buckle,
35
Maple Creemee Pie, 40
The Toll House Inn Chocolate
Chip Cookies, 28
Whoopie Pies, 36, 37
Nutmeg State. *See* Connecticut
nuts (toasting of), 15

O

Ohio
Buckeyes, 182
Oklahoma
Fried Pies, 155
Old Sturbridge Village
(Massachusetts), 32
Omaha, 196–197
Opal Pool (Yellowstone), 233
Oregon
Bing Bars, 302
Outdoorsman Bars, 234
oven temperature, 14
Ozarks, 150

P

Pacific Northwest, 284–305
Alaska
Baked Alaska, 305
Idaho
Ice Cream Potato, 298
Potato Macaroons, 301

Oregon
    Bing Bars, 302
Washington
    Mapleine Dreams, 289
    Nanaimo Bars, 292
    Seattle Coffee Crèmes, 297
Padilla, Hernan, 96
Palisade Peaches n' Cream Pie, 251
Palmer, Bertha, 175
Palmer House (Chicago), 13, 174, 175
Palmetto State. *See* South Carolina
Palm Springs, 258–259
Palm Springs Art Museum, 263
Parker House (Boston), 13, 22, 25, 26
Pass Picada Channel, 135
Pastel Vasco, 281
pastries
    Fried Pies, 155
    Kringle, 190–191
    Searcy County Chocolate Rolls,
      151
Peach Cobbler, 13, 90
Peach State. *See* Georgia
Pellerin, Brandon, 121
Penn, William, 53
Pennsylvania
    Irish Potato Candy, 56
    Shoofly Pie, 59
    Strawberry Pretzel Salad, 53
Perkins, Edwin, 199
Peter Paul, 44
petit fours, Blarney Stones, 216–217
P.H. Hanes Knitting Company, 102
Philadelphia, 56
Pie Crust, 17
Pie-O-Neer, 254
pies. *See also* icebox pies
    Buttermilk Pie, 128
    Chess Pie, 101
    Chocolate Haupia Pie, 282
    Hatch Chile & Cheddar Apple
      Pie, 255
    Hoosier Pie, 181
    Key Lime Pie, 94
    Palisade Peaches n' Cream Pie,
      251
    Shoofly Pie, 59
    Silver Miner's Pie, 278

Sorghum & Honey Pecan Pie, 87
Pike Place Market (Seattle), 13, 296,
    334
Pine Tree State. *See* Maine
Piñón, 96, 97
Piñón Tart, 273
Pittsburgh, 50–51, 322
Polvorones Rosas, 264
Possum Pie, 147–148
Potato Macaroons, 301
Potato Museum (Idaho), 301
Povitica, 209–210
Pralines, 13, 125
Prickly Pear Cheesecake, 274
The Pride of Deseret, 247
The Prized Lane Cake, 13, 139–140,
    326
Public Garden (Boston), 30
pudding, instant (mix), 16
puddings
    Bourbon Bread Pudding, 159
    Spoon Bread, 98
Puerto Rico
    Piñón, 96, 97

Q

quick breads. *See also* breads
    Black Walnut Bread, 163
    Cranberry Loaf, 30, 31

R

Racquet Club Estates (Palm
    Springs), 260, 262, 266–267
Redford, Robert, 147
Red Velvet Cake, 64
Reuben, Arnold, 61
Revolutionary War, 32
Reynolds Tobacco, 102
Rhode Island, Coffee Milk
    Cheesecake, 47
Rocky Mountains, 243, 250
rolled cookies. *See also* cookies
    Bizcochitos, 252
    Moravian Spice Cookies, 102

Rough Rider State. *See* North
    Dakota
Route 66, 254
Rumsey, James, 162
The Runza, 204–205
Ryman Auditorium (Grand Ole
    Opry), 157

S

Saguaro National Park, 274
Salt Lake Valley, 246
Sanders Confectionery Company,
    184
sandwich cookies. *See also* cookies
    Seattle Coffee Crèmes, 297
    Whoopie Pies, 36, 37
Savannah, 84–85
Schenley Plaza, 55
Searcy County Chocolate Rolls, 151,
    326
Seattle, 286–287
Seattle-Bainbridge Island Ferry, 294
Seattle Coffee Crèmes, 297
Shadd, Sallie, 71
Shield's Date Garden, 270
Shoofly Pie, 59
Show-Me State. *See* Missouri
Silver Miner's Pie, 278
Smörbakelser, 206
S'mores Crack, 243
Snickerdoodles, 43
Some Good Things To Eat, 138
Sorghum & Honey Pecan Pie, 13, 87
South, 80–163
    South Atlantic, 82–109
      Benne Wafers, 106
      Charleston Chewies, 109
      Chess Pie, 101
      Hummingbird Cake, 105
      Hush Puppies, 93
      Key Lime Pie, 94
      Moravian Spice Cookies, 102
      Peach Cobbler, 90
      Piñón, 96, 97
      Sorghum & Honey Pecan Pie,
        87
      Spoon Bread, 98

Southern Interior, 142–163
    Black Walnut Bread, 163
    Bourbon Bread Pudding, 159
    Fried Pies, 155
    Jam Cake, 160
    Nashville Goo Clusters, 156
    Possum Pie, 147–148
    Searcy County Chocolate
      Rolls, 151
    The Vanilla Wafers of North
      Little Rock, 152
South Gulf, 110–141
    Bananas Foster, 119
    Beignets, 114
    Buttermilk Pie, 128
    Calas, 122
    German's Chocolate Cake, 131
    Mississippi Mud, 132
    Mobile Bay Peanut Butter &
      Chocolate Chip Pie, 137
    Pralines, 125
    The Prized Lane Cake,
      139–140
    Texas Sheet Cake, 127
South Atlantic, 82–109
    Florida
      Key Lime Pie, 94
    Georgia
      Hush Puppies, 93
      Peach Cobbler, 90
      Sorghum & Honey Pecan Pie,
      87
    North Carolina
      Hummingbird Cake, 105
      Moravian Spice Cookies, 102
    Puerto Rico
      Piñón, 96, 97
    South Carolina
      Benne Wafers, 106
      Charleston Chewies, 109
    Virginia
      Chess Pie, 101
      Spoon Bread, 98
South Carolina
    Benne Wafers, 106
    Charleston Chewies, 109
South Dakota
    Butter Brickle Cake, 220

Kuchen, 219
Southern Interior, 142–163
    Arkansas
      Possum Pie, 147–148
      Searcy County Chocolate
        Rolls, 151
      The Vanilla Wafers of North
        Little Rock, 152
    Kentucky
      Bourbon Bread Pudding, 159
      Jam Cake, 160
    Oklahoma
      Fried Pies, 155
    Tennessee
      Nashville Goo Clusters, 156
    West Virginia
      Black Walnut Bread, 163
South Gulf, 110–141
    Alabama
      Mobile Bay Peanut Butter &
        Chocolate Chip Pie, 137
      The Prized Lane Cake,
        139–140
    Louisiana
      Bananas Foster, 119
      Beignets, 114
      Calas, 122
      Pralines, 125
    Mississippi
      Mississippi Mud, 132
    Texas
      Buttermilk Pie, 128
      German's Chocolate Cake, 131
      Texas Sheet Cake, 127
Southwest, 256–283
    Arizona
      Dateland Iced Oaties, 277
      Piñon Tart, 273
      Prickly Pear Cheesecake, 274
    California
      Chiffon of Grapefruit, 261
      Date Cream, 269
      Mojave Nuggets, 270
      Polvorones Rosas, 264
    Hawaii
      Chocolate Haupia Pie, 282
    Nevada
      Pastel Vasco, 281

    Silver Miner's Pie, 278
Splitlog, Mathias, 211
Spoon Bread, 98
Starbucks, 296
Steel City. *See* Pittsburgh
Stewart, Martha, 31
Strawberry Hill (Kansas City), 208,
    208, 209, 211
Strawberry Pretzel Salad, 53
stuffed breads
    The Runza, 204–205
sundaes
    Bananas Foster, 119
Sunshine Granola, 248

T

Tar Heel State. *See* North Carolina
tarts
    Kuchen, 219
    Piñon Tart, 273
Tennessee
    Nashville Goo Clusters, 156
Texas, 126
    Buttermilk Pie, 128
    German's Chocolate Cake, 131
    Texas Sheet Cake, 127
To Kill A Mockingbird, 138
The Toll House Inn Chocolate Chip
    Cookies, 28
toothpick test, 14
Tremé neighborhood (New Orleans),
    123
Troup, Bobby, 254
Tschirky, Oscar, 63

U

Utah
    The Pride of Deseret, 247
    Sunshine Granola, 248

V

Vaffeldagen, 206
The Vanilla Wafers of North Little
  Rock, 152
Vedauwoo, 235
Vermont
  Maple Creemee Pie, 40
Vieux Carré restaurant, 119
Virginia
  Chess Pie, 101
  Spoon Bread, 98

W

wafers
  Benne Wafers, 106
Wakefield, Ruth, 28
Waldorf Astoria, 63, 65
Waldorf En Stase, 63
Wallingford neighborhood (Seattle),
  288
Wampanoag, 31
Washington
  Mapleine Dreams, 289
  Nanaimo Bars, 292
  Seattle Coffee Crèmes, 297
Washington, DC, 74–75
  Watergate Cupcakes, 77–78
Watergate, 77
West, 224–305
  Mountain West, 226–255
    Bizcochitos, 252
    Chokecherry Homestead
      Muffins, 237
    Hatch Chile & Cheddar Apple
      Pie, 255
    Huckleberry Ice Cream, 244
    Huckleberry Scones, 231
    Laramies, 240
    Outdoorsman Bars, 234
    Palisade Peaches n' Cream
      Pie, 251
    The Pride of Deseret, 247
    S'mores Crack, 243
    Sunshine Granola, 248
  Pacific Northwest, 284–305
    Baked Alaska, 305

Bing Bars, 302
Ice Cream Potato, 298
Mapleine Dreams, 289
Nanaimo Bars, 292
Potato Macaroons, 301
Seattle Coffee Crèmes, 297
Southwest, 256–283
  Chiffon of Grapefruit, 261
  Chocolate Haupia Pie, 282
  Date Cream, 269
  Dateland Iced Oaties, 277
  Mojave Nuggets, 270
  Pastel Vasco, 281
  Piñon Tart, 273
  Polvorones Rosas, 264
  Prickly Pear Cheesecake, 274
  Silver Miner's Pie, 278
Westside Drive-In (Boise), 298
West Virginia
  Black Walnut Bread, 163
whipped cream (beating of), 15
whipped topping, 16
Whoopie Pies, 36
Wilburn Brothers, 133
Wilcoxson's, 244
William Ramsay House, 99
Winthrop, John, 25
Wisconsin
  Kringle, 190–191
Wolf's Bakery, 170, 176
Woodward Candy company, 221
Wyoming, 236
  Chokecherry Homestead Muffins,
    237
  Huckleberry Scones, 231
  Laramies, 240
  Outdoorsman Bars, 234

Y

Yellowstone National Park, 13, 242,
  228–229
Young, Brigham, 246

Z

Zion National Park, 248

ABOUT THE AUTHOR

B. Dylan Hollis is a #1 *New York Times* bestselling author and social media personality who dives headlong into the world of wacky recipes from yesteryear. Born and raised on the island of Bermuda and trained in jazz piano at the University of Wyoming in Laramie, he skyrocketed to online fame through his feverish passion for old cookbooks. With each dish, Dylan brings history to life, delighting millions of followers with his sharp humor and quick wit as he celebrates the quirks of the past in signature fashion.